*CIRCULATION POLICY
IN ACADEMIC, PUBLIC,
AND SCHOOL LIBRARIES*

CIRCULATION POLICY IN ACADEMIC, PUBLIC, AND SCHOOL LIBRARIES

Sheila S. Intner

New Directions in Information Management, Number 13

Greenwood Press

New York • Westport, Connecticut • London

Library of Congress Cataloging-in-Publication Data

Intner, Sheila S.
    Circulation policy in academic, public, and school
libraries.

    (New directions in information management,
0887-3844 ; no. 13)
    Bibliography: p.
    Includes index.
    1. Libraries—Circulation, loans.   2. Libraries,
University and college—Administration.   3. Public
libraries—Administration.   4. School libraries—
Administration.   I. Title.   II. Series.
Z712.I57   1987   025.6   86-14952
ISBN 0-313-23990-8 (lib. bdg. : alk. paper)

Library of Congress Catalog Card Number: 86-14952
ISBN: 0-313-23990-8
ISSN: 0887-3844

First published in 1987

Greenwood Press, Inc.
88 Post Road West, Westport, Connecticut 06881

Printed in the United States of America

The paper used in this book complies with the
Permanent Paper Standard issued by the National
Information Standards Organization (Z39.48-1984).

10   9   8   7   6   5   4   3   2   1

CONTENTS

PREFACE

Once upon a time, librarians chained books to the wall. This mode of disseminating information was in keeping with their perceptions of the purpose of the library—to accumulate and preserve our intellectual heritage—and goals of service, which tended to be minimal. Stories are told about the library of Harvard College being kept open but a few hours each week and being accessible only to faculty. Perhaps these stories are apocryphal, but they contain a core of truth, nevertheless. There are still places around the world where client use of materials is not the primary goal of the institution, and this is not in reference only to archives or private collections.[1]

Today, American librarians (and this includes our colleagues to the north and south) contemplate an array of methods for disseminating information to clients including, of course, circulation services, interlibrary loan (ILL), selective dissemination of information (SDI), materials by mail, bookmobiles, and many more. Of all the methods of getting library materials into the hands of clients, circulation remains the most often used, accounts for the largest numbers of items, and may sometimes be the *only* way people can obtain materials for use outside the library building.

This book is concerned with the policies for circulation services being followed in public libraries, school libraries, and college and university (academic) libraries in the United States, describing them in some detail for a representative sampling from the three groups. It also describes the methods for client borrowing being employed by each of the institutions, as well as some of the problems librarians believe need to be addressed in their libraries. The information was obtained by surveying a selection of public, school, and academic librarians.

The survey was conducted in the spring of 1983, with a few of the last replies received late in 1984. Respondents came from an initial selection of approximately twenty institutions in each category. The selection, while not a random sample, was made with a deliberate effort to include libraries of varying sizes, focuses, and geographic areas around the country. (The small number of libraries cannot furnish generalizable conclusions, but should include enough variety to enable readers to recognize similarities to their own local situations.) Each recipient librarian was asked to send documents used to convey circulation policy information to clients, or other relevant documentation. Many sent client brochures, flyers, and library guidebooks, some also sent staff manuals, and others sent only their staff manuals or excerpts from them. In addition, each was asked to fill out a survey questionnaire which explored circulation systems, policy-making, and planning for the future. (See Appendixes 1 and 2 for a list of the institutions surveyed and the questionnaire sent to them.) Their responses are most revealing.

After a brief introduction to the general background and structure of circulation systems, two chapters for each of the three groups follow—six chapters in all. The first chapter of each pair describes the policies and methods used by the libraries in that group and reproduces portions of published or publicly distributed borrowing information. The second chapter discusses the problems encountered in the institutions and thoughts about their resolution. In some libraries, the directors answered the questionnaire; in others, it was passed on to the person responsible for circulation services. In a few places, several people contributed to the responses. These distinctions are noted where it seemed relevant to do so. Chapter 8 is devoted to an appraisal of the future of circulation services in each of the three types of libraries.

This book is intended for all people concerned about the use of library materials, i.e., library staff members, both professional and non- or paraprofessional, professional educators, students of the information professions, and end users of the services described here—library clients. This last-named group may well benefit from the information between these covers, though they are least likely to be aware of its existence. If clients of libraries discovered the power they could wield by focusing their efforts at policy reform, the future of library service could be dramatically changed.

My thanks go to my editor, Mary Robinson Sive, who prodded and pushed the idea for the book out of me, as well as to my teacher and colleague, Jane Anne Hannigan, who introduced me to library research and gave endless encouragement. Thanks go to Carole Bailey of the Graduate School of Library and Information Science and her colleague, Shirley

Nordhaus, master problem analyst, both of UCLA. A different sort of thanks goes to my IBM-PC and the UCLA Office of Academic Computing, which, together, made the preparation of the text painless—even fun—using computerized word processing and text editing programs.

A final acknowledgment should be made to Selda Arnoff, Al Baman, Kathleen Barry, Pam Bristah, Judith Hunt, Ed O'Hara, and Lynn Reiff, who, as Columbia University's School of Library Service Class 8031 (Current Problems in Technical Services) during spring semester, 1984, listened and gave constructive criticisms for the Introduction of the book and provided a sounding board for many of its findings and ideas.

NOTE

1. See, for example, a humorous description of modern academic librarianship in mainland China: John N. Miller, "The Chinese Disconnection," *American Libraries* 15 (Jan., 1984): 22-24.

*CIRCULATION POLICY
IN ACADEMIC, PUBLIC,
AND SCHOOL LIBRARIES*

1   *INTRODUCTION*

Libraries of all types have been reluctant to devise written documents defining their policies in specific terms. They may create high-sounding mission statements that talk about "serving the public" or "supporting curriculum and research" or "providing for lifelong education." They are less likely to define exactly what is meant by *service* or *curriculum support.* Many professionals believe everyone knows what libraries are supposed to do and written policy documents are simply a waste of time. Others have never had any desire or demand for codifying the amalgam of traditions, ideas, and ideals into a written statement. There has not been a tradition in the practice of librarianship of using written goals and objectives as measuring sticks against which administrators can evaluate their accomplishments or lack thereof as there has been for some time in business and industry, as well as in some areas of government service.

One of the few library services where detailed policies have had to be defined and where some form of publicly distributed or published documents containing this information have been prepared is the circulation of materials outside library buildings.

Libraries have always had to decide *who* can borrow materials, *what* materials will be lent and for *how long,* and *what will happen* when someone does not return borrowed materials on time. These three components of the circulation operation, the identification of materials, patrons, and transactions, combined with the fine and fee structure, make up the areas requiring policy decisions.

Each component has many decisions associated with it. For example, consider several kinds of decisions concerning patrons: Most libraries first make a basic decision about their primary jurisdiction, i.e., who their constituents will be in terms of where they live, or their attendance in a school or college, etc., and next they will distinguish between different types of clients depending on their age, educational status, and other factors. Then they will make additional decisions regarding what special services they may provide to some, but not all of their clients, and also how they will handle persons who are not part of this primary constituency. Many libraries permit outsiders to receive borrowing privileges for a fee. Others have reciprocal arrangements with other institutions to serve one anothers' clients. Purely logistic decisions include what proof a library will demand from potential clients to prove their eligibility for service, how often people will have to register as borrowers, what information they will have to furnish to the library, and so on. A variety of different decisions will be made about materials—what will circulate, for how long, to whom—and the transactions themselves.

In practice, it has proved simpler to prepare a written list of rules governing circulation activity than to explain to each person coming into the library for the first time how the system works. This written list of rules has been an effective operating policy for circulation services. Sometimes in smaller libraries, of course, policies are implemented without written rules, but both the library staff and frequent borrowers are in agreement about the general rules governing most borrowable materials. It is only when an unusual request is made or when new people come into the library as clients or employees and have to be trained that questions arise about what should be done to which materials and for whom it can be done.

Normal kinds of transactions with familiar clients by veteran staff cause little need for examination of written documents. Often, even in libraries where written documents exist, they are not always consulted by new staff or as a result of an unusual request. Instead, other staff members are questioned about how to proceed. If senior staff members believe they know the rules, they will answer such questions without checking the policy documents. Sometimes, seniority on staff is enough to perpetuate misinterpretations of what the actual policies dictate for several generations of circulation department employees.

When an institution has no written rules to resolve the issue, it is likely to be decided according to a staff member's recollections or impressions of what can and cannot be done. Any one particular case will have little consistency with any other, and some previously established, but not written, policy probably will be distorted by faulty memory, the natural inclinations of the people involved, or fear of making a decision for which one might be held responsible. It is hard to lay blame at the door of staff in these instances since, without clear and definitive policies, any decision can be questionable. Sometimes the requests are so extraordinary that no policy could be expected to cover them. Sometimes the policies are not clear in a particular area. There are many reasons for staff members to be reluctant to interpret policies, whether written or unwritten, besides the natural inclination to "pass the buck."

CIRCULATION PROCEDURES

Until the advent of computer-based circulation control systems, only a few relatively simple methods were used in libraries to keep track of the people, materials, and transactions which, together, form the circulation service system. Libraries had many variations on these basic themes, but few of them were radically different. Materials were usually identified by means of book cards (also used for nonbook materials, and still called book cards), and patrons were also given library cards for identification. Transactions were recorded either directly on the book card, which then was retained by the library, or on a third kind of card, called a transaction card or a t-card or t-slip. The remaining component in the process was to record the date due for the borrower, usually with a rubber stamp on the book card, t-slip, and/or a special slip of paper affixed to the item.

Ideally, a library could keep track of its borrowed materials by means of a file in which book cards or other transaction records were kept. Files of transaction records could be arranged by main entry, or call number, or they could be put into chronological order either by their due dates or charging dates. Libraries could keep several transaction files if they wished so they could retrieve by date, or call number, or main entry. As long as at least one file was maintained, an item could be recalled at any time if it was requested by another borrower. This method is still the most popular manual circulation system in academic libraries.

Other libraries, usually public libraries, believed they could trust their clients unless they proved to be unworthy by not returning their books on time. Rather than maintain a paper file of borrowed materials, they merely recorded the transactions on film and retrieved only those records for which items were overdue. Two problems occurred with this type of system: First, they could not retrieve the transaction record for an item that was gone from the library but not overdue and, second, when they did become overdue, the process of retrieving and using the borrowing records was time-consuming and, therefore, costly.

Libraries of all kinds sought a method of exerting better control over borrowed materials without all the costly paper-pushing of maintaining paper files of circulation transactions. They also wanted to lower the costs of the overdue billing operation, reserve, and hold systems and speed up the recall system, if there was one. These goals seemed in absolute conflict until the application of computer systems to libraries in the early 1970s offered an opportunity to accomplish all of these at once with an online, interactive, computerized circulation control system.

AUTOMATED CIRCULATION SYSTEMS

In the mid-1970s, CLSI, the first turnkey library system vendor, began to sell libraries an entire circulation system based on a Digital Electronics Corporation minicomputer. Once the library had fed information about its clients, materials, and loan policies into the computer, it maintained complete control over the materials wherever they were; automatically checked materials in and out; maintained transaction files; produced overdue notices, recalls, and bills; and notified the operator if someone deemed ineligible to borrow materials tried to check them out.

In the 1980s there are much more sophisticated computerized circulation systems, both stand-alone systems and larger ones, in which the circulation component is but one subsystem in an integrated whole, covering all the operations involving basic bibliographic data, such as acquisitions, cataloging and public catalog displays, serials control, and interlibrary loans. Many vendors have joined CLSI, still the vendor with the largest number of customers, in marketing turnkey circulation systems. The last *Library Technology Reports* issue dealing with such systems described fifteen different systems, adding Data Phase, Systems Control, Inc., Cincinnati Electronics, Online Computer Library Center (OCLC), Avatar, Universal Library Systems, Geac, Gaylord, Computer Translations, Inc., and Sigma Data Computing Corporation to the ranks of turnkey vendors, and four software-only packages to all of these: DOBIS/LEUVEN, NOTIS, VTLS, and Maggie's Place.[1] Although some of these vendors are no longer part of the marketplace and others have joined it, this much increased number of participants in less than a decade indicates the magnitude of its expansion.

Every different system has its own capabilities and limitations, but all provide methods of storing, sorting, and retrieving circulation information without human filers and paper files. The amount of information and its retrieval characteristics differ depending on the system. The more computers do, however, the less people have to do; or, perhaps it is more accurate to say that the more computers do, the further people's jobs are removed from the traditional tasks of stamping, typing, filing, and unfiling pieces of paper.

As a result of the changes to traditional circulation brought about by computer applications, policies in those libraries with computers have been changing. Although even the earliest circulation systems were designed to accommodate a variety of loan periods, some libraries decided it was easier to compromise, maintaining a single loan period for all of their materials. They were forced to examine not only loan periods, but also every detail of their overdue and fine structures, special status collections (reserves, nonbook materials, periodicals, and serials), and client privileges and to ask themselves whether they wanted the computer system to duplicate what they had been doing or whether this change afforded an opportunity to do something new and different. Soon, even those libraries that had not yet purchased a computer to support their circulation department began to think about the possibility of altering their policies in preparation for implementing one, or making changes in policy without planning to computerize at all.

The desire to obtain the benefits of complete control over library materials and automatic tracking of loans, charges, and so on, led a number of smaller institutions to contemplate joining forces with their colleagues to computerize circulation together. This presented new and different problems and opportunities. The problems centered on the mechanics of joint purchases and joint responsibilities, while the opportunities tended to lead in the direction of broader access, collection sharing, and other expanded services to clients of each individual institution in the venture. Again, here was a reason to examine traditional policies and consider their implications for the public as well as think creatively about new and expanded services.

If the experience of CLSI is any indication, the early purchasers of turnkey circulation systems were mostly public libraries, for whom borrowing materials was perhaps their most important and highly visible public service. In contrast, college libraries in the 1970s were deeply concerned about different issues—the cost and speed of cataloging and acquiring enough materials for their needs—and they appeared to be less interested in computer support for circulation. The success of the OCLC in providing relief for the academic community's cataloging problems was phenomenal and led to the formation of a variety of computer networks. However, before long, it became apparent that public libraries with automated circulation systems were using them to provide a new kind of information beyond that which traditional card catalogs could provide. This new kind of information included the borrowing status of the item—whether it was on the shelf, charged out to someone, or merely on order or in process. Although early circulation systems had neither a complete bibliographic record nor subject access, they offered a much faster means of learning whether a person could have a desired item. This advantage seemed to offset the drawbacks of circulation databases as online catalogs and hastened the formulation of online catalogs to which item-specific information was added—one of the radical departures from traditional catalogs in card or book form.

As the 1970s passed, many academic libraries bought separate, or stand-alone, circulation systems. Many public libraries joined cataloging networks. The sophistication of computer systems continued to move ahead at an incredible pace. It was obvious that circulation and cataloging systems shared some of the same data and that both could benefit from a connection, or interface, between them. One such connection was developed in the late 1970s by a company called Innovative Interfaces that enabled a network cataloging record from the OCLC database to be entered automatically into a CL Systems (CLSI) circulation database. Another connection, developed by one of OCLC's pioneer institutions, Ohio State University, added item-specific information to an archival tape containing the library's cataloging records so that they could be used as the basis of a circulation system. These developments continued to progress, offering all kinds of libraries much more than a simple single-function system for much less cost than they might have believed possible only a few years before.

There are now a number of different kinds of choices in the marketplace for automated circulation systems, although no network has yet managed to implement its own circulation subsystem. There are, however, in addition to the stand-alone turnkey systems for circulation control, micro-computer-based systems and software-only packages which libraries can buy and mount on their own computers. There are also systems in which the library shares the capabilities of a vendor's mainframe computer for some, though not necessarily all, of its circulation functions, while performing other work on its own terminals or smaller mini- or micro-processors. These systems, like the minicomputer-based turnkey systems, have different capabilities and may serve all or only some of a library's needs depending on several factors, including (but not limited to) the size of the collections to be controlled, the types of records used for identification, the number of clients involved, and the level of activity the system is expected to support. While this variety has had many benefits for libraries with diverse needs, budgets, and environments, it has also become the source of much confusion.

To recapitulate, before automated systems were employed to do library circulation, there were few choices available. Libraries could not easily keep track of all their materials at all times. They could choose to maintain files of all borrowed materials in eye-readable form on cards or slips of paper, or they could keep them on microfilm, examining only those records that required overdue notices or bills.

The shelf-list plus the borrowing files offered inventory control, but, after a number of years enough error crept in to make it necessary to do a complete check of what was really still owned—on the shelf or in a current file of borrowed materials—and what had somehow been lost in the shuffle. It was hard, in public libraries, to tell a legitimate borrower from someone who possessed numerous overdue materials and owed large fines. These delinquents could keep coming in time and time again, taking out more materials and abusing their borrowing privileges. Even academic libraries, who could exert more pressure on their clients (at least their student-clients) to keep within the limits of proper behavior by preventing registration for classes or postponement of graduation, had a difficult time of keeping up with the labor-intensive procedures of filing and unfiling cards, typing bills and notices, and maintaining the special circulation collections such as reserves, overnight loans, and so on. They had unique troubles, too, controlling delinquencies on the part of faculty members, since they were typically accorded privileges which put them "above the law" in most institutions. The reserve collections, frequently involving thousands of items for hundreds of courses which changed each semester, was another problem peculiar to academic libraries costing large sums of money to support and maintain.

Computers were hailed as furnishing a solution to many, if not all, of these conflicting needs and problems. However, the application of computers required a much closer and more detailed examination of what circulation processes were doing and, more important, what they were expected to do in the future. Scrutiny of written policies and creation of new ones were part of the automation process. In institutions where no written policy existed, decisions had to be made and disseminated to all staff members who would operate the automated system. The result was a need for a written policy.

The effects of widespread implementation of computer systems in all types of libraries has been to highlight the need for written policies and procedures even when immediate automation is not contemplated. One motivating force is the growth of county, regional, and state networks in which even the smallest and least likely candidate for automation may be able to participate. Another is the desire to prepare for future automation projects. A third is to keep up with the most visible and innovative institutions whose experiences are featured in the literature and at conferences and meetings, inspiring others to follow along.

OTHER TRENDS AFFECTING CIRCULATION POLICY

At the same time, other trends in library and information service are contributing to changes in circulation policies. One of these trends is an emphasis on accountability to funding authorities or, in some cases, directly to the public. A second trend is the economic crunch in library budgets caused by inflation and soaring costs combined with fewer and smaller increases or downright cuts or elimination of monies from funding sources. A third trend is the broadening of service goals and information needs to clients. A fourth trend is the implementation of more complex and far-reaching cooperative projects, many of which have resulted in vastly expanded and/or dramatically different circulation patterns. It is worthwhile to examine these four trends and their relation to circulation policies in libraries before proceeding to an examination of actual policies and practices.

Accountability

While not a new term or a new concept in society, accountability as applied to libraries is relatively recent in origin. The accountability of elected officials to those who elected them and of other public servants, such as teachers and educational administrators, to the general public as well as to parents and taxpayers, was a flaming political and educational issue in the 1960s and early 1970s. It represented, partly, a new realization that enormously large sums of the taxpayers' money were being spent as directed by public officials and other public servants as well as being consumed by them. Public debts reached millions and billions of dollars, and seemingly small changes in public policies affected tens of thousands of people—to say nothing of large changes affecting millions of citizens. Public scandals from relatively small incidents, such as sliding scores on standardized educational tests, to larger and more spectacular ones, such as Watergate, contributed to a depreciation of trust in government and publicly run operations.

It was not that libraries were part of any specific scandals or direct accusations of misuse of funds, but rather that most libraries are, if not directly part of publicly funded services, at least part of the sector including nonprofit institutions, that caused them to be drawn into the process of being held accountable. After all, school, public, and academic libraries were the direct beneficiaries of taxpayers' monies under ESEA (Elementary and Secondary Education Act) and HEA (Higher Education Act) legislation. It is not at all surprising that eventually someone would get around to asking whether the investment was being well spent, particularly when the "Johnny-can't-read" syndrome and the lower averages on college entrance examinations were being publicized in many quarters.

Libraries traditionally offered accountability documentation in the form of annual reports to boards of trustees, university administrations, and school boards. Librarians were not expected to turn profits, and even the most discouraging performances could, somehow, be gussied up to pass muster when translated into numbers of people who walked in the door, whether or not they received any service, or numbers of books added to the collections, whether or not they were read. Considering that periodic nationwide surveys of public use of libraries have shown consistently that very few people use them and that those who do are part of what we usually define as an elite group, it probably has not been important that annual reports of libraries be good or bad, so long as they were provided. Furthermore, the quality of library service was particularly hard to define in measurable terms and eluded efforts to be evaluated.

The furor over accountability in the public sector filtered down to the library world, nevertheless, and some people began to ask for more than just glowing generalities in annual reports. They wanted factual data, measures that could be linked to budget allocations, and figures that could be examined to determine whether the job this year was more or less, better or worse, than the previous year.

Some librarians realized accountability could be turned into an asset, one whereby they could ask for more money, more equipment and materials, and more staff, and they produced a variety of statistics to prove how effective their agencies were in providing services to the public. Practices which were common throughout the private sector began to be more widely applied in the public or nonprofit sector too. We began to see, in all sorts of places, the translation of performance measures into library terms and the application of theories of financial, personnel, and operations management to libraries.

Whether pulled, pushed, or dragged, library managers began to see themselves and their staffs as managers, supervisors, and employees and their libraries as operations to be managed in many, if not all, of the same ways as corporations. Though the notion has been challenged, proponents of the extension of management theory to libraries consider information to be a product or a good to be managed, like any other. Management by objective and similar theories of evaluation were promulgated by library administrators anxious to prove their worth or forced to do so by higher authorities. Explicit policies, clearly documented in measurable terms, assumed a high priority in this process.[2]

Economic Crunch

The last part of the 1960s was an era of plenty for most of the nation's libraries, whether school, academic, or public. The federal government was contributing large sums of money to pay for the expansion of library buildings, materials, and services; colleges and universities were expanding to accommodate the babies born after World War II, and bigger and better libraries were at the heart of the expansion; schools were moving into a new era of learning by experiment and investigation rather than rote memorization, involving the acquisition and use of materials to support these methods; and public libraries experienced a fallout of demand from the increased proportion of educated people as well as their own efforts to reach out to people previously unserved or poorly served.

Unfortunately, the flush of increased income was not to last. Before the expansions of libraries and library services were completed, predictions abounded of a dire future beginning in the 1970s with falling school registers following the baby boom, falling registrations at colleges and universities, and failing municipal budgets with tax income insufficient to cover the cost of rising salaries and social services. Although the actual happenings were yet some years away, they provided an atmosphere of fear which began to be realized more quickly than might otherwise have been anticipated because of changes in general economic conditions, namely inflation, the energy crisis, and falling productivity. This combination of factors, especially inflation in the cost of books and periodicals—still accounting for the bulk of library materials—and heating oil for library buildings, hit libraries particularly hard in the last few years of plenty. Then, inexorably, the lean years set in with accompanying retrenchment—attempts to stretch limited dollars to cover clients' higher expectations, the explosion of information production, and professionals' heightened awareness of service possibilities.

One of the librarians' responses to continuing budget crunches in the 1980s was to establish priorities for materials and services so that, as cuts had to be made, they would affect the most needed and wanted items last instead of randomly affecting all items. This required looking at all budget items carefully and deciding what were important to retain, what could go, and what could be cut without destroying them entirely. It also made automation, with its promise of taking over costly labor-intensive procedures, look extremely attractive, provided the initial outlay of money for hardware and software systems could be made. For those who wanted to automate, policy examination was an important step. For those who could not contemplate automation, policy examination was part of the streamlining process whereby libraries could get the most out of their manual systems.

Broadening Goals

Part of the excitement of the 1960s was the speeding up of the research process, developments which began during World War II and resulted in the successful achievement of working computers to assist in research, as well as a host of other encouragements from government and industry to research activities. Not only were grants offered to scientific and technical researchers, but also to social scientists and historians, artists, musicologists and musicians, writers and dancers—people from all disciplines. Research and development organizations emerged, where scholars from many disciplines could interact, brainstorm joint problems, and pursue their own interests in the likelihood that something wonderful would result. Foundations joined the government and private industry in funding research. All of this activity resulted in the production of incredible amounts of information which needed to be disseminated so that they could, in turn, cause the wheel to turn again as the fodder for still more research.

The increase in numbers of college and university graduates quite naturally led to an increase in the pool of applicants for graduate programs—encouraged in part by the need for more teachers in expanding programs at higher levels as well as more scholars for multifaceted research projects and corporate and government development programs of all kinds and by the hope of realizing the American dream through the acquisition of advanced degrees. Production of periodicals and monographs, films, records, television, and the whole gamut of materials communicating ideas flourished wildly, moving at a faster and faster pace throughout the decades of the sixties and seventies.

More and more people began to realize how important information was to their lives. They expected libraries to provide it, too, especially in academic settings, but also in public institutions. The more information there was and the faster it could be disseminated by new electronic means, the higher the expectations grew and the greater the desire of librarians was to respond. Librarians quickly became aware of the impossibility of libraries continuing to expand. They could not grow large enough to own everything and do everything because there were physical limitations, but also because of money problems, preservation problems, organization problems, logistic problems, and other problems as well. Nevertheless, their goals were broadened by the growth of information and the recognition of its importance to all people, not just a scholarly elite.

Cooperative Ventures

The computer network offered one kind of solution for some of the problems of too much information and too little money, space, and staff. As a result, OCLC exploded from a small group of Ohio college libraries in 1970 to perhaps 3,000 institutions of all kinds located all over the world (but mainly in the United States) just ten years later. Computer capabilities continue to grow as does the recognition on the part of professionals of how to employ them in efforts to cope with current events. One lasting effect is the broadening of library goals for service. The 1980s are witness to all kinds of networking, sharing, and other cooperative activities by librarians in all kinds of libraries made possible or enhanced by computer communications but engendered primarily by the realization that, in order to survive, they must work together to be effective in answering the needs of the 1980s.

The computer is the focus of much cooperative activity. For the first time in library history, there is a way to build union catalogs without doing twice as much (or more) work; libraries in distant places can have immediate access to the same information; large numbers of catalog entries—in the millions—can be manipulated with relative ease; and costs can be divided among all who share in the system. No longer do we have to wait for some great library to publish its catalog in book form to know what its holdings are. The minute it catalogs its newest acquisitions online, the information is available to all other members of the network. The power of the computer to provide instantaneous communication is also harnessed to send a message to that hypothetical great library that its material is wanted by another institution—the interlibrary loan subsystem—enabling any participating institution to circulate materials held by other libraries almost as easily as it circulates its own holdings.

On a much smaller scale, computer networks have been formed by fewer than a dozen libraries to share the cost of the computer system and access to more materials than any one owns. Simple turnkey circulation systems have been used in this way, for instance in the LEAP libraries in southwestern Connecticut.[3] In between the small local area network and the national bibliographic utilities are networks of all sizes, some merely providing support for one utility or another and others offering a variety of services in addition to utility support.

The interest in cooperation among libraries in a geographic region, with a common subject interest or of a particular type, and the constant reminders in the literature and at conferences of the advantages of cooperation and the difficulties of going it alone have encouraged many non-computer-based cooperatives to form or expand. Any library can gain from association with other libraries for some common purpose.

The identification of a common purpose and the acceptance of the limitation of individual control over policy are two conditions for successful cooperation. Both of these conditions assume or require that goals and policies of individual libraries must be clearly identified and, usually, carefully documented. It may not be difficult to cooperate, but it usually demands that activities to be shared must be written down and agreed upon before commencing. Joining a bibliographic utility or one of its regional networks requires that more formal and complex agreements be arranged and contracts be signed. Thus, cooperative projects depend not only on knowledge of policy in the individual agencies, but also on their willingness to commit some part of their control over it to the common territory covered by the cooperative or network. The LEAP libraries, in sharing one computer, had to decide whether to form a separate entity to own and maintain their hardware, to agree to pay shares of the ownership and maintenance without such an entity allowing the host library to be the designated owner, or to become a multiple purchaser with all the libraries designated as owners. In this case, a new entity was formed, LEAP, with each town sharing in the membership. Acquisition of the circulation control system required policy decisions to be made about far more than just who may borrow, what they may borrow, and for how long. Fortunately for the participants, no insurmountable problems arose to negate the project. It demonstrates, however, how important the definition of policies becomes when cooperation is contemplated.

SUMMARY

Written circulation policies covering borrowers, materials, and the rules of borrowing and return have been quite common in libraries of all kinds for many years. This is true despite the traditional lack of written policies in other areas of library service. It may be that it was simply easier and more efficient to put down the rules and publicize them than to have to explain them to every new person who walked in the door; or, it may be that, even in libraries of relatively modest size, the written document ensured consistency of understanding and treatment between staff members and the public.

Only a few methods have been employed to circulate materials over the years, though there are probably many variations on each basic theme. In one method, cards identifying the material and its borrower are filed in the library for each item circulated. Librarians could locate any one item at any time, although sometimes this might require a lengthy search. In another, no attempt is made to maintain usable files of the records of borrowed items until they become overdue. At that time, microfilmed records of transactions are examined to produce overdue notices. While it is true that the microfilms contain all transaction records and could be searched to find an item at any time, no one who intends to locate materials before they are due (e.g., for a recall system) would consider this an efficient substitute for any eye-readable file of transactions in main entry order, even if the main file were divided into daily or weekly subfiles.

The application of computers to library circulation in the early 1970s demonstrated how control could be maintained over all materials, whether they were on loan or shelved in the library, as well as how the seemingly conflicting objectives of exerting *more* control with *less* effort—staff time, energy, and cost—could be accomplished. A new era in library circulation began.

Not only has the automation of circulation services required a careful examination of policies being implemented in order to reproduce them in the automated system, but also the capabilities and limitations of the automated system have worked to alter librarians' ideas about circulation policy. In addition, four trends in recent years have motivated librarians to examine and reformulate existing circulation policies. These trends are (1) the accountability of library administrations for services and expenditures, (2) budget problems and the need to deal with financial retrenchment, (3) broadening service goals for libraries emerging perhaps from a combination of factors including the explosion of information production and the realization that no one institution could be self-sufficient, and (4) cooperative ventures entered into by all kinds of libraries for all kinds of reasons sometimes, but not always, based on automated systems.

All of these related factors interact to influence circulation policies and procedures. The chapters that follow provide a selection of existing policy statements from academic, school, and public libraries. From these and from the comments of librarians from these and other institutions about circulation policy, a picture of the state of the art (or process) may be drawn.

NOTES

1. Richard W. Boss and Judith McQueen, "Automated Circulation Control Systems," *Library Technology Reports,* 18 (March-April, 1982): 125-266.

2. Joseph A. Ruef, "MBO and the Public Library," *Public Library Quarterly*, 2 (Spring, 1980): 23-26.

3. LEAP stands for Library Exchange Aids Patrons. It includes the public libraries of Hamden, Cheshire, North Haven, North Branford, and West Haven. It now supports not only circulation and interlibrary loan, but also provides online catalog access for the public.

2   *ACADEMIC LIBRARY POLICIES*

Circulation policy documents from seven private and seven public colleges and universities are examined in this chapter. A summary of each policy, illustrated with excerpts from the documents sent by each institution, is described in terms of the three main questions with which circulation is concerned: Who may borrow? What may they borrow? How may it be borrowed? Special mention is made of unusual or atypical provisions as well as the methods used to deal with perennial problems: nonreturns, nonaffiliated borrowers, collections other than regular circulating materials including reserves, and so on.

The institutions included here represent all kinds of academic settings. Some are universities with a multitude of undergraduate, graduate, and professional programs. There are four-year colleges with graduate departments and community colleges with two-year programs designed to provide career training as well as preparation for advanced study at a four-year college. Most of the institutions are decentralized multiunit library systems; however, in a few cases, both policies and facilities are centralized in a single unit.

One of the libraries described serves only a graduate professional school within a large university. Gutman Library of Harvard University, the library serving Harvard's Graduate School of Education, is one of the decentralized units in the Harvard University Libraries system. Though it is autonomous in many respects, Gutman's connection to the other Harvard units impacts on some of its programs and policies. Thus, it represents a different sort of organizational structure than do the other libraries.

For convenience, the institutions whose publicly distributed policy documents are described and reproduced here either in part or in full are discussed first. They are divided into two groups: private universities and colleges and public universities and colleges. The private universities and colleges include Emory University's Woodruff Library, Columbia University's Butler Library, Harvard University's Graduate School of Education's Gutman Library, Agnes Scott College's McCain Library, the Nazareth College of Rochester's Wilmot Library, the University of Bridgeport's Wahlstrom Library, and Whitworth College's Cowles Library. The public group includes Mankato State University's Memorial Library, the University of North Florida's Thomas G. Carpenter Library, Queens College of the City University of New York's Paul Klapper Library, and the University of Wisconsin's (Whitewater campus) Andersen Library.

Following the descriptions of these academic libraries is a description of the policy implications contained in the staff manuals of three more institutions: the Bank Street College of Education in New York City; the Pima Community College in Tucson, Arizona; and the Stony Brook campus of the State University of New York. These three institutions sent only their staff manuals. Naturally, these documents tend to be more detailed and include information rarely reproduced in handouts for the public. They are also completely functional, without the kind of illustrations, photographs, or fancy graphics intended to make them especially attractive or easy to use. Examination of the three staff manuals indicates, among other things, the differences in approach and orientation inherent in staff-only materials.

The final section of this chapter compares the different options for service employed by the academic libraries included here. Each institution has its own unique approach to the issues of circulation: who may borrow; what they may borrow; and how they may borrow it. Each has its own set of priorities which may be interpolated from the documents, although some are quite clear and direct about their purposes and reasoning. Naturally, the policies of public institutions are more directly affected by legislation and other state policies concerning education and libraries. These influences may not be specifically identified, but they undoubtedly set the context in which the libraries in public colleges and universities operate.

CIRCULATION POLICY IN DOCUMENTS FOR THE PUBLIC

The variety of publications used in the eleven academic libraries included in this section to inform clients—primarily students and faculty—of their circulation policies is astonishing. Some institutions employ several kinds simultaneously. These publications range from attractive, costly, well-produced and formatted library handbooks along the lines of traditional college catalogs complete with photographs to typed and duplicated information pieces of all sizes and shapes, including bookmarks, standard 8½-by-11-inch flyers, legal-sized sheets—sometimes folded and sometimes not—and other smaller, nonstandard sizes.

Several institutions sent publications directed specifically toward faculty or students. A few pieces of literature sent were titled "Circulation Policies," "Policies and Procedures," or some variation on this theme; however, the majority made no explicit reference to *policy*, but instead bore such titles as "Guide to the Library," "Library Handbook," or "Rules and Regulations." Some included one piece of material giving basic information on the three major questions and were supplemented by other sheets on special topics. Others did not send any general circulation information publications, though this does not necessarily mean they do not have them.

Presumably, this variety among the small sample of academic libraries included here reflects a similar diversity in the larger universe of colleges and universities throughout the nation. With that in mind, a closer examination of each policy item can help gain an understanding not only of *what* these documents say, but also *how* they say it.

PRIVATE ACADEMIC INSTITUTIONS

Emory University

Emory University in Atlanta, Georgia, provided a handsome, copiously illustrated booklet titled "General Libraries Handbook,"[1] giving all the basic information for its main library, the Robert W. Woodruff Library, including a brief history of information service at Emory. The booklet also explains some of the services of two other general campus agencies, the Candler and Chemistry Libraries which serve, respectively, as audiovisual media center and a center for the disciplines related to chemistry apart from its science department. One is referred to specialized brochures for information about Emory's special collections, for example, the medical, law, and theology libraries. The booklet directs clients to still another brochure for specific details about Candler Library's materials and services. A detailed table of contents and an index make the handbook especially easy to use.

What does this general guide have to say about borrowing and other circulation services? The first subheading under "Main Floor" services is "Circulation Department," where they are succinctly described:

All materials that circulate must be checked out at the circulation desk. A valid University identification card permits users to borrow library materials. Eligible library borrowers are faculty, staff, students (including Oxford College students), alumni, University Center students (who must have a valid interlibrary use card and proper identification), persons with a Visiting Scholar card, persons issued Local Researcher cards, and other authorized individuals.

Loan Periods: Books may be checked out to Emory faculty, staff and students for four weeks. The most recent issues of periodicals do not circulate. Bound periodicals shelved on the Main floor do not circulate. Bound periodicals shelved in the stacks may be borrowed for one day and are not renewed. If books are not overdue or have not been recalled by another patron, they may be renewed at the desk or by telephone. Borrowers must bring books to the circulation desk to renew after the third renewal. Only five books may be renewed per phone call.

Overdue Materials: The fine for overdue books is ten cents per day for each overdue book. The fine increases to fifty cents per day for an overdue book that is not returned when it has been requested by another borrower. The fine for each overdue periodical is fifty cents per day.[2]

In addition to the summary of policies above, there are references to special materials, services, and clients, scattered throughout the booklet:

1. New Books: Recently acquired books are shelved in the General Reference Reading Room. New books can be checked out at the Circulation Desk for two weeks.

2. Material in the pamphlet file may be borrowed from the library and may be checked out at the reference desk.

3. Books and serials shelved [in the Science Department] may be located through the card catalogs on the Main floor, and checked out at the circulation desk.

4. Those government documents which circulate can be checked out at the Documents reference desk.

5. Materials housed in Special Collections do *not* circulate outside the department, where there is ample reading space for researchers. . . . Some photocopying from the collections is permitted, subject to the regulations of the department.

6. Candler Library serves primarily as an audiovisual learning resources center for Emory College and the Graduate School of Arts and Sciences. In this capacity it provides a wide range of materials, equipment and services which may be utilized both within and without the classroom. . . . It includes a small general collection of printed materials, a reading room and an area where materials are kept on reserve for special circulation.

7. Interlibrary Loan: Emory students and faculty may request from other libraries materials not owned by Emory. Forms for requesting loans of books and purchases of journal articles are available at the General Reference Desk on the Main floor and in the Interlibrary Loan office nearby.

8. Interlibrary Use: . . . Emory belongs to a consortium of colleges and universities in the Atlanta-Athens area known as the University Center, Inc. This membership permits librarians in the General Reference Department to issue cards to Emory students and faculty authorizing their use of the libraries of member institutions. Such interlibrary use includes the privilege of borrowing materials subject to the circulation policies of the lending institution.

9. Service for the Handicapped: Handicapped persons are provided a number of special library services. Some of the special services provided by the General Libraries staff include . . . proxy checkout of library materials.[3]

Reserve room materials, a special circulation service particular to academic libraries, are treated in two ways: open and closed reserve. The handbook explains,

Reserve materials are withdrawn from regular circulation and placed in the Candler Library reading room, where they are made available to users in the following ways, as designated by the instructor. . . . Books placed on open reserve are located on designated shelves in the reading room. They may be used freely within the reading room or brought to the circulation desk [i.e., the Candler Library circulation desk] to be checked out for either one or three days. . . . Materials placed on closed reserve are located behind the circulation desk in the reading room. These materials may be checked out for two hours, one day, or three days, as designated. Most books and articles on two-hour closed reserve may be checked out overnight after 11 p.m. No audiovisual materials may be checked out overnight.[4]

Supplementing and further defining this information from the handbook are individual printed sheets covering general borrowing regulations for three categories of clients: Emory students and employees (Figure 2-1)[5]; faculty, trustees, librarians, and officers of the university (Figure 2-2)[6]; and guests (Figure 2-3).[7] Another four-page typed handout explains the interlibrary use policy in greater detail.[8] Although it would appear to permit faculty, staff, and students from any of the eleven participating institutions relatively free access to all the collections, many of its provisions require clients to prove their scholarly needs to the satisfaction of "authorized librarians."[9] User's cards have definite time limits with a twelve-month maximum for full-time faculty, the most privileged category, and allow individual libraries to put restrictions on access to their materials well beyond their normal practices.

For Emory students and faculty, the primary client groups using Woodruff Library, there are four major differences in privileges:

1. the need to present a valid identification or library card—students must but faculty do not

2. the extension of library privileges to spouses or proxies—mentioned only for faculty

3. the payment of fines—faculty are not fined except for nonreturn of books that have been recalled

4. the length of loan periods—faculty may keep ordinary circulating materials for a year, whereas students have four weeks. Of course, renewals extend the initial loan period to some degree, and there are certain specified exceptions, which are the same for all users.

Figure 2-1
Circulation Information Flyer

THE ROBERT W. WOODRUFF LIBRARY

Borrowing Regulations for Emory Students and Employees

I. **Classification**
   - A. Emory University students.
   - B. Emory University employees.
   - C. Oxford College students.

II. **General Borrowing Regulations**
   - A. Students must present a valid University identification card in order to withdraw library materials.
   - B. University employees must present a valid library card when withdrawing library materials. Staff library cards can be obtained at the Circulation Desk after employment verification.
   - C. Borrowing privileges are not transferable and do not extend to children of borrowers in this classification.
   - D. Students in this category may secure a University Center Interlibrary use card from one of the Reference Librarians. These cards are provided primarily to augment individual research when needed research material is not available at Emory.
   - E. All material checked out is subject to recall and must be returned by the specified date.
   - F. Students in this classification who need to use a library in another city may request a letter of introduction from the Reference Department.
   - G. Borrowers are responsible for material checked out until it is returned to the Library or section of the library from which it was borrowed.
   - H. Borrowers in this category may use any library on campus subject to the regulations governing that specific library.
   - I. Borrowers may have access to the stack floors. Upon presententation of a University ID card (students) or a staff card (employees), borrowers may purchase a coded card for admission to the restricted stack floors.
   - J. Books may be renewed if no one else has requested them.

III. **Loan Periods**
   - A. Books are checked out for four week loan periods.
   - B. Specialized journals other than the current issue, may be checked out for **one** day and are not renewable. Some journals do not circulate.
   - C. Books may be renewed by telephone if:
     1. books are not overdue;
     2. borrowers restrict themselves to renewing only five books per call;
     3. the books have not been recalled;
     4. the borrower agrees to bring the books to the Circulation Desk after the second phone renewal.
   - D. Government documents in the Document Center may be borrowed for two weeks and are renewable. Some documents are for reference only.

IV. **Overdue Books and Fines**
   - A. A fine of ten cents per day is charged for each overdue book.
   - B. Failure to return an overdue book requested by another borrower results in a fifty cents per day fine.
   - C. A fine of fifty cents per day is charged for each overdue periodical.
   - D. Student library records must be cleared by the end of each semester.
   - E. University employees with more than a $5.00 library record must clear their account or have their library privileges revoked.

V. **Lost or Damaged Books**
   Lost or damaged books must be paid for or replaced by the borrower.
   - A. Replacement charges for lost books: $15.00 plus $5.00 processing fee.
   - B. Damaged books: cost of repair; if not repairable, price of lost book as above.
   - C. Borrower may replace a lost or damaged book with a copy acceptable to the Library. plus $5.00 processing fee.

STUDENT REGISTRATION AND/OR TRANSCRIPTS ARE WITHHELD FOR OVERDUE BOOKS NOT RETURNED, FINES NOT PAID, AND LOST OR DAMAGED BOOKS NOT PAID.

Figure 2-2
Circulation Information Flyer

THE ROBERT W. WOODRUFF LIBRARY

Borrowing Regulations for Faculty, Trustees, Librarians, and Officers of the University

I. Classification
   A. Members of the Board of Trustees. (See Official List)
   B. Officers of the University. (See Bulletin)
   C. Members of the instructional staff with the rank of instructor or higher. (See Bulletin or Directory)
   D. Clinical faculty of the School of Medicine. (See Medical School Bulletin or Medical Library ID card)
   E. Emory University Librarians.
   F. Emeritus faculty. (See Bulletin)
   G. Postdoctoral fellows working under Emory faculty.
   H. All spouses of the above mentioned patrons.

II. General Borrowing Regulations
   A. Borrowers in this classification wishing to withdraw library materials must:
   1. present a valid library or University identification card;
   2. be listed in the appropriate directory or bulletin;
   3. present a letter from their department chairman or their dean;
   4. present a note from the professor under whom they are working (for postdoctoral fellows).
   B. Wives and husbands of borrowers in this category must apply for library privileges with their spouse who must have valid authorization.
   C. Borrowing privileges are not transferable and do not extend to children of patrons in this classification. If for some reason the borrower cannot come to the library, the Circulation Department will approve a proxy letter to a member of their staff, but the person signing the authorization is responsible for the return of all material and is expected to respond to all recall notices, replacement bills, and other queries.
   D. All material checked out is subject to recall and should be returned by the specified date. Patrons not adhering to this policy will be referred, as appropriate, to their Department Chairman, the Dean of the School or College, or the Vice-President and Dean of Faculties.
   E. Borrowers in this category may request a letter of introduction from the Reference Department for other libraries which they need to use for research purposes.
   F. An interlibrary use card may be secured from a Reference librarian for borrowers who need to use other University Center libraries for materials not available at Emory.
   G. Borrowers are responsible for material checked out until it is returned to the appropriate library or department.
   H. Borrowers may use any library on campus subject to the regulations of that specific library.
   I. Borrowers may have access to stack floors. Upon presentation of a University ID card, borrowers may purchase a coded admission card at the Circulation Desk for entrance into the restricted stack area.
   J. Borrowers in this classification are not assessed overdue fines, except for recalled books requested by another borrower.

III. Loan Periods
   A. All circulating material is subject to yearly renewal.
   B. Limited circulation:
   1. specialized journals, other than the current issue, may be checked out for **one** day and are not renewable. Some journals do not circulate.
   2. government documents in the Document Center may be borrowed for two weeks and are renewable. Some documents are for reference only.

IV. Overdue Books and Fines.
   1. Failure to return an overdue book requested by another borrower results in a fifty cents per day fine.

V. Lost or damaged books must be replaced by the borrower.
   1. Replacement charges for lost books: $15.00 plus $5.00 processing fee.
   2. Damaged books: cost of repair; if not repairable, price of lost book as above.
   3. Borrower may replace lost or damaged book with a copy acceptable to the Library, plus $5.00 processing fee.
   4. If not paid or replaced, the request will be referred, as appropriate, to the Chairman of the Department, the Dean of the School or College, or the Vice-President and Dean of Faculties.

Figure 2-3
Circulation Information Flyer

THE ROBERT W. WOODRUFF LIBRARY

Borrowing Regulations for Guests

I. Classification

A. A person having Alumni status at Emory.
B. University Center students with a valid interlibrary use card and proper school identification.
C. Persons issued Visiting Scholar cards.
D. Persons issued Local Researcher cards.
E. Friends of the Library.
F. Student or Staff Spouse.
G. Other authorized groups.

II. General Borrowing Regulations

A. Borrowers in this classification must present a valid guest card which is issued at the Circulation Desk or by the appropriate Library Department. Local Researcher cards are issued to qualified applicants by Reference Librarians, the Supervisor, and the Associate Supervisor of Circulation Services.
B. Borrowing privileges are not transferable and must be exercised personally.
C. Borrowing privileges do not extend to periodicals.
D. Only five books may be checked out to persons in this category.
E. Books requested for recall must be returned by the specified date.
F. Borrowers are responsible for material checked out until it is returned to the Library or section of the library from which it was borrowed.
G. Persons not adhering to borrowing regulations will have privileges revoked.
H. Borrowers in this category may have access to the stack floors if they present the proper, valid identification.
I. Books may be renewed if no one else has requested them.

III. Loan Periods

A. Books are checked out for two week loan periods.

B. Books may be renewed by telephone if:

   1. books are not overdue;
   2. the books have not been recalled;
   3. the borrower agrees to bring the books to the Circulation Desk after the second renewal.

C. Government documents in the Document Center may be borrowed for two weeks and are renewable. Some documents are for reference only.

IV. Overdue Books and Fines

A. A fine of ten cents per day is charged for each overdue book.
B. Failure to return an overdue book requested by another borrower results in a fifty cents per day fine.

V. Lost or Damaged Books

Lost or damaged books must be paid for or replaced by the borrower.
A. The replacement charges for lost books: $15.00 plus $5.00 processing fee.
B. Damaged books: cost of repair; if not repairable, price of lost book as above.
C. Borrower may replace a lost or damaged book with a copy acceptable to the Library, plus $5.00 processing fee.

LIBRARY PRIVILEGES WILL BE WITHHELD AFTER ACCRUAL OF MORE THAN $5.00 FOR FINES AND/OR PAYMENT FOR LOST BOOKS.

Other than these, all client groups are treated alike: All must purchase stack entry cards to gain access to the books, all are charged the same fees for lost materials ($15.00 per book plus a $5.00 processing fee), and all have the same access to periodicals. If faculty neglect to pay for lost or damaged materials, they are threatened with referral to their department chairs or deans; if students do not pay, they face blocking of registration or transcript services.

Guest privileges, extended to Emory alumni, friends of the library, student/staff spouses, visiting scholars, local researchers, interlibrary use card holders and others, are extended if a guest card is obtained. Guests are limited to five books for two weeks, which may be renewed if the books have not been requested by another borrower.

Emory answers the circulation question of who may borrow rather liberally, even extending some privileges to students' spouses and outsiders. Essentially, they may borrow books, with newer titles limited to half the regular loan period. The removal of periodicals, government documents, and audiovisual materials from the library is strictly limited. The question of how materials are borrowed is answered in very different ways for the three client categories, with greater privileges and convenience for the faculty than for the students. If student renewal privileges are counted, the gap between their loans and faculty loans is narrowed somewhat. Guests are extremely limited in their borrowing, however, in both the number of items and the length of loans.

Columbia University

Columbia University in New York City is a private institution with diverse clients and collections, is an Association of Research Libraries' member, and is located in a large city. Columbia provides, however, a far less dramatic-looking general circulation brochure titled "Circulation and Borrowing Information." This concise black-and-white foldout explains the basic policies (Figure 2-4).[10] The document also contains tables summarizing borrowing privileges for its three primary clienteles, which are somewhat different than Emory's: (1) students and staff, (2) doctoral candidates, and (3) faculty and officers. These circulation rules are in effect at Barnard College, Teachers College, and twenty-eight departmental libraries, in addition to Columbia's main general agency, Butler Library. Fine schedules, hours of service, and telephone extensions are included in the brochure. Full borrowing privileges are extended to Columbia University ID cardholders at the Union Theological Seminary as well as at Barnard and Teachers colleges.

A smaller brochure prepared for visitors lists five categories of visitor, including alumni of Columbia and its three affiliates, "qualified" residents or nonresidents of the New York City metropolitan area, visiting scholars,

Figure 2-4
Client Circulation Brochure

Circulation

and

Borrowing

Information

Avery • Biological Sciences • Burgess/
Carpenter • Business/Economics • Chemistry
• Circulation • College • College Study Hall
• Columbiana • Documents Service Center •
East Asian • Engineering • Geology • Geo-
science • Health Sciences • Interlibrary Loan
• Journalism • Law • Lehman • Library Infor-
mation Office • Library Service • Math/
Science • Microform Reading Room • Music
• Paterno • Periodical Reading Room •
Philosophy • Physics/Astronomy • Psychology
• Rare Book & Manuscript • Reference (Butler)
• Social Work • Barnard College •
Teachers College • Union Theological Seminary

Research Library Group (RLG) participants, and participants of the New York Metropolitan Reference & Research Library Agency (METRO).[11] The basic privilege being extended to four of the five visitor categories is the use of materials within the building, called reading privileges. Only visiting scholars—persons with official status conferred by virtue of being appointed by a dean or department chair—may actually borrow materials without the payment of additional fees. City residents and consortia members are expected to determine whether the holdings of the New York Public Library will satisfy them before they approach Columbia, and, even when reading cards are issued, they carry time limits of two weeks. Alumni have a year's reading privileges free and they may renew them. Other visitors must pay $75 a month when their two weeks expire, and the fee does not include interlibrary loan, database services, or blanket use of the affiliates.[12]

Columbia University Libraries have many printed brochures and bulletins, frequently formatted as flyers, but also in other formats. One pamphlet describes Columbia's participation in RLG, METRO, and the Center for Research Libraries (CRL) and contains a brief description of privileges accorded to Columbia clients at other RLG libraries:

On-Site Access. Columbia faculty, students, and staff are eligible for service at other RLG libraries upon presentation of a Columbia ID validated for the current semester or academic year. Readers who plan to visit another library on weekends, evenings, or during holiday periods should first check with local reference staffs so that special arrangements may be made if necessary. Specific requests may be sent ahead via an RLIN [Research Libraries Information Network] Electronic Mail System to ensure that material will be available for use on a specified date. Columbia users at other RLG institutions will be given the same reading and stack access as local readers of the same academic status or affiliation, with the possible exception of stack access for undergraduates. Borrowing privileges are not included in the on-site access program, but may be arranged in accordance with local library policies.[13]

Turning again to Columbia's primary clientele, students and faculty, a comprehensive, liberally illustrated, eight-page insert in the *Columbia University Record,* a weekly campus newspaper, titled "An Introduction to the Columbia University Libraries," explains most services including instructional programs, database services, reserves, specialized collections and materials (which are also described more fully in a handsome pamphlet costing $1.50), services to the handicapped, and outside resources available through cooperative programs.[14] This handy booklet concentrates on introductions and does not attempt to outline or duplicate the information in the circulation booklet. It does tell readers where to find the additional rules and regulations and includes hours, phone numbers, and a map for easy access to the buildings and collections. Individual topics are covered in a plethora of flyers, e.g., schedule of fines,[15] copying services,[16] and reserve room procedures.[17] Some of these are also reproduced in smaller size, such as bookmark size, either by reducing the size of the original or by consolidating the information into more concise terms, as shown in Figures 2-5A and 2-5B.

The primary difference among the three categories of client appears to be the length of time for which materials can be borrowed. Sometimes these differences are very slight: a student may borrow a book from the East Asian Library for four weeks; a doctoral candidate, for one semester; and a faculty member, for three months—depending on the timing, doctoral candidates may actually be granted a longer or shorter borrowing period than faculty or students. Many items do not circulate to anyone. Renewals may or may not be permitted depending on the item and the collection.

Fines are not levied on faculty, although this is not explicitly stated in the basic documents. Unlike at Emory, faculty must present their ID cards to be served, perhaps because of the larger size of the institution with its larger faculty. Though the circulation brochure indicates punishments only for students (prevention of registration, receipt of diplomas, and transcript services), Columbia's staff manual deals at length with treatment of faculty who do not cooperate by returning materials when requested by others or who keep materials long past a required due date. Though the emphasis was on inducing the person to cooperate, measures designed to bring pressure to bear included notification of department chairs or deans and blocking the person's ID number.

Borrowing at Columbia University Libraries was extended beyond its primary clientele with reluctance and only upon payment of fees. Within the university family, doctoral students were accorded special privileges, though not as many as faculty; students were given the least flexibility and the fewest privileges.

Graduate School of Education, Harvard University

Circulation information disseminated by the Monroe C. Gutman Library at Harvard University in Cambridge, Massachusetts, serving its Graduate School of Education, was much simpler than Emory's or Columbia's (see Figure 2-6).[18] This could be expected for a single unit within a large university library system, especially one in which there were no undergraduate students.

Gutman's stated rules give any client a virtually unlimited length of time with materials by permitting unlimited renewals for anything that circulates regardless of the client's status, although additional privileges could be granted to faculty of the school and the university. The only limitations on these liberal borrowing policies are that the items cannot be overdue or

Figure 2-5

A. Client Flyer, Information Reduced in Size

B. Information Summarized

LIBRARY	Monday-Thursday	Friday	Saturday	Sunday
Avery, x3501	9 am-11 pm	9 am-5 pm	12 noon-6 pm	2 pm-10 pm
Biological Sciences, x4715	9 am-9 pm	9 am-5 pm	12 noon-5 pm	2 pm-10 pm
Burgess/Carpenter, x4710	9 am-11 pm	9 am-7 pm	12 noon-5 pm	2 pm-10 pm
Business/Economics, x3383	8:30 am-11 pm	8:30 am-10 pm	10 am-6 pm	12 noon-8 pm
Study Hall	8:30 am-9 am. Business/Economics is open for Study Hall only			
Chemistry, x4709	9 am-9 pm	9 am-5 pm	12 noon-5 pm	CLOSED
Circulation, Butler, x2235	9 am-11 pm	9 am-7 pm	12 noon-5 pm	2 pm-10 pm
College, x5327	9 am-11 pm	9 am-7 pm	12 noon-5 pm	2 pm-10 pm
College Study Hall (no services — ID required)	11 pm-2 am	—	5 pm-11 pm	10 am-2 pm & 10 pm-2 am
Columbiana, x3786	1 pm-5 pm	1 pm-5 pm	CLOSED	CLOSED
Documents Service Center, x5002	9 am-9 pm	9 am-5 pm	12 noon-5 pm	2 pm-10 pm
East Asian, x4319	9 am-9 pm	9 am-5 pm	12 noon-5 pm	CLOSED
Engineering, x3206	9 am-9 pm	9 am-5 pm	12 noon-5 pm	CLOSED
Geology, x4713	10 am-6 pm	10 am-5 pm	2 pm-5 pm	CLOSED
Geoscience, x95-208	9 am-5 pm	9 am-5 pm	CLOSED	CLOSED
Health Sciences, x92-3692	8:30 am-11 pm	8:30 am-11 pm	9 am-5 pm	12 noon-10 pm
Interlibrary Loan, x3542	9 am-5 pm	9 am-5 pm	CLOSED	CLOSED
Journalism, x3860	9 am-10 pm	9 am-5 pm	10 am-5 pm	1 pm-5 pm
Law, x3743	8:30 am-12 midn.	8:30 am-12 midn.	9 am-7 pm	12 noon-12 midn.
Lehman, x5087	9 am-11 pm	9 am-7 pm	12 noon-5 pm	2 pm-10 pm
Library Information Office, x2271	9 am-6 pm	9 am-6 pm	12 noon-5 pm	CLOSED
Library Service, x3543	9 am-11 pm	9 am-7 pm	12 noon-5 pm	2 pm-10 pm
Math/Science, x4712	9 am-9 pm	9 am-6 pm	12 noon-5 pm	CLOSED
Microform Reading Room, x5328	9 am-11 pm	9 am-7 pm	12 noon-5 pm	2 pm-10 pm
Music, x4711	9 am-9 pm	9 am-5 pm	12 noon-5 pm	CLOSED
Paterno, x2307	10 am-6 pm	10 am-6 pm	CLOSED	CLOSED
Periodical Reading Room, x4704	9 am-11 pm	9 am-7 pm	12 noon-5 pm	2 pm-10 pm
Philosophy, x2259	9 am-9 pm	9 am-5 pm	12 noon-5 pm	CLOSED
Physics, x3943	9 am-10 pm	9 am-10 pm	12 noon-5 pm	CLOSED
Psychology, x4714	9 am-10 pm	9 am-5 pm	12 noon-5 pm	2 pm-10 pm
Rare Book & Manuscript Manuscript Reading Room, x2231	9 am-5 pm	9 am-5 pm	CLOSED	CLOSED
Rare Book Reading Room, x3528	9 am-5 pm	9 am-5 pm	12 noon-5 pm	CLOSED
Reference, Butler, x2241	9 am-11 pm	9 am-7 pm	12 noon-5 pm	2 pm-10 pm
Social Work, x5159	9 am-11 pm	9 am-7 pm	12 noon-5 pm	2 pm-10 pm

LIBRARY	Monday-Thursday	Friday	Saturday	Sunday
Barnard, x3953	*8:45 am-10 pm	8:45 am-6 pm	12 noon-5 pm	*1 pm-6 pm
	*Barnard Reserve Room stays open until 11 pm Sunday through Thursday nights			
Teachers College, 678-3494	**10 am-9:30 pm	10 am-6 pm	10 am-6 pm	1 pm-5 pm
	**Instructional Materials and Media Center closes at 9 pm, Monday-Thursday			
Union Theological Seminary, 662-7100	9 am-10:00 pm	9 am-5 pm	9 am-5 pm	CLOSED

HOURS CHANGE DURING EXAM, INTERSESSION AND SUMMER SESSION PERIODS. CONSULT POSTED SCHEDULES.

At the Circulation Desk...

Books circulate for 4 weeks.
    They may be renewed indefinitely
    so long as no one else requests
    them. Telephone renewals will
    be taken for up to three titles;
    otherwise, bring the books(s) or
    a list of the call numbers to
    the Circulation Desk.

    Fines will be reduced by half
    if they are paid at the time you
    return the overdue item(s).

Most reserve books circulate for
    2 hours, although a few are on
    longer loan periods. They may
    be checked out overnight 1 hour
    before closing time, and are
    due at 9am the next morning.

    Fines for reserves are posted
    at the Circulation Desk.

Interlibrary loan service is
    provided for books or journals
    not available within the
    Harvard library system.

Circulation Desk telephone number:
    495-3423.

Remember--The Circulation Desk
Closes 15 minutes before the
posted Library closing time.

needed for reserves or another request and that the number of phone renewals cannot exceed three. A list of more than three titles to be renewed is honored at the desk to eliminate the need for dragging in a large number of heavy tomes every four weeks.

The fine schedule at Gutman, reflecting the liberal thrust of its borrowing policy, is confined to flat fees per item per notice (Figure 2-7). It becomes truly punitive only when notices are ignored—the charge for a lost item is $35 including processing fees. Debtors' borrowing privileges are suspended. Though not explicitly stated, faculty are exempt from fines and, therefore, also from other punishments associated with nonpayment of fines.

Agnes Scott College

Policies directed at specific clienteles using the McCain Library at Agnes Scott College, a private, four-year, liberal arts institution for women located in Decatur, Georgia, appear in its "Faculty Handbook" and "Student Handbook."[19] The primary difference in service between the faculty and students is the length of the borrowing period. Faculty have an unlimited amount of time; students are given two weeks with an option to renew the books, in person only, unless the books are requested by another person. Faculty are expected to return requested items promptly, and, since there is no due date, there are no faculty fines. A browsing collection containing new books has a limited circulation of two weeks for all clients, without options to renew. According to the "Faculty Handbook," "A fine of ten cents per day was [to be] collected for overdue books,"[20] presumably for items with due dates (books from the browsing collection) or materials that have been recalled.

Placing books on reserve at McCain Library is not a complex process, and faculty are urged to give the library such desired titles "several days before the books were needed,"[21] in contrast to the much more elaborate procedures required at Columbia and Emory where forms must be filled out weeks in advance of actual use. At Columbia and also at Harvard's Gutman Library, where they are processed by computer, reserve lists must be submitted several weeks before a semester begins. Sometimes, the items are not permitted to circulate normally even during semesters when the classes for which they are designated are not being taught. At Emory, reserves are not located in the Woodruff Library, but in a nearby building, the Candler Library. Thus, for these institutions, reserve collections involve major relocation and processing of materials.

McCain Library, like the larger university libraries, charge students more for overdue reserve books than for ordinary circulating or browsing collection materials, with charges mounting by the hour instead of by the day.

Figure 2-7
Fine Policies

MONROE C. GUTMAN LIBRARY

GENERAL CIRCULATION PROCEDURES

* CIRCULATION ITEMS: Books, theses, and microfiche circulate for four weeks.
  These items are subject to recall after ten days, if needed by another
  borrower, or immediately, if needed for reserve. (Beginning on the eighth
  day after notification, recalled books are fined at the rate of $1 per day
  when needed by another patron, and $2 when the book is recalled for reserve.)

* NON-CIRCULATING ITEMS: Periodicals, reference books, and Qualifying Papers
  must be used in the library. With special permission, periodicals may be
  signed out for up to three hours during the day for the purpose of
  photocopying.

* RENEWALS: All circulation items can be renewed indefinitely if not needed
  for Reserve or for another borrower. A renewal should be requested within
  a day or two of the due date, since an overdue notice is sent when a book
  is several days overdue.

  A telephone request is honored only if no overdue notices have been sent.
  Since we can handle only a few books by phone, if you have many books to
  renew, please bring in a list of the books, including call numbers.

* OVERDUE BOOKS AND FINES

  FIRST NOTICE of an overdue book is sent when an item is four to eleven days
  overdue. There is a fine of $2 per book for the first overdue notice.

  SECOND NOTICE of an overdue book is sent two weeks after the first notice.
  There is a fine of $5 per book for the second notice.

  PLEASE NOTE: ALL OVERDUE FINES WHICH ARE PAID IN PERSON PRIOR TO
                BILLING WILL BE REDUCED BY 50%. (Fines will be $1 for
                the first overdue notice, and $2.50 for the second.)

  If the book is still not returned within two weeks of the second notice, you
  will be billed for the book as though it were lost. Lost books are billed at
  $35 per book, which includes the cost of replacing the book, processing fees,
  and late fines. If you return a book after you have been billed for it, you
  will be liable for the $5 late fine and $10 searching, term billing and
  crediting fee.

* SUSPENSION OF BORROWING PRIVILEGES: Borrowers who have not returned overdue
  books and/or who have fines outstanding will have their borrowing privileges
  temporarily suspended until the indebtedness is satisfied.

* MISSING BOOKS: Please check at the Circulation Desk for any book you cannot
  find in the stacks. We can tell you if the book is on Reserve or checked out.

* RESERVATIONS: If a book has been checked out for at least ten days, we can
  recall it for you. The borrower is given one week in which to return the
  book, or a $1 per day fine is incurred. You will be notified when a book
  is being held for you.

* SEARCHES: We will be glad to look for any book you are unable to find. You
  will be notified of the results of our search.

9/83

Nazareth College of Rochester

Like Agnes Scott College, the Lorette Wilmot Library of Nazareth College of Rochester, New York, has simpler rules for circulation, which are summarized in a brief printed handout for students (Figure 2-8).[22] The four-page foldout brochure does not distinguish between faculty, staff, and students, indicating only the need for a college ID to borrow books. Fine rates are low, but they double when a second week of overdue status is reached—from five to ten cents per day. The overdue fine for reserve books is 25 cents per hour. A look at the library's floor plan indicates that nonbook media, including periodicals which, with a few exceptions, do not circulate, occupy nearly half of the library's space. Both the importance of noncirculating materials and the simplification of rules for those that could be borrowed indicate Wilmot Library's greater emphasis on service over materials, with the amount of effort (and money) spent on the functioning of a circulation operation kept to a minimum.

University of Bridgeport

A similar simplification can be found in other private institutions, too. Examination of the University of Bridgeport's (in Bridgeport, Connecticut) publicly disseminated circulation policy statement demonstrated this (Figure 2-9).[23] In this policy statement, two categories of borrower and two categories of material are recognized. Renewals are permitted only once and only for faculty/administration borrowers. What is distinctive about the University of Bridgeport's policy is the incorporation of guests— presumably including local residents or business people, students from nearby colleges and universities, and others—into the category with students, support staff of the university, and interlibrary loan borrowers. While such major institutions as Columbia, New York University, and Princeton are becoming more restrictive in their policies regarding physical access beyond primary clienteles, others, like the University of Bridgeport, are finding it advantageous to permit or even encourage use of their collections by persons totally unaffiliated with the institution but either living or working within its environs.

The University of Bridgeport's Wahlstrom Library, like Gutman Library, revokes library privileges when rules are ignored for more than six weeks, making it difficult to build up large amounts of either materials or fines owed. This would seem a relatively simple method of dealing with one of academe's worst offenders, the faculty member who abuses circulation privileges. Like many other academic libraries, Wahlstrom charges a $5 processing fee for lost books, in addition to a sliding scale of replacement charges for all materials ranging from $2 to $30 unless a price is listed for the work in *Books in Print.*

THE LORETTE WILMOT LIBRARY

Welcome to the Lorette Wilmot Library, the learning resources center of Nazareth College of Rochester. We hope you will use the books, periodicals, media resources, facilities and services of this library freely and often. We ask that you observe a few simple regulations:

- No food or drink in the library except in the Late Night Study area.

- No smoking in any part of the library.

- Use your ID to borrow all materials; you will be responsible for all use made of your ID.

- Please be considerate of your fellow students in using the building and the collections.

HOURS: Regular Term

Monday-Thursday	8:00 a.m. - 11:00 p.m.
Friday	8:00 a.m. - 10:00 p.m.
Saturday	10:00 a.m. - 10:00 p.m.
Sunday	12:00 noon - 11:00 p.m.

Media Center hours are now the same as library hours. Media materials are obtained at the new Media Materials Desk. Please arrange for media equipment loans, duplications, and room reservations at the Media Center Office.

The LATE NIGHT STUDY is open every night until 2:00 a.m. unless otherwise posted. HOLIDAY AND VACATION HOURS are announced at the entrance.

Figure 2-9
University of Bridgeport
Magnus Wahlstrom Library:
The University Library Circulation Policy

<u>Circulating Materials</u>

One month, no renewal   UB Students, UB Support Personnel,
                                        Guest Borrowers, Interlibrary Loan

One semester, one renewal   UB Faculty, UB Administrative Personnel

<u>Reserve Materials</u>

UB Students and Personnel need appropriate ID

Non-UB need appropriate ID: e.g, Driver's License

Two Hours   Reserve Reading Room only

Overnight   Borrowed two hours prior to closing and returned
                 one hour after opening the following morning.

One Day   Borrowed any time during the day or evening. Due
                 any time the following day or evening.

Three Days   Borrowed any time during the day or evening. Due
                 any time on the third day or evening.

<u>Overdue Fines</u>

Circulating materials - 10¢ per day not to exceed $30. If the material is
overdue six weeks after the due date, borrowing privilege will be revoked
and Bursar will be notified to freeze transcript.

Reserve materials - $1.00 per day not to exceed $30. When the material is
overdue six weeks after the due date, borrowing privilege will be revoked
and Bursar will be notified to freeze transcript.

<u>Lost Material Fines</u>

Book - Price of the book listed in Books in Print plus a $5 processing charge.
If not listed in Books in Print, $30 will be charged; $10 for Curriculum materials,
Juvenile books, Paperback books.

Tapes and Records - $10 will be charged.

Reserve Photocopy Articles - $2 will be charged.

<u>General Information</u>

Materials are subject to recall if needed for Reserve or when requested by another
user. Materials must be returned within one week of the date of the Recall notice.

Reserve materials must be returned no later than 15 minutes befdore the Library
closes.

Circulating materials must be checked out no later than 15 minutes before the
Library closes.

9/83

Whitworth College

A brief, but attractive library guide from Whitworth College's Cowles Library in Spokane, Washington, summarizes circulation policy on the cover page, following the hours of service:

General books circulate for two weeks and may be renewed. Renewed books may be recalled upon request. Most periodicals circulate for two weeks, and are not renewable. There is no limit on the number of books that may be borrowed by eligible persons. Your student ID card is also your library card. Anyone may use the library materials in the building. Borrowing privileges are extended to all registered students, faculty, alumni and employees of the College, as well as registered students at cooperating colleges. Non-members, however, must have special cards in order to borrow library materials. An annual fee of $5.00 is charged for this privilege, and cards may be obtained at the Loan Desk.[24]

On the fourth and final page is Whitworth's fine policy. In keeping with a generally liberal policy, *no fines* are charged for non-reserve materials kept longer than the designated due date. Only if three overdue notices, the final one including information about charges for nonreturn, are ignored, is a bill issued and transcripts restricted. Reserve materials are divided into two categories: those designated for two- or three-hour loans generate overdue fees at the rate of 25 cents per hour and those circulating for a day or more are charged at the rate of 25 cents per day.

All information from Whitworth College applied specifically to students. It was not indicated whether the same rules applied to the other borrowers mentioned (faculty, staff, and nonaffiliated clients), but the student rules were very nearly the same, except for the length of the loan period, as privileges extended only to faculty by other academic libraries. Even the fee for borrowing required of "non-members" was minimal, to say the least, and would hardly constitute much of a deterrent to use.

An interlibrary loan document from Whitworth provides for a great variety of requests with or without accompanying forms. Telephone and electronic mail requests are honored as are telephone renewals. The only restricted materials are those in the college archives and musical scores.

On the whole, Whitworth's policies are uncomplicated and service oriented. Charges are minimal, and the primary goal for them appears to be to get materials back or, if that is not possible, to obtain the wherewithal to replace them.

All of the libraries in the academic group discussed thus far are part of private institutions. They include colleges and universities; single-sex and coeducational student bodies; very diverse communities as well as relatively homogeneous ones; and graduate-only, graduate and undergraduate, and undergraduate-only clienteles. The next section discribes five public institutions whose attributes, while not as diverse, represent differences in sizes and programs.

PUBLIC ACADEMIC INSTITUTIONS

Mankato State University

Mankato State University, located in Mankato, Minnesota, has prepared attractive, illustrated, color-coded guides to the library in blue/gray/white for students[25] and in orange/gold/beige/white for faculty.[26] Organized a little differently for each clientele, both brochures end with very different expositions of policies and procedures governing circulation (Figures 2-10 and 2-11). Faculty at Mankato State are, indeed, more privileged, not only in having no mention made of fines or other penalties for infraction of the rules, but also in being able to borrow periodicals (overnight) and all other circulating items for a full quarter instead of the one-day to three-week loans (depending on the material) accorded to student borrowers.

Figure 2-10
Mankato (MN) State University

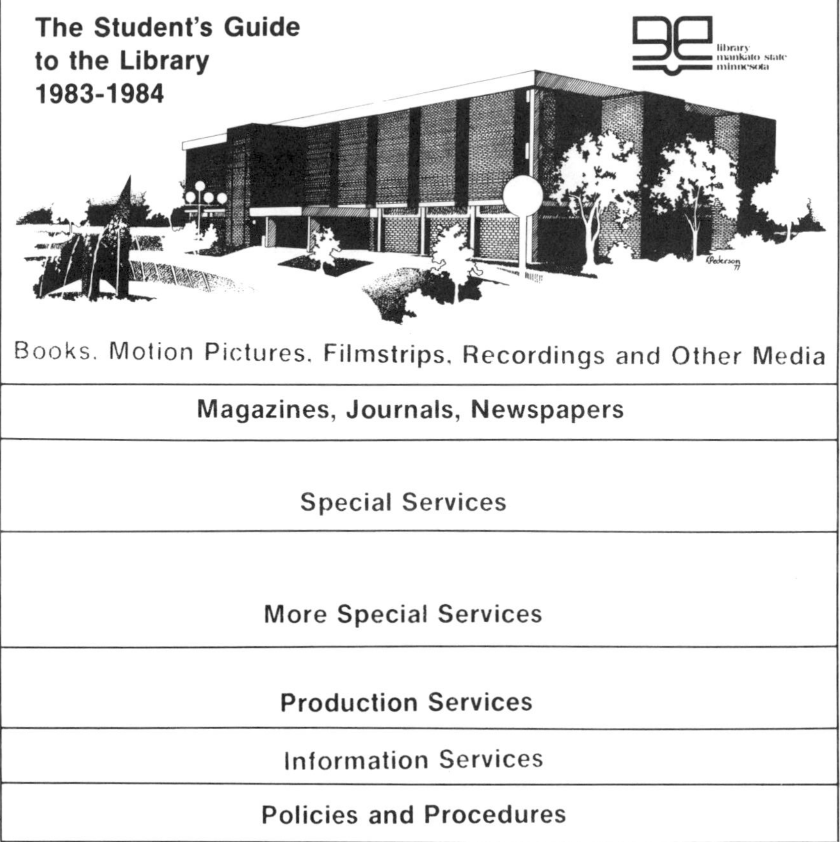

A number of interesting points are covered in these policies. First, any person with a valid *public library* card is served at Mankato State, as well as students and staff from *all* Minnesota colleges and universities, whether public or private. Everyone is given borrowing privileges, not just reading privileges (use of materials within the building), in contrast to the private universities' extension of borrowing privileges only after payment of fees.

Second, the borrowing periods seem extremely complex and, in general, rather limited, though renewals are permitted. Fines, on the other hand, appear to accumulate to the replacement cost plus $5, making it an unprofitable exercise to hold items overdue. Students are threatened with the usual triple whammy of withholding registration, transcripts, and grades.

A large proportion of the information in the faculty brochure is devoted to putting onto faculty shoulders and removing from the library all

Figure 2-11
Mankato (MN) State University

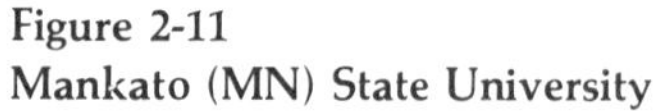

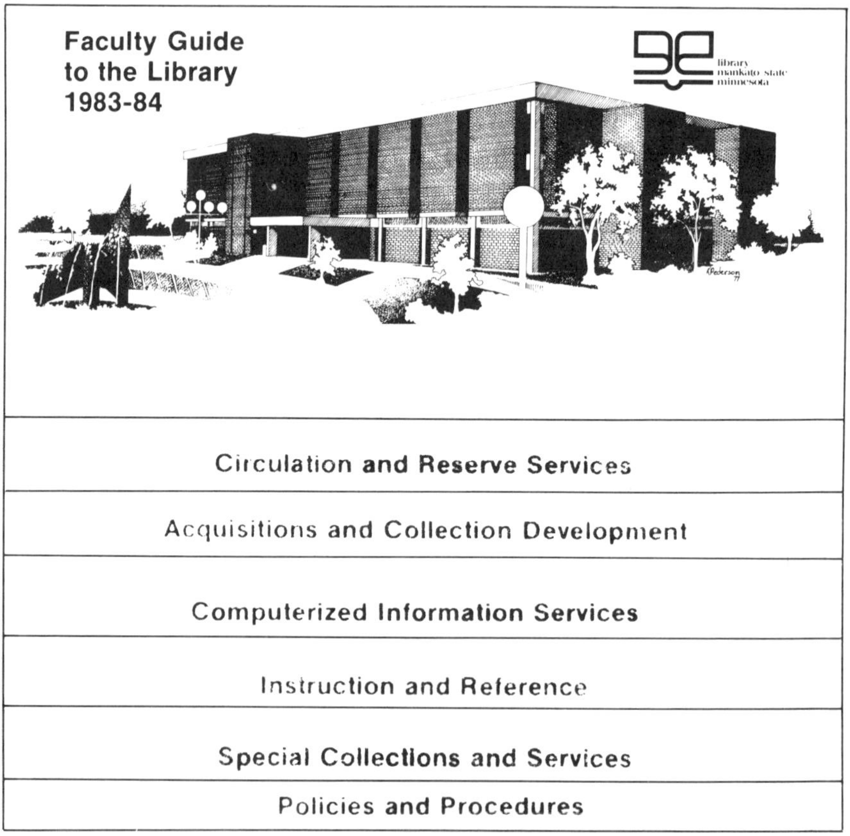

Faculty Guide to the Library 1983-84

library mankato state minnesota

Circulation and Reserve Services

Acquisitions and Collection Development

Computerized Information Services

Instruction and Reference

Special Collections and Services

Policies and Procedures

obligations and responsibility for compliance with the copyright code in connection with reserve materials. Also, the library maintains the right to remove any materials from reserve that were not used at least five times in a quarter. Though several other institutions explicitly declare only *required* readings are to be put on reserve, Mankato monitors use and takes steps to ensure it. One humorous note is a sentence that reads: "Only required, non-textual readings should be placed on reserve," which could be taken to mean picture books only, rather than non-textbooks, as intended.

One final departure from the usual are the several references to borrowing equipment including audiovisual, microcomputer, and television equipment as well as microreaders. Many academic libraries solve the problem of lending nonbook hardware by restricting the use of the software to a media laboratory or center. Mankato State has made the more liberal decision to allow these items to circulate along with the necessary playback/projection equipment.

Throughout these brochures, the importance of nonbook media materials and their equality with books as information resources are evident. In the faculty guide, a section enumerating circulation staff and their various responsibilities lists books simply as one of six different categories, including government publications, maps, periodicals, audiovisual and Minnesota materials. Under the reserve services list, "printed materials" followed "audio tapes/learning kits,"[27] which might lead one to speculate on the relative importance of the two categories. In the student guide, the first section titled "Books, Motion Pictures, Filmstrips, Recordings, and Other Media,"[28] is devoted to an explanation of the omnimedia online catalog in which entries for all of these types of materials appear. Mankato's commitment to an integration of resources in all physical forms is clearly reflected in its circulation policies.

University of North Florida

At the Thomas G. Carpenter Library of the University of North Florida, in Jacksonville, Florida, a six-page foldout brochure titled "Borrowing Regulations, Policies and Procedures (Summarized from the University of North Florida Lending Code)"[29] contains the library's policies and procedures (Figure 2-12). The brochure democratically declares that "All borrowers, including faculty and staff, are subject to library fines and charges."[30] The only special privileges accorded faculty are term-long borrowing periods; others receive only two-week loans. Of the six pages in the summary handout, more than three (or over 50 percent of the text) are devoted to a discussion of fines, payments, and appeals, leading this researcher to believe that this was a topic of greater importance at this university than at most of the other institutions described.

BORROWING REGULATIONS, POLICIES AND PROCEDURES

(Summarized from the UNF Library Lending Code)

Under Florida laws and regulations the Library is accountable for its inventory. This accountability is transferred to the borrower at the time material is checked out and remains with the borrower until the material is both returned and the check-in transaction is completed. While the materials are checked out to a borrower the financial responsibility and accountability for the property lies with the borrower. The application process must fully demonstrate accountability before borrowing privileges will be extended.

LIBRARY CHARGE CARDS are issued quarterly to all eligible University of North Florida borrowers. Researchers who are not currently affiliated with UNF should apply at the Circulation Desk. Quarterly application is required so that the Library may maintain accurate records for accountability. Library registration records are protected as confidential information under Florida statutes.

Library charge cards are not transferable. Use of the charge card by proxy is reserved for UNF faculty and the physically handicapped upon advance notice. Other identification in addition to the Library card may be required before materials may be checked out.

Lost Cards. Until the Library is notified of a lost library card, the borrower is responsible for all loans made with that card. Limits of liability are defined by the prevailing credit laws.

Some other departures from practice elsewhere are the explicit refusal to renew books unless they are physically brought to the original chargeout point (probably more of a hardship on faculty and graduate students than on undergraduates); the grace period of eight days before overdue fines are charged; the statement that sending overdue notices was *not* a library obligation, but merely a courtesy, putting the entire burden of responsibility for returning things on time clearly in the client's lap; the declaration that clients are held responsible for that elusive category of material, the "claims returned" (the items a person claims to have returned but the library has not discharged); and, finally, notice that fines and other charges are paid to the university's financial offices, not to the library. This far brisker, no-nonsense, "business-is-business" approach is a remarkable departure from the gentler tenor of most academic library policy statements.

All of these policies are based on an opening declaration of accountability for library inventory required under the laws of the State of Florida. Since it has been in force for more than three years (as of this writing) without alteration, one can only conclude it has been successfully implemented.

Beyond those points already mentioned, two other features of the University of North Florida's policy stand out: First, the place of the library card and, second, the role of the computerized circulation control system. These elements are, to some degree, related to one another. The policy summary includes a rather detailed description of the issuing and use of library cards (see Figure 2-13).[31] Carpenter Library issues library cards quarterly—a costly and, one would imagine, a largely redundant operation over the course of a single academic year of three or four quarters—unless continuing faculty, students, and staff are allowed to retain the same card. Most academic libraries allow the university ID card to double as a library card, saving themselves a major registration effort apart from that already required by the institution for the usual purposes. The reason for Carpenter's unusual number of re-registrations is stated as follows: "so that the Library may maintain accurate records for accountability."[32] Like a credit card, the library card is not transferable and carries a certain amount of liability if it is lost. Also like a credit card, one must present proof, not only of one's eligibility for the service being sought—by virtue of attendance or employment at the university—but also of one's "financial responsibility and accountability for the property."[33]

They are dead serious about circulation at this library. A borrower is responsible *until the material is checked in,* and the burden of proof in case of doubt or dispute is on the borrower.

In several places in the summary document the presence of the computer is noted. First, it is directly named under the heading "Audit Trail," which says: "In addition to the computer record, the Library maintains a stamped listing of due dates and return dates in each book checked out . . . to substantiate appeals by documenting machine errors."[34] Second, a bar-code

Figure 2-13
Sample Library Card

label for machine scanning is affixed to the library card in the box provided. Third, the presence of the grace period and emphasis on *dis*charging is more typical of automated systems than manual ones. For example, in a manual system, one can tell a check-in assistant to treat book drop material as if it had been returned the night before. A computer, however, is too literal for such a simple ruse, and once its internal calendar says that it is, say April 1, it cannot be tricked into acting as though it were still March 31. In order to get a computer to ignore such time lags in checking materials in after a night, weekend, or holiday, a grace period must be programmed, allowing library staff a specified number of days or hours in which to get around to the check-in tasks without penalizing borrowers. A grace period is a double-edged sword, however, because it also enables borrowers the same time period penalty free beyond the stated due dates.

The amount of material a faculty member may place on reserve for a course at the University of North Florida is twenty-five items. In addition, copyright obligations are spelled out clearly on the request form (a separate form must be filled out for each item), and the library reserves the right to refuse a request considered improper. Two handouts on the "fair use" provisions of the copyright law explain its applicability to reserve materials, and a third handout informs the faculty member how to obtain permission to duplicate material from its copyright holder. These all indicate continuing control of the reserve system as well as a real commitment on the part of the library to fulfill its legal obligations in full, passing on to the faculty whatever is seen to be their responsibility.

Like Mankato State University, Carpenter Library welcomes local residents, stating in its "Library Guide," "We welcome any adult resident of the Jacksonville area."[35] Although not as free as Mankato about granting borrowing privileges, they are not denied either: "Borrowing privileges are granted . . . upon special application, subject to approval."[36] Accountability to the public (or at least the taxpaying public) of the state is further acknowledged at the end of this document with the following statement: "This public document was promulgated at a total cost of $185.50, or 6.2 cents per copy, to inform the University of North Florida community of its Library's resources."[37] Perhaps more than other public institutions, the University of North Florida acknowledges subordination to its state government and tailors its library policies to fulfilling complete satisfaction of all financial obligations that might be attributed to it as an agency of the university. This may appear to make library policies unduly strict and rigid, but it also protects the library administration and staff from two common pitfalls: First, they cannot be charged with treating clients favorably or harshly according to the personal whims of desk clerks or other staff members and, second, they provide precise and easily applied rules and penalties so that it is never necessary to interpret what was actually intended.

Queens College, City University of New York

Queens College of the City University of New York, a senior college in the extensive CUNY system, located in Flushing, New York, provides a brief summary of circulation rules in its illustrated library guide pamphlet titled *This Is Your Library: A Guide to the Paul Klapper Library, Queens College, CUNY*[38] and a flyer, containing more details, titled "Main Circulation Desk," in which basic information appears.[39] Klapper Library distinguishes, first of all, among three categories of borrowers: students, part-time faculty and staff, and full-time faculty. Of the five different categories of materials enumerated, borrowing periods (or lack thereof) for three types of materials are identical for all clients. Regular circulating materials from the stacks, however, have a sliding scale giving students three weeks, part-time faculty and staff four weeks, and full-time faculty eight weeks. Students are confined to one three-week renewal; the other two categories of borrowers can renew their materials indefinitely unless the titles are requested by another person. The last category of material having varying loan periods comprises sound recordings, which may be borrowed for four weeks by full-time faculty and for only one week by everyone else. The only nonrenewable materials are in a collection called the "Good Reading Collection,"[40] a title which begs the question "Are the rest Bad Reading?" Humor aside, these books, which consist of selected titles from among newly published scholarly works, have a three-week-only loan period for all clients.

Only full-time faculty are exempt from payment of fines, and an accumulation of $2 or more in overdue fines results in withdrawal of borrowing privileges. Although not stated on any publicly disseminated information, faculty paychecks are withheld for nonpayment of library fines at the end of the semester. No threats to students, typical of most general literature, appear in either of Queens College's publications. A paragraph headed "Lost Books" does not refer to books on loan lost by clients, but rather to books listed in the catalog which cannot be found on the shelf, on loan, in the reserve collection, or in storage.[41] (In such a case, if further search for the item is fruitless, a new copy is ordered for the client's use.) This service orientation is a pleasant departure, even though the usual penalties for incurring debts to the library—holding transcripts, diplomas, or preventing registration—are not lacking. The only punishment mentioned is the loss of the privilege of borrowing more materials, and the low debt of $2 which initiates it seems innocuous in the face of our current economy. Once an item is overdue for more than six weeks, it is considered lost, and a bill for replacement is generated. Again, this will result in a loss of borrowing privileges. The difference between this charge and the $2 charge mentioned before is between money owed on materials *not* returned and that owed on materials already returned, but overdue. The distinction

Figure 2-14
Client Circulation Flyer

Main Circulation Desk
PAUL KLAPPER LIBRARY
Queens College, Flushing, N.Y. 11367

BORROWING PRIVILEGES

All Queens College faculty, staff, and students are eligible to borrow books and other materials from Paul Klapper Library. Borrowing privileges are also extended to students attending the Graduate Center, as well as to faculty and students at most City University units. Students from other CUNY units must present a currently validated I.D. card from their home school.

IDENTIFICATION

The College Identification Card, with a current semester validation, is to be used by all College borrowers. A staff member at the Main Circulation Desk will affix a zebra label to your ID card. This card will be used for all loan transactions. Once you obtain a zebra label, you will not need another one for the duration of your stay at Queens College.

REGISTRATION

All borrowers are expected to have current address and telephone number on file at Paul Klapper Library. Please report any change of address to the Main Circulation Desk.

LOAN PERIODS

Type of Material	Students	Part-time Faculty and Staff	Full-time Faculty
Regular stack books	3 weeks	4 weeks	8 weeks
Good Reading Collection	3 weeks	3 weeks	3 weeks
Phonorecords & cassettes	1 week	1 week	4 weeks
Periodicals & reference books	Non-circ.	Non-circ.	Non-circ.
Microforms	Non-circ.	Non-circ.	Non-circ.

RENEWALS

Patrons may renew books (except those in the Good Reading Collection) for three weeks. Full-time faculty, part-time faculty, and staff may renew until the item is recalled.

RECALLS AND HOLDS

If the author card in the card catalog does not indicate RESERVE or STORAGE, and you cannot locate the book in the stacks, go to the Main Circulation Desk and fill out a hold request form. If the book you need is out to another patron, a "hold" will be placed for you. When the book is returned, you will be notified that the book will be held for you at the Circulation Desk for seven days.

If you receive a recall notice, please return the book on or before its due date. Prompt response to recall notices will help to make more materials available to other patrons.

(over)

is a function of the computerized circulation control system used at Queens, which has three methods of blocking client loan services—by the amount owed on books outstanding, by the amount owed on materials returned but overdue, and by the total number of overdue items in a client's possession.

The presence of the computer is noted in the matter of identification, which describes the machine-readable, bar-coded label assigned to each borrower. (Klapper's information sheet calls these *zebra labels* because of their black and white striped appearance.) It is also mentioned with regard to the generation of bills. Otherwise, the policy statements do not focus on the computer system at all.

In the matter of non-college affiliated borrowers, both the guide and the information sheet discuss outside borrowing, but from different points of view. The circulation desk sheet states that students from the Graduate Center in Manhattan as well as faculty and students from most other CUNY units may borrow materials from Klapper Library upon presentation of a validated ID card from their home institution.[42] The guide, on the other hand, indicates to Queens College students that *they* may have borrowing privileges at other CUNY libraries.[43] That a cooperative borrowing program should exist among the units of a university system located in one city comes as no surprise. What is surprising are the cautionary statements in the guide, dated 1982, that several units do not participate and that students should check at Klapper before trying to use another CUNY library. No mention is made at all of local residents or of scholars from outside institutions, which may not indicate their exclusion but would certainly imply a less-than-welcoming attitude toward them, unlike the policies and information brochures of the University of North Florida and Mankato State University.

University of Wisconsin-Whitewater

The Harold Andersen Library of the University of Wisconsin-Whitewater has a concise six-page foldout that summarizes its circulation policies (Figure 2-15).[44] Much of the text in the document is concerned with services other than circulation, such as the availability of individual carrels or group study rooms, the lost and found, and typewriter and computer rooms—all also included as a matter of course in the library guides or handouts of other institutions—as well as information about the electronic security system and the need for books to be desensitized before leaving the building, closing procedures, and special collections. Rarely has a security system been so publicized, perhaps because part of its effectiveness is thought to lie in its invisibility, or because it is taken for granted in most places. Here, however, students (toward whom most campus publications are directed, unless otherwise noted) and faculty are forewarned as well as informed that

HAROLD ANDERSEN LIBRARY
CIRCULATION POLICIES

1. INDENTIFICATION REQUIREMENT: Loans are made
with the presentation of a validated I.D. card.

2. LOAN PERIODS: Undergrads may borrow from
the general stacks for 2 weeks. Grads may borrow
for 4 weeks, and faculty may borrow books for
a semester. All books normally fall due on
Monday or Thursday (loan periods may vary near
the end of a semester and during vacation
periods).

3. DATE-DUE SLIPS: A date-due slip is inserted in the pocket of all books charged out. It
MUST be returned with the book or a fine of $1.00
will be assessed.

4. RENEWALS: Renewals may be made provided that
no one else has requested the book. Undergrads
may renew a book twice; Grads may renew a book
once. After a book has been renewed, it may be
recalled if another patron requests it. There
are NO telephone renewals. Books may be renewed
by mail by sending in the date-due slips. The
letter must be postmarked on or before the due
date. OVERDUE books will not be renewed unless
fines are paid.

5. FINES: Fines are 10¢ per day. A 50% discount
is allowed if fine is paid when material is
returned and before overdue process is started
(normally after 2 weeks, but sooner at the end
of the semester). Fines not paid at the time of
return will be processed through Student Billing
and payable only at the Cashiers Office. If the
book has been requested by another patron and a
recall notice has been sent to the borrower, the
fine rate is 25¢ per day until the book is returned. No discount on recalls.

reports are filed with the university administration if the alarm is tripped by a client.

Overdue fines that reach the notice-generation stage at Whitewater are handled through university financial systems, as at the University of North Florida. Like some other libraries, however, immediate payment is rewarded with a 50 percent discount. The only threats made to students are the possible loss of library privileges and, in the case of overdue reserve materials, notification of their instructors. This latter penalty seems both appropriate and fair, since instructors assume reserve materials are always available to all students in a class when, as a result of one person's negligence, they may not be. Reserves seem exceptionally complicated, too, with the several kinds of loans each having different return requirements.

Clients are directed to use their validated ID cards to borrow materials, with a sliding scale of loan periods for ordinary circulating books from the stacks. Students, of course, are on the lower end, with undergraduates receiving two weeks, graduate students four weeks, and faculty a semester. Like a number of other institutions, due dates are usually scheduled for a specific day of the week—in this case, on Mondays or Thursdays (Nazareth College of Rochester's books fall due on Wednesdays—making it possible for discharging work to be scheduled regularly, too. The renewal system brings undergraduate and graduate students' privileges into greater balance, with the former permitted two renewals and the latter only one. No mention is made of faculty renewals. The policy states that recalls are made after renewal, indicating they might not be made during the initial loan period.[45] This is somewhat atypical, since most academic libraries institute recalls after some minimum specified time a book is out on loan, usually less than a full borrowing period. If the policy is applied as stated, it means that no student (or faculty member, for that matter) can recall a book taken out by a faculty member for at least one full semester. This policy hardly seems fair, despite the commonly observed special status of faculty. Also, like a few other libraries, Whitewater avoids renewals by telephone, although renewals may be made by mail.

Most of the information contained in this policy information booklet is reproduced in small sections on different colored bookmarks, which are undoubtedly widely available and could be inserted in books along with due date slips. Emphasis is placed on retaining due date slips—a fine of $1 is charged for losing one and mail renewals require sending them in to the circulation desk. This is a function of a manual circulation file geared to due dates, i.e., filed chronologically. While it is a frequent method of operation, it has its drawbacks, particularly the time-consuming and, therefore, costly process of searching an item *without* its date slip either upon return or for renewal or recall. Automation, a project in progress in Wisconsin's state university system as of this writing, would be a valuable asset in exerting greater control with less effort.

CIRCULATION POLICY IN STAFF MANUALS

Three academic institutions sent only their staff manuals, which cover circulation policies and practices, rather than the materials distributed to and intended for the public. The private institution, Bank Street College of Education, is described first, followed by the two public institutions, Pima Community College and the State University of New York at Stony Brook.

Bank Street College of Education

The policy manual of Bank Street College, located in New York City, dated 1981, is fifteen pages long and has eight sections, which cover user registration, borrowing rules for materials and equipment, transaction procedures, filing, overdues and billing, and a statement of the distribution of authority titled, "Who's in Charge of Circulation?"[46] This final paragraph names as the person in charge of circulation a single professional on the library staff working under the director's supervision, whose *persona* could change as staffing needs change.[47] This most atypical treatment of responsibility is matched by a most refreshing opening charge to staff members (not necessarily professional) who attend the desk (Figure 2-16).

The Circulation Desk is one of the primary communication units of the Library. . . . Those who work at the desk act as representatives of the library and the College to patrons and the visiting public, and must be prepared to answer a million questions, only some of which will have to do with books and libraries.[48]

Admonitions to "REMAIN CALM" and "Under no circumstances should you be seen . . . just sitting in a catatonic daze" reflect a good-humored approach often lacking in libraries and librarians as well as their policy documents.[49] In no way, however, does it deny or alter the gravity of the job to be done. Other directives demand responsibility, industriousness, and careful preparation for understanding and handling a busy desk with demanding clients who are "always in a hurry."[50]

Seven categories of clients are identified: (1) students of the college, (2) staff including college faculty, (3) alumni, (4) parents of students in the school, (5) students of the school, (6) fee-paying outsiders, and (7) individuals who borrow materials on ILL, who are referred primarily by the METRO regional network. In the case of certain adult materials, a client's category determines the length of loan periods, e.g., single issues of periodicals may be borrowed for use in-house up to five days by staff members only, while teachers at the Bank Street School are given year-long loans for classroom materials. Many materials may be used in-house only, including reference books, reserved books, heavily used books, periodicals, audiovisual software, Bank Street College archive materials, tests, and some theses. Other materials circulate for one week (recommended reading,

Figure 2-16
Staff Policy Manual

CIRCULATION POLICIES AND PROCEDURES OF THE BANK STREET LIBRARY
1981 REVISION

INTRODUCTION

The Circulation Desk is one of the primary communication units of the
Library and of the institution. Those who work at the desk act as representatives of the library and the College to patrons and the visiting public, and
must be prepared to answer a million questions, only some of which will have
to do with books and libraries.

You will be busy answering the telephone, taking messages, answering patrons'
questions, slipping and checking out materials, typing overdues, keeping track
of where everybody's going and when they're coming back. ("You mean Martin is
still in the storage room?")

Patrons are always in a hurry. Sometimes they get upset because they can't
find a book on the shelves, or they have received an overdue notice and they
know that they returned the book, or they can't take out a book because they
didn't return a long overdue book, etc. Sometimes what's really bothering them
is something else, and you're getting the flack. REMAIN CALM. Try to understand
what it is they want and explain the procedure that they must follow to accomplish
same. If you can't figure it all out, call on a librarian for help.

You should make yourself responsible for knowing when you are scheduled at
the desk, and appear on time. Under no circumstances can you leave the control
desk unattended. Find someone to take your place if you need to leave, even
for a few minutes. Under no circumstances should you be seen doing your home-
work, reading a book, sitting with the phone casually cradled on your shoulder,
or just sitting in a catatonic daze. If you don't know what work is to be done,
ask the Administrative Assistant.

The circulation area must be kept clean and neat at all times. There are
many overlays, stickers, cards, forms and other objects needed for various
processes. If things are left out of place or allowed to pile up, chaos is
inevitable. Slip books as soon as possible; remove tape and plastic overlays and
shelve last copy materials immediately. Keep the top of the desk uncluttered;
check and clear snags at least once a week. Make sure that enough supplies are
available and that the circulation machine is in working order and up to date.

textbooks, and some theses) or, at most, for four weeks (books not in heavy demand or the other above-named categories). Juvenile materials are borrowed for four weeks unless they are part of a special Children's Literature Collection consisting of two copies of each title, one for reference and one for circulation. The circulating copies of the Children's Literature Collection have one-week loan periods. Media hardware is not handled by the circulation desk, but rather by a media coordinator who is responsible for its scheduling and use. Renewals are allowed unless someone requests the item and it could not be done by telephone. Recalls are not mentioned—highly unusual for an academic library. Bank Street College is, indeed, an unusual institution.

Overdues for college students and fee-paying clients appear to be a matter of getting the materials back or paying a $15 lost item fee. No daily charges are mentioned, but grades or transcripts can be withheld if outstanding bills are not paid. Children in the school are offered the option of working off their debts in the library, and they lose their borrowing privileges if they do not clear up their lost-book problems. Staff are urged by personal contact to return materials or renew them. No penalties are mentioned with regard to staff.

The fundamental assumption of a client's honesty is clearly indicated in the "claims returned" procedure. The library urges the client to search again for the item in question but does not, in the final reckoning, hold him or her responsible for it, absorbing the loss after holding the account open for two years. Other institutions make no such assumption (Columbia requires the signing of a statement of legitimacy, which could become the basis for a legal action, and the University of North Florida assumes that the client is responsible unless or until they prove themselves without fault).

The Bank Street College library, which deals with a varied clientele, is obviously geared to a more personalized library staff-client relationship, which is demonstrated by their phoning people who have special materials overdue, by their contacting staff members personally about non-returns, and so on. The notion of having students work off their debts and not charging daily overdue fees are among Bank Street's unique practices—with possibility for more general application elsewhere. Most of its policies, however, seem appropriate primarily in a very small, tightly-knit organization, a profile not encountered with much frequency among academic libraries.

Pima Community College

A circulation policy of the District Library Committee of Pima Community College (PCC), in Tucson, Arizona, dated 1982 and amended in January, 1984,[51] outlines five basic elements: (1) eligible borrowers, (2) materials limitations, (3) transactions, (4) overdues, and (5) lost books. It is refreshing that overdues and lost books account for the shortest sections, whereas borrowers and materials account for the longest. In all, the policy is a bit over two pages including the amendment, which concerns new ID cards bearing the owner's photograph. If status is measured by placement on the list of items covered in the policy, people are first; if status is measured by placement on the list of person categories, students are first. The 1982 version of the policy permits students to show a number of different identification documents once they are registered in the computer system. The 1984 amendment, however, requires the presentation of the photograph-ID unless the person is not currently a student, in which case, other documents, including driver's license, social security card, or military ID, may be substituted.

Four other categories of borrower follow: (1) faculty, (2) associate faculty and staff, (3) off-campus borrowers, and (4) primary and secondary school students. Cards are issued to off-campus borrowers for six months, expiring at the end of June and December. The cards can be renewed as often as needed. This group of people is limited to borrowing a maximum of five books at one time, and they can keep them for only two weeks. Faculty and staff are supposed to present their college IDs to receive service; younger students are served without being issued cards at all.

Though PCC students are at the top of the list, they do not have the maximum borrowing privileges. These are reserved, as usual, for faculty and staff, who are given semester loans and who may borrow reference materials, sound recordings, and some microforms. Students may borrow books of all kinds for two weeks, but they cannot borrow periodicals either in hard copy or microform, sound recordings, or reference materials. Audiovisual materials mentioned, other than sound recordings and microforms, include posters, games, tapes (not identified as audio or video), filmstrips, kits, and slide sets. Though these may be loaned one at a time to off-campus borrowers, how they circulate to campus affiliates is not defined, possibly because they do not differ from the circulation of books (two weeks, or one semester, depending on the client's status).

Renewals are permitted for all materials as long as they are not overdue and the borrower was not "encumbered," the PCC term for withdrawal of service. (At Columbia, this was called "blocked." Other institutions probably have their own terms, though they were not mentioned in the documents examined here.) Telephone renewals are allowed as long as the proper ID numbers for clients and materials are furnished. Any transaction could be done at any of the PCC district agencies, again, a refreshing departure from the policies of most institutions where materials must be renewed or returned at the same location where they were borrowed. In some cases, the additional days required to transport materials from another location to the owning department/building is held against the client in terms of higher overdue fees.

No daily overdue charges are mentioned, but borrowing privileges are rescinded when more than one item is held more than two weeks overdue. This penalty is applied to faculty and staff as well as to students and outside borrowers. The policy also states that "Chronic and unresponsive offenders will be referred to the appropriate administrative officer."[52] Lost materials are charged at a replacement cost determined by the item's entry in the circulation database plus $5 for processing, a fairly typical charge.

Brief and businesslike, with responsibility for materials placed on the borrower, but without a complicated system of penalties and threats, this policy depends on the availability of a great deal of information from PCC's computer database, mentioned in several places in the statement. The existence of several campuses and several categories of nonaffiliated borrowers would make these liberal policies difficult to control without the aid of an automated system.

State University of New York (SUNY) at Stony Brook

Like the staff manual of Bank Street College, the circulation manuals of the Frank Melville, Jr., Memorial Library at SUNY's Stony Brook campus are designed to indoctrinate new staff members into personnel practices and technical procedures used in the library as well as to inform them of institutional policies concerning the borrowing of materials.[53] Two thick volumes contain the entire manual, the first of which covers borrowers, loan periods, and so on. In all, there are over 100 pages, including many pages of maps, samples of all forms used, examples of the circulation-related documents of other departments used by clients, and explanations of the automated system including a section titled "How Does the Computer Think," which explains preprogrammed circulation routines performed without input from an operator. Most of the text is typed, but handwritten corrections, additions, and deletions, as well as hand-lettered material on maps and other illustrations, mar the professional image of the document. New staff are given a deadline of one week to learn the first half of the manual and are examined before being permitted to begin the second half; however, slow learners can borrow the first half for additional study at home. The many little details, while not particularly complicated by themselves, add up to a great deal to integrate totally into one's consciousness in one week.

The introductory unit has a brief and useful definition of circulation (Figure 2-17).[54] In this definition, the borrowing and return cycle is described as the client service it really is. The distinctions between "desk" and "stack" duties and their interrelations are also made clear. Among the

Figure 2-17
State University of New York, Stony Brook
Staff Manual "Introduction"

1b

<u>WHAT IS CIRCULATION?</u>

The purpose of the Circulation Department is to charge-out, discharge, and shelve books and to maintain records and assist patrons.

1) The Stack assistants shelve the books in the proper call number order, so that the patron can find the book wanted.

2) The Circulation Desk assistants on the 3rd floor charge out books and keep records, so that we know where the book is. They also decide if the patron has a valid punched I.D. so that s/he is eligible to take books out.

3) The Circulation Desk assistants discharge the books when they are returned.

4) The Stack assistants re-shelve the discharged books, so that they are again available to our patrons.

As you see, the circulation process is a kind of circle, as the book goes out and returns. All the things we do, even many of our little extra services, are efforts to make this circle as complete and convenient to our patrons as possible.

Sometimes this circle is broken, because the patron cannot find the book wanted. Then the 3rd floor Desk assistants try to help him/her to find the book. First, they check the Computer Charge Printout and our small manual file to see if the book is already out. If so, the patron can put a "Hold" on it, so that s/he can get it when it is returned. Second, if the book is not charged out, the assistants try to find out if the patron has looked in all possible and logical places to find the book, sometimes going to the maps of the Stack areas or even to the shelves themselves, to help the patron, <u>if permitted by the supervisor</u>. Third, if the book cannot be located, they help the patron to fill out Search Requests for the book. Supervisors help in these problems.

Books may be renewed if a "Hold" hasn't been placed on the book.

When the book is returned, it should be placed in the book slots in the 1st floor Circulation Lobby. If this is closed, the book drops by the South entrance should be used, or the book drops at the curb near the Student Union.

In addition to charging, renewing and discharging books, Circulation Desk assistants are expected to help with the shelving when needed, search, file, stamp date due slips and help with special projects.

*   This figure represents an actual reproduction of the document.

policy responsibilities of desk assistants are decisions about the validity of client ID cards for borrowing privileges.

Five categories of borrowers are defined: three different student categories (Stony Brook undergraduates, graduates, and continuing education students), faculty and staff, and courtesy and open access borrowers. Members of the first four categories must have their official IDs in hand in order to make loans, and no one is allowed to use another's ID. The courtesy and open access group includes alumni, visiting teachers, families of Stony Brook affiliates (including students' families), other SUNY affiliates (there are some exceptions here), and researchers from Brookhaven National Laboratory. Doctoral candidates and masters students writing theses were granted extended privileges, similar to those accorded to faculty. Stony Brook students not actually enrolled or preregistered at the time a loan is being made are not eligible for service—apparently a particular problem during the summer. Intersession borrowing seems to be a complex issue in which every possible precaution is taken to prevent unauthorized loans, even requiring letters from instructors for students completing work from the previous term.

The loan period for students, staff, and outside borrowers is one month; semester-long loans are granted to faculty and graduate students writing dissertations or theses. Although almost all books from the stacks circulate, periodicals—whether bound or unbound—do not, nor do specially marked quasi-reference and/or serial works such as library catalogs, almanacs, dictionaries, and similar publications. (One might ask why these are kept in the stacks instead of in the reference collections if they are not intended to circulate.)

Fifteen circulation rules (Figure 2-18) cover transactions and penalties as well as returns, study facilities, copying service, and prohibitions on eating and smoking except in designated areas.[55] Included in these rules are renewals (once only if the book has not been requested by another client) and recalls (made after an item has been on loan for two weeks). Overdue charges are billed after five days, and they continue to accumulate until a ceiling of $5 is reached. Lost books are charged at a standard rate according to the category of the book plus a $5 processing fee. Overdues and fines must be paid to the university's financial offices even though they are billed by the library. The procedures for handling complaints about overdues, bills, or books claimed returned are prefaced by the admonition to "act as if *you know what you are doing* in this matter, even if it is a problem that will eventually stump you."[56] Several pages give exact directions for a host of common processes and complaints, e.g., the exact billing system process, answers to the claim that a book was returned and the client is still receiving notices, answers to claims that the client did not receive previous notices, and so on. All problems are to be referred to supervisors. Whether

UNIVERSITY LIBRARIES
State University of New York at Stony Brook

CIRCULATION RULES

1. Everyone may use books in the Stacks, but only library users with punched,
   validated I.D. cards may borrow circulating books. All I.D.'s must be
   validated for the current term. In order to protect library patrons, no
   person may borrow a book on another person's I.D. card.

2. Patrons with Library cards without pictures are asked to show some additional
   personal identification.

3. In order to borrow books during intersessions and summer vacations, evidence
   of pre-registration for the coming semester must be shown by all students
   including graduate students. Be sure to pre-register.

4. All periodicals and certain reference and serial volumes do not circulate.

5. The loan period is for 30 days (SUSB faculty and graduate students writing theses,
   one semester). There is no limit on the number of books which can be borrowed.

6. Any book is subject to Recall for another patron after two weeks (immediately if
   needed for Reserve). A person receiving a Recall notice must return the book
   wanted at once.

7. Any book may be renewed one time. Special permission may be given for additional
   renewals. No renewals can be made during the last 15 minutes that the Stacks are
   open.

8. Overdue books accumulate fines at 10¢ a day up to $5.00 maximum per book. Fines
   are not collected for the first four days. On the fifth day the fine billed is
   50¢, and the bill continues accumulating at 10¢ per day for each book. Instruc-
   tions for payment are printed on the bills.

9. Lost books are charged according to the average cost of that type of book plus
   a $5.00 processing fee.

10. Books charged out from the Stacks may be returned to the book slots in the first
    floor Circulation Lobby. When the Main Library is closed, outside book drops on
    both the North and South side of the Library may be used.

11. Study spaces in the Stacks are intended for the use of non-circulating books and
    materials. Other areas of the Library have many more attractive general study
    facilities.

12. If you can't find your books or have any problem, see the supervisor at the Circu-
    lation Desk. It may be possible to place a Hold or a Search Request on books
    which you cannot find.

13. Please do not eat or drink in the Stacks. This rule is designed to protect the
    books against infestation by insects or fungi.

supervisors have written policy and procedure manuals to handle the various issues is not made clear in this document. Special billing supervisors (as contrasted with circulation supervisors) are charged with determining eligibility for crediting client accounts. Application of lost book charges for all categories of borrower, including faculty and staff, is emphasized by a client document reproduced in the manual titled "Borrowing a Book from the Main Library,"[57] but faculty are exempted from overdues. Students are warned to clear up any outstanding charges before graduation.

At Stony Brook, a batch-processed computer printout supplies relatively up-to-date and accurate information for controlling circulation. It is mentioned frequently in the pages of the manual. Stony Brook appears to have streamlined most of its policies and to have eliminated a great many variations, particularly regarding loan periods. Of course, special collections, such as maps and government documents, and departmental libraries, such as the Health Sciences Library, have their own rules and regulations which differ from those of the main library. There are also separate rules for reserve materials, with several loan periods assigned by the faculty member designating the titles for reserve. There are no limits on the number of items placed on reserve. In the faculty handout on reserves, 90 days lead time is requested by the library, and a statement is included to demonstrate that the library complies with copyright laws by paying copying royalties or by obtaining reprints or whole issues of journals rather than copying articles. In an interesting and unusual reserve book arrangement at Stony Brook, most titles are on open shelves, enabling users to avoid the long lines during peak hours at reserve desks where students may spend thirty minutes or more just waiting to obtain needed material. Only articles, personal copies, or special materials are held behind the desk. Also, all reserved material is returned to original locations at the end of each semester. These policies seem eminently sensible, especially for large, heavily used reserve collections, and indicate the operation of an efficient reserve system capable of handling constantly changing collections.

ISSUES AND ANSWERS IN THE ACADEMIC LIBRARY

The basic questions of circulation—Who? What? How?—have been answered in different ways by the academic libraries included in this chapter. Certain issues stand out and bear additional discussion.

Nonaffiliates

The provision of loan service to persons not affiliated with the college or university, especially local residents, is usually, though not always, viewed with hostility. Some private institutions *do* extend service to area residents (the University of Bridgeport); some public institutions *do not* (SUNY at

Stony Brook). On the whole, public colleges and universities express more feelings of responsibility to the taxpaying public than do the private ones and they make some effort to serve the public, although rarely without limitations designed to ensure that their primary constituents—students and faculty—are not inconvenienced. Pima Community College District appears to be one of the most flexible about outside borrowers, permitting even younger students to use the libraries. Columbia University is, perhaps, among the most restrictive of the academic libraries, requiring payment of substantial fees for any borrowing service beyond occasional ILL referrals. Many institutions do not specify whether the general stacks are open or closed and whether identification must be shown in order to enter the building. For years, Columbia has not required showing an ID to enter Butler Library except on weekends, when security is minimal, though desk staff are supposed to check them before permitting entry to the stacks. Anyone can use materials on open shelves in the reference department, periodical room, and other collections without interference. This policy is changing, however, and security guards are beginning to screen out *all* outsiders all the time, which is already being done at such other research university libraries as Princeton and New York universities. One library, which responded only to the circulation survey and was therefore not included in this chapter, sent the results of a survey of seventy-two academic libraries concerning fees for nonaffiliated users. Of the total, 51 (71 percent) extended library service to outsiders free of charge, and 28 (39 percent) required the payment of a fee. The fees were relatively modest, as the report stated:

A review of printed policies . . . indicates returnable deposit fees for the few libraries requiring them [of] $21.00; non-returnable deposits average $3.00. Twenty-five dollars is the average yearly fee for granting borrowing privileges. . . . [M]ost libraries in California's university system were now charging non-students $50.00 and students enrolled in another academic institution (public or private), $24.00 per year for direct loan service.[58]

Public colleges and universities in their sample were more likely to have reciprocal borrowing arrangements with other libraries than were private institutions, though more than half of the private institutions did so. As a result of the survey, the library initiating it decided to continue studying two plans: one excluding all nonaffiliates except alumni, who would be charged a fee, and one permitting all nonaffiliates to receive service for a fee, with alumni paying 50 percent less than others.

Special Privileges for Faculty

The extent of special privileges granted to college or university faculty members and sometimes to administrative staff as well varies considerably from one institution to another. Usually, the two main perquisites of faculty are extended loan periods, usually a term in length with liberal renewals, and exemption from overdue charges. Few faculties are exempted from lost book fees, though horror stories I have heard from colleagues who tried unsuccessfully to deal with professors holding materials years beyond due dates demonstrated the ability of faculties to evade or ignore the rules neverthelesss. Very few institutions are as businesslike as the University of North Florida about overdue/fine charges against faculty members. Even when sanctions are applied, as they are at CUNY's Queens College, they are rarely made explicit. Pima Community College District's policy *seems* to be most objective and evenhanded in this regard, as does Mankato State University's, although in practice they may not function exactly as stated in policy documents. In some libraries, faculty may also borrow materials denied to others (periodicals, reference materials, and audiovisuals), use production facilities and equipment, and borrow without ID or library cards. Sanctions against faculty are couched in the most diplomatic terms, with every effort made to avoid confrontation and to persuade cooperation.

Selective Restrictions on Materials

Restrictions on the types of materials that may be borrowed vary widely. Circulation is very complicated in some places. Among the materials frequently restricted to use in the library only or with specially limited loan periods are periodicals, microforms, maps, music, other nonbook materials and associated equipment, government documents, textbooks, new books, reserve materials, early imprints, and manuscripts. Periodicals, especially, are in great demand for research in all disciplines, and librarians hate to let them out of their hands before completing and binding a whole volume. The switch to microform periodical backfiles, with its great space-saving advantages, often involves even more restrictive access. Copying in microform is usually more expensive, and fewer microform duplicating machines are made available, discouraging use of these most desirable materials even further. The chief kind of grist for the circulation mill is older books, called stack books in many places because they are usually shelved in open stacks rather than in specially designated areas or collections. Most reference collections never circulate, even to faculty, and periodicals are often nearby or are located in the reference department to keep them close to the indexes used with them, which do not circulate either.

Loan Periods

Loan periods on stack books may be set anywhere from a minimum of two weeks or less for outsiders to a maximum of a term or more for faculty. More and more libraries are streamlining the number of loan periods they maintain simultaneously, perhaps to make it easier for new staff to learn or, possibly, to accommodate computer-based systems with limits on the number of different loan periods that can be preprogrammed. There is a great turnover in circulation staff since in large measure it depends on student help. It is also easier for clients to remember fewer loan periods. Distinctions in normal loan periods between undergraduates and graduate students are made by only one institution, Stony Brook, although many others have special loan periods giving more time to doctoral candidates (in this group, Columbia and Stony Brook made specific reference to them). Distinctions between full- and part-time faculty are sometimes reflected in loan periods, too, and university staff are sometimes given faculty loan periods, sometimes student loan periods, and occasionally totally different loan periods.

Materials other than stack books often varied even more widely in loan periods, from a few hours or overnight to a term, with the great preponderance being of a week's duration or less. Loan periods of one day or three days are frequently used for special materials, reserves, and periodicals.

Overdue Charges

The amount charged for overdue materials and the existence of ceilings, grace periods, discounts, and limits to what is considered overdue and gone for good makes up another set of issues with many different responses. The number of libraries charging minimal amounts daily is diminishing, with 25 cents to $1 per day more typical than ten cents or less. Virtually all the libraries included in this chapter charge for processing lost books as well as for replacing them, and several put time limits on the overdue period after which a replacement is ordered and must be paid for. Overdues for reserve materials are charged hourly, not daily, and rates are usually twice as high (or higher) as they are for ordinary circulating materials. In almost every case, however, regular overdue rates are scarcely more per week than it would cost to copy half a dozen pages or a chapter and probably do not deter many students who believe they need the materials to pass a course. Substantial discounts are offered by several institutions if overdues are paid in cash immediately upon return of the materials, though some libraries have turned collection tasks over to university financial offices. Most libraries threaten students with withholding grades, diplomas, and transcript services, and some also do not permit registration unless library bills have been settled. Few publicly distributed documents threaten faculty, but notification of deans or department heads is typical in those that do. While teaching as an adjunct at Queens College, this author was warned to return all materials before the end of the term so their policy of withholding the final paycheck until obligations were settled would not be exercised. It may be that other institutions do the same, but do not publicize it. Perceptions of overdue fines as punishment seem pervasive. Only Stony

Brook mentions the cost of billing. The fine structures of most institutions are too low to recover the full costs of maintaining the billing system. On the other hand, charges for lost materials are realistic, and all seem geared to cover costs. Some libraries offer clients the option of buying a copy of a lost item rather than paying a replacement charge, though they are still held responsible for a processing fee—most popularly $5. Such an alternative certainly expedites the replacement process.

Renewals

Policies on renewals follow no discernible patterns among these institutions. Most liberal of all is Harvard's Gutman Library, which has no limitations on renewals unless there is a request from another client for an item and which does not require that materials be brought to the library for renewal. Many libraries require that materials not be overdue when renewed while others permit renewals after payment of fines. Some policies permit one renewal, some permit no renewals at all, and some insist that renewals be done in person. Though online circulation control systems make renewals simple and automatic at any terminal, the University of North Florida requires that materials be brought back to the place where they were charged out and prohibits mail and telephone renewals. The decision on whether to encourage or discourage renewals ought to be based on evidence of material use patterns, cost to administer, and similar facts. Instead, it seems to be an arbitrary choice made without any scientific foundation. No statements that limited collection size, heavy demand, or insufficient personnel to administer renewals are made to explain the stricter regulations, although it may be that any or all of these are the reasons behind them.

Client Notices

Notices and bills are timed variously from the fifth day an item was overdue to several weeks afterward. Two notices or one notice and a bill seem to be the most popular combination of client notification patterns. Some institutions require payment for a replacement copy automatically as soon as, or a specific amount of time after, a bill is rendered. Most libraries seem to take it for granted that sending overdue notices is part of their circulation system, and automated systems are geared to produce them ready for mailing. The University of North Florida considers them a courtesy.

As one of the most costly and time-consuming parts of any manual circulation system, the possibility of eliminating one or more notices should be attractive, provided book returns do not suffer. More libraries may adopt North Florida's stance on notices if, on balance, slower returns do not outweigh the savings derived from cutting down on the number or speed of their notices. A number of libraries (Stony Brook, North Florida, Wisconsin-Whitewater) do not collect fine money themselves, though it may not mean these amounts are not credited to library accounts. In fact, many libraries collect fines and turn them over to a general fund over which they have no special influence or control.

Policy Centralization/Decentralization

Some libraries have very cohesive governance and policy structures for most, if not all, of their component departments. Others indicate that every special department or collection "does its own thing" regarding circulation of materials. Science and health science libraries often are separated administratively from central or main libraries, as are the libraries attached to professional schools (theology, law, social work, journalism, etc.) and collections of special formats (maps, microforms, manuscripts, audiovisuals, etc.). The proliferation of separately determined, differing hours, borrowing rules, eligibilities, and services poses a bewildering array to clients with eclectic or multidisciplinary research interests and needs. The problem is exacerbated when collection development policies attempt to minimize duplication of titles or overlap between collections. While it may be hard, politically, to reach agreement on uniform policies and campus-wide library regulations, it has merit in terms of increasing client services and greatly simplifying staff training and client education.

Philosophy and Approach

Perhaps the greatest difference between policies, especially those in larger institutions, is in their approach to borrowing in general. First, some appear to presume that clients will abuse their privileges and will fail to obey the rules. Policies from these institutions focus on overdues and other penalties. Others, who seem to presume client cooperation, focus on services. These policies do not ignore fines, but they do not emphasize them. Second, some policies emphasize what clients *can* do; others emphasize what they *cannot* do. Third, some policies reflect a broad and liberal interpretation of the library's position toward borrowers, materials, and transactions; others are much narrower in their definitions of clients and services. It would be easy to distinguish between client-centered and library-centered policies if clear-cut patterns in each of these policy styles were followed. However, a library with broad and liberal definitions for clients can also have rigid and restrictive rules about materials with elaborate, punitive fine structures (see Tables 2-1 and 2-2). Naturally, since these policies were written by people, they tend to reflect their creators' views and tone. In the next chapter, there is a discussion of *who* creates policy and *how* it is done, shedding some light on the process by which these policies come into being, or, at least, how they are evolving now.

Table 2-1
Table of Academic Library Circulation Policies: I

SCHOOL	# OF CLIENT CATEGORIES	INCLUDES OUTSIDERS	# OF MATERIAL CATEGORIES	RANGE OF LOAN PERIODS	STUDENT LOAN PERIOD
EMORY	3	YES	2-3	1 DAY-1 YR	4 WKS
COLUMBIA	3	NO	1-4	OVERNIGHT-1 SEM.	4 WKS
GUTMAN	-	-	3	3 HRS.-4 WKS	4 WKS
AGNES SCOTT	2	NO	2	2 WKS-NO END	2 WKS
NAZARETH	-	-	3	2-3 WKS	2-3 WKS
BRIDGEPORT	2	YES	-	1 MO.-1 SEM.	1 MO.
MANKATO ST.	2	YES	25	OVERNIGHT-1 QUARTER	1 OR 3 WKS
NORTH FLORIDA	3	YES	1+	2 WKS-1 TERM	2 WKS
QUEENS/CUNY	3	YES	5	1 WK-8 WKS	3 WKS
WISCONSIN/AT WHITEWATER	3	NO	1+	2 WKS-1 SEM.	2 OR 4 WKS
PIMA	4	YES	7+	2 WKS-1 SEM.	2 WKS
BANKS STREET	7	YES	7	1 WK-4 WKS	4 WKS
STONY BROOK/ SUNY	5	YES	1	1 MO.-1 SEM.	1 MO.
WHITWORTH	5	YES	2	2 WKS	2 WKS

Table 2-2
Table of Academic Library Circulation Policies: II

SCHOOL	RENEWALS	PHONE/MAIL	OVERDUE	LOST BOOK	# NOTICES	DISCNT
EMORY	YES	NOT STATED	.10	$20	NOT STATED	NO
COLUMBIA	YES	NOT STATED	$1-$2	REPLACEMENT + PROCESSING + FINE	1	50%
GUTMAN	YES	YES	$2-$5	$35	2	50%
AGNES SCOTT	YES	NO	.10	NOT STATED	NOT STATED	NO
NAZARETH	NOT STATED	--	.05	NOT STATED	NOT STATED	30%
BRIDGEPORT	0-1	--	.10	REPLACEMENT + $5.00	NOT STATED	NO
MANKATO	YES	MAIL	PRICE + $5.00	ALL COSTS	NOT STATED	NO
NORTH FLORIDA	YES	NO	.25	REPLACEMENT + $3.00	NOT STATED	NO
QUEENS	YES	NO	.10	NOT STATED	1+	NO
WISCONSIN	2-1	MAIL	.10	$20	1	50%
PIMA	YES	YES	NOT STATED	REPLACEMENT + $5.00	NOT STATED	NO
BANKS STREEET	YES	NO	NOT STATED	$15.00	1	NO
STONY BROOK/ SUNY	YES	ONLY FACULTY	.10	AVERAGE COST IN PUBLISHER'S WEEKLY	2	NO
WHITWORTH	YES	NOT STATED	NONE	NOT STATED	3	--

NOTES

1. Emory University, "General Libraries Handbook" (Atlanta, Ga.: the University, n.d.), 32 p.

2. "General Libraries Handbook," pp. 7-8.

3. "General Libraries Handbook," pp. 9-11, 19, 22, 24.

4. "General Libraries Handbook," p. 23.

5. "Borrowing Regulations for Emory Students and Employees," (Atlanta, Ga.: The Robert W. Woodruff Library, n.d.), 1 p.

6. "Borrowing Regulations for Faculty, Trustees, Librarians, and Officers of the University," (Atlanta, Ga.: The Robert W. Woodruff Library, n.d.), 1 p.

7. "Borrowing Regulations for Guests," (Atlanta, Ga.: The Robert W. Woodruff Library, n.d.), 1 p.

8. "University Center in Georgia: Interlibrary Use Policy," (Atlanta, Ga.: the Center, 1983), 4 p.

9. "University Center, " p. 1.

10. "Circulation and Borrowing Information," (New York: Columbia University Libraries, 1983), 10 p.

11. "Use of the Columbia University Libraries: Visiting Readers," (New York: Columbia University Libraries, 1983), 5 p.

12. "Use of the Columbia University Libraries," p. 3.

13. "Cooperative Services at the Columbia University Libraries," (New York: Columbia University Libraries, 1983), 11 p.

14. "An Introduction to the Columbia University Libraries," *Columbia University Record*, 1983-1984, 8 p.

15. "Schedule of Library Fines," (New York: Columbia University Libraries, 1983), 1 p.

16. "Photocopiers/Microform Copiers," (New York: Columbia University Libraries, 1983), 1 p.

17. "Answers to Some Often Asked Questions," (New York: Columbia University Libraries, n.d.), 4 p.

18. "Monroe C. Gutman Library: General Circulation Procedures," (Cambridge, Mass.: the Library, 1983) 1 p. Some of the information from this typed flyer was reproduced on a bookmark titled "Gutman Library Circ Desk," which was sent in addition to the flyer.

19. Copies of pages from these documents that were sent were marked "Student Handbook, 1983-85" and "Faculty Handbook, 1983-84."

20. "Faculty Handbook," pt. IV, p. 12.

21. "Faculty Handbook," pt. IV, p. 12.

22. "Nazareth: The Lorette Wilmot Library," (Rochester, N.Y.: the Library, n.d.), 4 p.

23. "The University Library Circulation Policy," (Bridgeport, Conn.: the Magnus Wahlstrom Library, 1983), 1 p., 1-p. fine schedule.

24. "This Is Your Library Guide," (Spokane, Wash.: Whitworth College, n.d.), 4 p.

25. "The Student's Guide to the Library, 1983-1984," (Mankato, Minn.: Mankato State University, 1983), 15 p.

26. "Faculty Guide to the Library, 1983-84," (Mankato, Minn.: Mankato State University, 1983), 15 p.

27. "Faculty Guide," p. 4.

28. "The Student's Guide," pp. 1-2.

29. "Borrowing Regulations, Policies and Procedures (Summarized from the UNF Library Lending Code)," (Jacksonville, Fla.: Thomas G. Carpenter Library, University of North Florida, 1981), 6 p.

30. "Borrowing Regulations," p. 3.

31. "Borrowing Regulations," p. 1.

32. "Borrowing Regulations," p. 1.

33. "Borrowing Regulations," p. 1.

34. "Borrowing Regulations," p. 3.

35. "Library Guide," (Jacksonville, Fla.: Thomas G. Carpenter Library, University of North Florida, 1982), [p. 1].

36. "Library Guide," p. 1.

37. "Library Guide," p. 7.

38. "This Is Your Library: A Guide to the Paul Klapper Library" (Flushing, N.Y.: Paul Klapper Library, Queens College, n.d.), 12 p.

39. "Main Circulation Desk," (Flushing, N.Y.: Paul Klapper Library, Queens College, 1980), 2 p.

40. "Main Circulation Desk," p. 1.

41. "Main Circulation Desk," p. 2.

42. "Main Circulation Desk," p. 1.

43. "This Is Your Library," [p. 12].

44. "Harold Andersen Library Circulation Policies," (Whitewater, Wis.: Library Learning Resources, University of Wisconsin-Whitewater, n.d.), 6 p.

45. "Harold Andersen Library Circulation Policies," [p. 1].

46. "Circulation Policies and Procedures of the Bank Street Library," (New York: Bank Street College of Education Library, 1981), 15 p.

47. "Circulation Policies," p. 15.

48. "Circulation Policies," p. 1.

49. "Circulation Policies," p. 1.

50. "Circulation Policies," p. 1.

51. "Pima Community College District Circulation Policy," (Tucson, Ariz.: the College, 1982), 3 p.; District Library Committee, Minutes of meetings, Aug. 17, 1983 and Jan. 20 1984.

52. "Pima Community College," p. 2.

53. Circulation Manuals, 1981/82 (Stony Brook, N.Y.: the University Library, 1981), 2 vol.

54. After a description of the purpose of the circulation department, it said, ". . . the circulation process is a kind of circle, as the book goes out and returns. All the things we do . . . are efforts to make this circle as complete and convenient to our patrons as possible." Circulation Manuals, vol. 1, p. 1 b.

55. Circulation Manuals, vol. 1, [p. 2]-2a.

56. Circulation Manuals, vol. 2, p. 24a. Emphasis in original.

57. Circulation Manuals, vol. 1, unit 6.

58. From a sample letter to survey participants, unsigned and undated, originating at the University of Vermont's Bailey/Howe Library.

_3_   *ACADEMIC LIBRARY*
RESPONSES TO THE
CIRCULATION QUESTIONNAIRE

In an effort to learn more about policy issues, decision making, and the process of policy formulation, as well as the ways in which circulation policies are changing, especially as libraries automate their circulation systems, a questionnaire was sent to a selected sample of academic libraries. A copy of the questionnaire may be found in appendix 1. All the libraries whose policy documents were described in Chapter 2 replied, as well as eight more who chose not to send any circulation documents.

Questions focused on four different themes: (1) the circulation system itself and its operation, (2) policy-making in the institution, (3) current problems being encountered, and (4) future plans for circulation. The first part of this chapter is divided into four sections to cover each of these themes; responses are discussed without reference to the specific institutions making them.

THE CIRCULATION SYSTEM

Contrary to the feeling one might get from a review of the professional literature in recent years, namely that online circulation control systems are common, most academic institutions answering this survey did not have online systems. Many libraries had more than one system operating concurrently. Out of a total of twenty-seven systems, only seven employed computers, and, of these seven, only four were online. The four online systems included two CL Systems, Inc. (CLSI) LIBS 100 turnkey systems, one Library Control System (LCS), and one system developed within the institution itself and mounted on university, not library, hardware. The other three automated systems were offline, batch-processed systems also dependent on university time-shared computers.

The LCS user employed it for "routine monographic circulation" only, using a manual card-based system for reserves, periodicals, government documents, and interlibrary loans. OCLC was used as part of the interlibrary loan procedure, too. In the manual system, only one card per item was filed, limiting staff access routes to materials for recall or other functions. One of the CLSI users specified having a separate batch-mode listing for reserve materials, produced by the institution's computer center. In this library, the turnkey system was used only for regular circulating materials. Both of the libraries having batch-mode operations mounted on their university computing systems for their main library circulation used manual charging for their branches and/or departmental units.

Nine of the manual systems were not named specifically but were described as being based on book cards and/or transaction cards. A tenth system was described generically as *photocharging*. The ten named manual systems included four libraries using the McBee keysort, three using Gaylord, two using Demco, and one using a Brodart product. In all, the twenty manual systems represent 74 percent of the group.

One of these libraries added that an in-house developed computer system was nearly completed, with implementation scheduled in the next semester. If all went according to schedule, this library should now have an automated system in place.

Questioned about plans to purchase, develop, or implement a different circulation system in the foreseeable future, sixteen libraries responded affirmatively, including the one that was about to be installed. Only six libraries had no plans to change their systems in some way. Included in this smaller group were both libraries with CLSI systems, two very small libraries, one library in a large university that reported having other priorities ahead of circulation, and one library that reported being willing to wait until its bibliographic utility designed a circulation module. (This last institution may have a long wait since the utility's policy has not included adding such a module.) The libraries with batch-mode processing systems were at some stage along the road to obtaining a new system.

One of the most frequently mentioned features in new circulation systems being planned is integration with acquisitions and online catalogs. Several comments indicated the desire to provide status information as part of catalog entries now possible with integrated systems:

Circulation is seen as an extension of the online catalog, displaying local holdings and current status.

We are in the final negotiations . . . to obtain this integrated library system in which circulation, cataloging, the online public access catalog and other subsystems will all be based on the same bibliographical record.

The Library is interested in a system which can eventually become an integrated one, leading to an online catalog.

We hope that if our current [online public access catalog] pilot project is successful and moves into full production we will be able to acquire . . . a circulation module which will be integrated into the OPAC system.

We are in the final negotiations . . . to obtain this [system].

The library [is] about to implement a new automated system designed to "interface with our online catalog."

Libraries with batch processing want their new systems to be online. A library using an online system mounted on the university computer wants an integrated turnkey system—one over which the library will have complete control as well as one that will perform all the functions of an integrated system of technical services.

Many libraries using the manual systems require clients laboriously to fill out charging forms, as in the following descriptions:

The user must give the complete bibliographic information, call number of the book, plus his name and local address on each circulation card. . . . This system is cumbersome for the library clientele . . . in terms of the time spent filling out circulation cards.

Patron signs name and student number/faculty department/office on 2 book cards.

The student fills out name, address, and social security number. We check a student ID to verify the social security number.

When one contemplates borrowing only one or two items, such systems pose a minor inconvenience; however, when the time required to fill out one or two forms with personal and bibliographic information is multiplied by five, ten, or fifteen, it can amount to a significant length of time. The staff suffers, too, because client scrawls are often hard to decipher, especially weeks after they have been interpreted by one desk attendant and are being re-read by another. One enterprising student who borrowed many books from the library during a three-year graduate program had a stamp made up with her name, address, and student number (the social security number was used in her institution), saving her many hours over the length of her academic career.

One circulation librarian's biggest complaint was "the frustrations encountered because of the handwritten circulation system utilized by the department." Having staff fill out forms—rarely encountered in academic library circulation departments—is no antidote to these problems either since it is equally time consuming and offers no guarantee of greater legibility.

The signed card system may require only personal information to be provided by a borrower or both personal and bibliographic information for the desired materials. As the comments above indicate, a few institutions require the signing of more than one card, although two-part forms are available where one signature imprints a duplicate simultaneously. These are also available in triple or quadruple carbons, like multipart order forms used for acquisitions.

Some of the manual systems rely on client number imprints from an embossed card or plate (Gaylord and Demco) saving clients the trouble of writing in their personal data, but these impose an added burden on the library staff. Records must be kept and searched each time the name and address to which a number is linked has to be used by a staff member. In photocharging, used by one library in the sample, a picture is taken of client and material identification, again, saving clients the trouble of manually providing either or both kinds of information but forcing library staff to use a laborious procedure to recapture data for use.

Regardless of the client input required by manual systems, only the photocharging system does not create one or more transaction files that have to be maintained constantly by the circulation staff in the library. (The photocharging system does create a file in microform and staff members do have to store and consult it, but it is more or less automatically generated.) A few librarians said they used only one card; therefore, they must maintain only one file. A few specified they kept more than one transaction file in order to have several points of access. One reply stated, "1 [book card] by call number and so can't check by user name to see how many books [the user] has checked out." Another replied to the same question, "Biggest complaint is probably the checkout procedure itself. Student must fill out a card for each book with call number, author and title. If they are checking out several items it can take a relatively long period of time." A third reply said one of the patrons' biggest complaints is the library's "inability to provide patron information—to quickly inform a patron what he/she has out at the time, etc." This was echoed by several other librarians.

The drawback to filing book cards chronologically is that it is harder to locate any specific item, either in answer to a question concerning its whereabouts or for recall. To determine whether an item is actually in a client's possession or is lost, misshelved, or otherwise in process when it is listed in the catalog but is not on the shelf, it first has to be searched in each day's circulation file. On the other hand, if the file is maintained by call number or main entry, each day's or each week's overdues have to be located some other way. Sometimes this is done by having holes punched in the book card so that a needle inserted through the holes will pull up the desired cards—the McBee system employs this methodology. Neither a chronological file nor a call number/main entry file, however, will aid in finding out what a particular client has, at any moment, charged out to him or her. This information is important not only to the client who cannot remember what he or she has out, but sometimes also to staff members trying to determine eligibility or lack of it for additional services. When asked what services not currently offered by their circulation systems respondents most wanted to add, eight replies were for information on the status of materials—the largest single reply. Two of these also included a way for clients to access this information themselves, and two more wanted remote access to it available, i.e., from outside the library itself. Other services named by four libraries each were obtaining lists of borrowed materials by client name and automatically generating notices. Thus, of the added services most frequently named, data on materials status and client holdings were two which typical manual files either cannot provide at all or provide only partially.

The desire for self-service operations and automated checkouts, named by two and three survey respondents respectively, not only obviates the need for handwritten identification of clients and/or materials, but is also a response to a felt need to speed up circulation operations and to make them more responsive to the needs of all users, both clients and library staff members. Added spinoff bonuses to the library would be the opportunity to reap some savings in desk staffing and to make circulation records more accurate. Together with automated production of notices (holds, overdues, bills, recalls), which also speed operations and save staff time, these were the highest priority services not currently being offered. One automated library did not yet have self-service checkouts—its only response to what new services it wanted.

The need in the field to streamline operations and save staff time was highlighted by one library with a manual checkout system which had automated its overdue system by putting it onto a self-programmed Apple computer. Naturally, the size of its overdue operation had to be small enough for a microcomputer-based application, but, more important, the emphasis for this library was on reducing the clerical work occupying staff rather than exerting greater control over materials. For very small libraries, control is probably much less critical than managing operations with a limited (often limited to one person) staff.

In sum, few of the academic libraries queried had automated systems, and most wanted to change to new systems. Most complained about a lack of information, primarily information about where materials were but also about what individual clients had on loan. Many complaints focused on the tediousness of handwritten transactions and the corollary problems of inaccurately written call numbers, authors, and titles as well as illegible names and addresses. Though few people complained specifically about massive filing maintenance tasks accompanying manual circulation operations, they were in agreement that their manual files were unable to provide the access they wanted, either for staff inquiries or for client service.

For several libraries, circulation is no longer perceived as a separate service department but as part of an entirely integrated system of bibliographic (or technical) and public services which need to be treated as a whole. It is easy to see the nature of integrated systems from the technical service point of view. Acquisitions, cataloging, and circulation are a life cycle, so to speak, of library materials, and the bibliographic identification will vary from one function to another but will never be absent altogether. It is much more difficult to recognize the public service nature of catalogs and cataloging, yet combining circulation information into an online catalog furnishes a bridge between these traditionally separate "public" and "technical" service operations. Three respondents to the survey specifically named online catalogs as the service they would most like to provide with their circulation systems.

Automated systems were few, with three commercially marketed systems—two CLSI and one LCS—and four self-designed systems mounted on university computer hardware. Interest is high in stand-alone integrated systems though several librarians were not sure how their budgets could be stretched to pay for them, or if they could muster support for such a project from their institutions over and above their normal expenditures. Others were investigating regional or university-wide networking (two libraries), letting Requests for Proposals (RFPs) or negotiating with vendors (two libraries), or on the verge of implementing an online system (one library).

The McBee keysort system was the most popularly used commercially marketed manual circulation system (four libraries) probably because it allows for one transaction file to be arranged by call number or main entry rather than chronologically while still providing for easy access to overdues. Gaylord was also relatively popular (used by three libraries), and Demco and Brodart were also mentioned (in two libraries and one library, respectively). Signed book cards—sometimes more than one or multiple forms—were used by all but one of the rest (nine libraries), and photocharging was employed in the last library.

POLICY-MAKING IN THE INSTITUTION

Several questions on the survey elicited information about who made contributions to circulation policies, how often policies were reviewed, and who conducted the policy review. The answers revealed as wide a variation in policy-making practices as in the policies themselves.

First regarding policy review, usually a prerequisite to policy changes, five brave and confident librarians said there were no circulation policy reviews in their libraries. One commented, "No written policies ever existed. In virtually all cases the question, 'Why does policy X exist?', cannot be answered. With the advent of a new administration in Fall 1983, each circulation practice is being examined and reformulated when the need arises." This director is involving the circulation staff and other professionals as well as himself in creating, for the first time, a set of written policies. Comments from the others indicated in one library a full review would be made before implementing an automated system; in another, that problems were considered as they arose but policy was not reviewed (there may be some semantic problems here); and in a third, that the current administrator was trying to institute a review though one had not been done for about six years (antedating his regime). The fifth negative reply offered no comment at all to explain the lack of policy review.

Six librarians reported that they regularly reviewed circulation policies, and all did so annually. In each case, however, the review process was somewhat different. One circulation librarian said that the review was informal, consisting of his noticing suggestions for change that routinely appeared in the annual reports of various department heads. Beyond that, a review could be prompted by a specific problem. Other libraries have far more formal procedures which usually are performed or directed by circulation heads, public services heads, or the library directors. In two places, the entire circulation staff participated; in two others, one or two persons were responsible for the entire annual policy review. In a sixth library, the Head of Reference, under whose authority the circulation department was placed, conducted the annual review, after which the University Librarian and Librarians' Council—which sounds like an advisory board or administrative cabinet—took up final decisions on changes to existing policies. This was the most complex system of policy review described and also the most politically astute review process, involving the circulation department's chief administrator, other professionals, and the University Librarian. It would seem to insure that policy changes were approved, if not by a complete consensus, at least by many more than a single group or person within the organization.

One librarian replied that circulation policies were under continuous review and evaluation. She elaborated on their system:

Most procedural changes are made by the circulation department staff with input from the Director of Public Services when this is deemed necessary. Policy changes are handled by the library administrators with input from a designated committee and staff members. Major changes are usually made during the slower summer months. Implementation of these changes generally takes place at the beginning of the fall term.

She also reported,

Generally when circulation policy is being formulated, a committee is designated. Membership on the designated committee includes circulation staff employees, employees from other departments, and top library administrators as the need dictates. All policies are reviewed and acted on by the faculty Library Policy Committee.

Though several respondents mentioned the presence of faculty committees, this was the only one requiring official action by the committee before changes were instituted.

The remaining ten libraries either indicated their circulation policies were reviewed irregularly or gave no answer to the question. Perhaps the most realistic and incisive comment came from a community college librarian who said: "No we do not regularly review policy—we regularly *discuss* reviewing the policy and make small changes as needs arise—small policy changes are suggested and reviewed by the circulation staff and supervisors at the two branch campuses." As previously mentioned, plans to automate circulation often engender a thorough policy review. One library director replied, "[Circulation policy is not reviewed] on a regular schedule. All policies will be reviewed prior to and, perhaps, during implementation of automated system."

Two librarians who said they reviewed policy but not regularly, as well as another who said there was no policy review, and still others who had regular reviews, all said they handled policy issues on an "as needed" basis. The fact that some librarians perceive treating problems as they arise as "policy review" and others see this as a separate activity related to, perhaps, but not the same as policy review indicates no clearly defined distinctions are made in the field between establishing policy principles and interpreting them in various applications. As the director who inherited a policy-free library pointed out, it is the *why* things are done in a certain way that constitutes the basis of policy. There were all sorts of rules in his library, but no service goals or objectives tied them together or explained the purposes they were meant to serve. Circulation rules themselves should be designed to implement the policy goals and objectives of the library. Seen in this light, the strict rules of the University of North Florida make good sense since their policy is to be fully accountable to state authorities for the library's inventory. Other libraries' rules freeing university faculties from overdues and other restrictions on borrowing serve a policy in which these privileges are part of faculty perquisites contributed by the library to the university at large. These special considerations take precedence over other principles, such as strict accountability for property or equal access to materials for all, including students. Most often, it is a policy in which curricular preparation and research use of materials—the reasons that faculty use library materials—have higher priorities than other kinds of uses, such as supplementing textbooks. Some might point to reserve materials as being specially designated to supplement textbooks for students; however, our current mode of teaching supposedly encourages students to search out and discover facts on their own, and this methodology relies on information being freely available to them. Northwestern University has a selected collection of approximately 50,000 titles for use by undergraduates, called its core collection, kept separate from its other materials intended for use by graduate students and faculty researchers. A number of other institutions have separate "college libraries" though these are not always interpreted in the same manner as Northwestern's. Nevertheless, where faculty and other special categories of users are granted more privileges than undergraduate students, the result is to put undergraduates at some disadvantage when they compete for the same materials. Since extensive faculty privileges are a widespread phenomenon, it can only be concluded they are serving a policy widely accepted by most of academe.

There was a much wider spectrum of contributors to circulation policy than reviewers of it. As previously discussed, policy review is largely a function of middle to top management, though it may also involve committees, the circulation staff as a whole, or staff from many library departments. Generally, library directors reserve the right to the final decision on policy changes resulting from a review, though, in one place, the last word was reserved for a faculty committee and, in another, it was wielded by an interinstitutional committee. When it comes to suggestions for change, formal or informal, the door seems to be wide open. Three librarians indicated that everyone in their institution contributed to making circulation policy, including circulation librarians and support staff, other library staff members, administrators, faculty, and students. Three more said that all library staff made contributions to policy; twelve said the entire circulation staff participated. In addition, administrators were named specifically by twelve respondents, committees by seven, and circulation department heads by five. One librarian who did not have regular policy reviews said everyone would be involved if reviews were done. One can also assume contributions would be sought from all sources as well in this library. Thus, participating by making suggestions or questioning the validity of any policy and initiating an evaluation with a possible change ultimately resulting from it is the province of a much broader circle of people than might have been thought. It is a campus-wide prerogative in several places and, in others, at least a library-wide or department-wide function.

For some libraries, all library policies, not just circulation policies, are subject to the committee-review system. Of the seven replies that committees contributed to making circulation policy, composition of the committees varied quite a bit depending on the size and composition of the institution in which each library exists. One community college, part of a larger college district, had a District Library Committee made up of the heads of each campus library and the heads of each technical services department, which reviewed all library policies. Another smaller and completely self-contained university had a Librarians' Council made up of all professional staff reviewing all policies. One university had both a Policy, Planning and Services Committee and a standing Library Faculty Committee to review changes to established policy. In this case, library faculty probably refers to the professional staff, who may be awarded faculty status in academic libraries. One library submitted policy changes to its university's Educational Services Committee. A committee with broad representation putting its stamp of approval or endorsement on a change in policy can be a great asset. It generates commitment to the new policy principles from beyond the circulation department or the individual administrators concerned with circulation to the entire library and/or the larger university community. It provides an opportunity for objections to be raised and implications of the changes to be explored. It also acts as a communication channel to the various constituencies represented on the committee, as well as from them. Often, a policy change alters the balance of benefits and liabilities among the several campus constituencies, and representatives of student groups, faculties, and university staff members serving on library committees can react to the proposals before they become a fait accompli. Even library-only committees expand opportunities for communicating questions, cautions, or objections among persons from outside the circulation department itself.

The committee review system can also have a different effect, that of resisting changes of any kind and protecting the status quo. Naturally, this is always a possible result of enabling a diverse membership to review policies. Some groups or persons may object to any suggested change in policy and might conceivably defeat it—the end result being that few, if any, changes would survive review. Though certainly a danger when entrusting policy decisions to a committee, it implies the people involved feel no responsibilities to improving their systems and services and no larger sense of purpose beyond the narrowest kind of self-interest. In effect, a committee can function well if its members have confidence in their ability to make changes and a sense of responsibility to help maximize library service, even though ideas about what might constitute maximum service might differ from one person to another. If, on the other hand, the members see themselves as ineffectual against opposing groups or as serving only their own constituency, it is unlikely they will contribute much to overall library service. Some committees may feel bound to echo an administrative "party line" or be extremely hesitant about going against tradition. Most, however, take their charge seriously and do the best they can with the issues and concerns of the campus community with which they are faced. They will undoubtedly be swayed by their group loyalties. Students might, for example, oppose extending faculty privileges or increasing fines only to students, while faculty might be in agreement with those changes. They may be persuaded by dynamic administrators whether in the library or the university, but, on the whole, committee members can be expected to try to see beyond those influences to the general good. Getting committee members to be sufficiently interested in policy issues so they carefully analyze and evaluate proposed changes is probably the most pressing problem. As one survey reply stated: "We are trying to get subcommittees together to do a review this year, but not having very good luck."

PROBLEMS CURRENTLY FACING CIRCULATION DEPARTMENTS

Two questions on the survey addressed current problems from two points of view: What is the library's biggest circulation problem and what are the clients' biggest complaints? The answers to these questions were sometimes the same and sometimes different, indicating that survey respondents tried to consider more than their own immediate concerns.

For several librarians, an inconvenient and unresponsive manual circulation system was the biggest problem for everyone, as noted in the following comments:

The biggest circulation problem is the frustration encountered because of the handwritten circulation system . . . [and], the patron's biggest complaint is frustration with the current circulation system.

Biggest complaint is probably the checkout procedure itself.

Quick and accurate access to circulation information was another major circulation problem; the patrons' complaint was

Inability to provide patron information . . . [and our] inability to quickly identify location of item not on shelf.

The major complaint is the tediousness of filling out the manual checkout cards.

"Manual files, identifying where any given item is at a given time," was the circulation department's biggest problem in one library while patrons complained most "They can't find the book they want. Manual files sometimes[s] make it hard for us to find them [i.e., the books] for them."

A second major issue is the extension by faculty of their already extended privileges as embodied in the following remarks: "Our relative ineffectiveness in recalling materials from [faculty] who are not fined or 'blocked', as are students and staff," was patrons' biggest complaint, while the staff felt their biggest circulation problem was "return of recalled items."

Others agreed:

Faculty non-returns are still a problem, however.
Faculty members' low level of responsibility in renewing books.

"Faculty who do not return materials," was the biggest circulation problem in another library, while patrons complained about "other patrons who don't return items that they are waiting for."
    Other problems were:

Getting faculty to return or replace items they borrow.
Staff complains about large number of faculty overdues (by years and years . . .).

Some libraries are dealing with this problem by rescinding the faculty's freedom from overdue charges. One director commented on this,

We have successfully introduced a policy of withholding part-time faculty paychecks at the end of a semester until books are returned and/or fines for lost books are paid. Full-time faculty are billed for overdues and lost books in the same manner as students.

Two other libraries hold faculty responsible for fines, too. One circulation librarian stated that policies were being changed in order to "establish control over faculty borrowing the same way we have control over student borrowing." A feeling of helplessness pervades some of the replies, as evident in these statements responding to the question about the biggest circulation problems:

No control of chronic abuses of library privileges. No way to determine if a particular student has overdue books when he leaves the college (e.g., at graduation).
Inability to identify delinquent patrons easily.
Inability to stop non-compliers at charge desk.
Community users consider fines and replacement charges a "cost of doing business—provides no incentive to return materials. . . . Abuse by non-affiliated users. . . . Theft, vandalism."
The delinquent borrowers who are not students/faculty at the university, but who have purchased or been given special borrower's cards are not directly billable, and because we do not have an automated system it is difficult to flag them when they come in to take more items.

    The fact that faculty and non-affiliated borrowers constitute major groups of problem clients is leading otherwise service-oriented professionals to reconsider their status and to change the regulations permitting abuses. It is also motivating the installation of automated circulation control systems in place of manual systems that would otherwise be tolerated, despite their many drawbacks.

Other issues named as major problems by survey respondents were that:

- Manual production of overdue notices was slow and inefficient.
- The limitations of reserve material circulation were vexing to their users.
- Desired materials were not on the shelves or available quickly enough.
- There were too many duties for the staff to perform leading to a sense of frustration.
- Circulation of noncataloged materials could not be controlled.
- There were ineffective fine schedules, inaccurate records, poor stack maintenance, improper renewals, and inconsistent enforcement of circulation rules among several branches.

Part of the unresponsiveness of manual circulation systems is their inability to produce notices except by tedious, labor-intensive procedures of examining each overdue record, transcribing the data by hand or typewriter, and then mailing the resulting notice—usually after stuffing, sealing, and stamping an envelope. While lack of information about overdues was cited by most people, seven of them felt the cost and length of time it took to prepare notices (including bills, recalls, and holds) was the worst problem. A corollary to cost and length of time were the additional difficulties caused by inaccurate records. One librarian said their biggest problem was, "Getting across to our student staff and to staff in other areas the importance of making sure the whole call # is listed on the charge cards"; another echoed, "Incorrect information recorded on charge card, [i]ncomplete information needed for circulation purposes (copy, edition), [i]naccurate discharging of books." A third found problems locating "the correct, current, local address of students from an out-dated Registrar's list. The Library should either receive printouts more frequently or be on-line with the University's computer." In all, five librarians complained about inaccuracies in record-keeping as a major circulation problem.

Computer systems may overcome some kinds of record errors such as transcribing numbers, names, or other data incorrectly and misfiling records, but they will not be infallible since errors in human data entry will be compounded throughout the system. A classic computer cartoon shows two white-coated computer scientists standing in front of an enormous computer console, while one remarks to the other, "Imagine that! It only took microseconds to compound your little error to the 4,387,524,683, 201,724th power!"

Though it is inevitable in circulating collections that materials will be out on loan, seven librarians felt their worst problem was that books were not on the shelf when clients looked for them. Two more found stack maintenance a problem, with misshelved books making it even harder for clients to find what they wanted. Some professionals believe a trek to the stacks for a particular item ending in disappointment (because it is not there) is a client's worst frustration, far more disturbing than paying fines or writing charge cards. Two respondents noted they interloaned missing materials, but admitted the time lag in receiving them made ILL a poor substitute for having desired items available in the first place. Some of the library guides made a special point of telling clients the number of weeks it took to obtain materials from another library, with one such paragraph headed "Plan Ahead" in big, bold letters. Contributing to the absence of materials on the shelf by keeping them in circulation for longer periods of time are renewals, sometimes permitted to continue indefinitely with few restrictions. Some libraries have begun restricting the number of renewals allowed in order to get materials back on the shelf, where they can be found without waiting for recall, hold, or ILL procedures. Indeed, many clients never ask for materials to be recalled or loans from another library because, as one person put it, "I need it *now* (preferably yesterday)!" Nevertheless, two librarians reported restrictions on renewals were a major client complaint, with one specifying that lack of telephone renewal service was the problem. Clients sometimes complain, too, about the more restrictive loan periods for reserve materials, especially if the item is needed by a graduate student for research or thesis work rather than by an undergraduate in the class for which it was reserved. Students in large classes often find themselves competing for one or two copies of required readings with most or all of their classmates just before an examination; while commuting students resent having to spend long hours in a crowded reserve room instead of being able to examine materials at home or while traveling. Textbooks on reserve are sometimes assigned the shortest possible loan periods, usually two hours, as well as the least flexibility about extending it, e.g., as an overnight loan when closing time approaches. No doubt this is because too many such texts disappear forever or are not returned promptly enough for others in the class to use them. The high cost of many textbooks places them outside the reach of students with already tight budgets, and more and more they must rely on reserve collections for access.

At the same time, several librarians indicated their displeasure with long reserve lists which take the circulation staff hours of preparation to search, pick from shelves, duplicate if necessary, reprocess, and house, only to have no one use them before the whole process has to be undone at the end of a term. Faculty occasionally forget to delete anything from their reserve lists, but they add to them every time they repeat a course. Others use the shotgun approach, figuring that if they put everything they can think of on the list, some of it may be read. Still others feel that everything on a syllabus reading list, whether required or merely recommended, should be made available on reserve. Some faculty members pride themselves on their excellent bibliographies which, at some moment in the future, may prove useful to a (former) student. Multiplied by a faculty of hundreds (or even thousands in a large university) these behavior patterns translate into a monumental task with revolving collections in the tens of thousands. (If each of 200 faculty put 50 items on reserve, it would equal 10,000 items.) Regardless of their desire to furnish students with a broad range of pertinent materials, faculty need to consider the burden this places on a library's staff. Circulation librarians respond by limiting the total number of reserve items permitted or eliminating readings that are not required and monitoring use in order to winnow out items that are not circulating. The reserve system, with its complex of hourly, overnight, one-, two-, or three-day loans and more, is a nightmare to program for an automated system, especially when the fine schedule varies with the type of materials as well as the loan period, the status of the borrower, and the time of day.

Surprisingly, problems with fine schedules were generally not emphasized; only three librarians listed them as an issue of concern. Two others noted in passing that fines were not a problem in their libraries. A belief in fines as psychological motivation to return books on time rather than as penalties with clout sometimes results in keeping the daily charges very low. Setting them too high, on the other hand, encourages theft of materials, since it proves cheaper to pay for replacement. Ceilings on the accumulation of overdue charges are encountered frequently, but floors were mentioned in only one place, specifically because of the cost of sending notices to recover fines amounting to less than fifty cents. Enforcement is also a problem, regardless of the amount charged for nonreturn of materials. One librarian said clients felt enforcement was too strict; another believed that variations in enforcement at different locations was most aggravating to clients.

A staff complaint voiced in two survey replies, but not really confined to circulation departments, is that staff have to perform many complicated tasks. Like many other library functions, circulation procedures may be rife with exceptions and include responsibility for services and/or materials that do not fall easily into any one department, such as supervising coin-operated duplicating machines, ILL, etc. Complicated procedures make training difficult and tasks time consuming. Worrying about regular loans, reserve loans, holds, recalls, shelving, overdues, and billing, especially in libraries with manual systems, is probably taxing enough without making change for copiers, calling for repairs, and filling paper trays, or filling out ILL forms, searching union catalogs, and so on. One library director said her circulation desk attendants were "responsible for messenger service between [our library] and [a nearby college library] with which we have a fee-based borrowing arrangement." More and more, circulation services are becoming true document delivery services, with the larger variety of methods and tasks involved in providing more than a passive client-initiated checkout. The same director added, "Our next biggest problem is SPACE. The circulation area was designed, along with the rest of the library, with little input from librarians. It is appalling—small and cramped, making the execution of a variety of tasks more difficult and confusing."

Current emphasis in college and university teaching on having students survey the literature on a topic—sometimes an introduction to an original research project and sometimes an end in itself—means students will continue to rely heavily on library materials, many or most of which will be borrowed, whenever possible.

FUTURE PLANS FOR CIRCULATION

Automating circulation for libraries with manual systems and extending automated systems currently in place figure prominently on the list of librarians' future plans. Sixteen of the twenty-two academic libraries participating in the survey were at some stage in planning for or obtaining a computerized circulation system, preferably one that would interface with other systems currently planned or implemented. (Since the survey, some of these libraries may have obtained automated systems.) A number of replies indicated that the planning was at a very early stage:

The Library has tentative plans to join a regional system.

The University of———is working on an RFP for System-wide use. No details are as yet available, but an automated circulation system is, hopefully, in our future plans.

Task Force has been formed to study various systems.

A computerized system is being investigated at this time. No definite decision has been made about which system we will eventually install.

We are currently exploring various on-line circulation systems.

A few libraries are going as far as possible with their planning, although no budget or specific timetable has yet been committed. One reply described this situation well: "A Committee consisting of [library] staff at all levels has spent the last couple of years defining what we need in a new system. . . . The powers that be in our college, in the state community college system, and in the state government have not made the financial resources available for any type of new system so the project is currently somewhat in limbo." Another reports, "We are hoping to automate circulation. Have begun retrospective conversion of holdings." Academic libraries using computerized networks for cataloging are able to prepare for other computer applications by building their database of bibliographic information. Another preparatory step is the bar-coding of materials—reported by two libraries—and issuing library cards. One librarian wrote: "We are planning on acquiring a turnkey integrated system which will use code-labelled patron ID cards. Consequently, we have started to require plastic photo IDs—which are issued on a voluntary basis by the College—for materials check-out. IDs were not required so stringently until we became computerized."

Two libraries reported being farther along in the process of automating: "We have just finished an extensive 'Invitation to Bid' that will be distributed to interested vendors," and "an on-line integrated library system will be selected this year, which will include a circulation/reserve module." A third reply indicated a system was already selected, but planning to evaluate its purchase was now under way. Two more libraries were well into the programming or negotiation phases for new online systems.

Libraries using computer systems for part of their circulation indicated plans to extend them or to add to them for more materials or departments: "NOTIS, acquired about one year ago, will be used for Reserve Circulation eventually," and "we hope that . . . we will be able to acquire within the next year a circulation module which will be integrated into the OPAC [Online Public Access Catalog] system. . . . If these plans prove not to be feasible, alternative plans to extend the current system to several selected department libraries will be implemented."

Corollary to automating the borrowing process is linking it with other systems, either by adding modules for acquisitions, serials control, and public catalog display, or developing interfaces between systems performing these functions. Two libraries specifically mentioned selecting a particular turnkey system because it claimed to provide this integration of functions, and a third was continuing to develop, in-house, a circulation module as part of a total system of technical services.

Asked about proposed policy and service changes being contemplated in the near term, many topics were mentioned. Heading the list of desirable new services was *immediate access to status information*; some of the eight librarians listed it specifically as a self-service activity clients could perform not just as information available to staff. Several elaborated on their primary interest in having the catalog show where copies of a title were (on the shelf, out in circulation, or in process); others wanted to be able to identify items charged out to individual borrowers. Most saw this as a service to clients; indeed, one librarian said this information should be available to clients in their offices, dormitories, or homes, but it could also be useful to staff in determining client status (having too many materials charged out to be given more).

Remote access to circulation data from outside the library and the *ability to charge items or place requests without the need for assistance by library staff* were named desired services by three and four librarians, respectively. *Speeding up the charging process*, though not necessarily by means of self-service procedures, was listed by three more people.

Other services sought by at least one respondent included campus-wide document delivery, selective dissemination of information (named as desirable but not a circulation service by a second librarian), and better statistical reports for management information services.

Most believed automation would help provide these services, particularly access to information about materials and clients, which seems to be at a critical point in many academic libraries.

Policy changes currently being sought centered most frequently on changing loan periods. Six librarians were pursuing such changes, with faculty loans, reserve loans, and periodical loans being mentioned in particular as needing change.

Five librarians each said they wanted policy or procedural changes designed to get faculty to return materials or to control delinquency more effectively. Another library added that policies "to dispel the 'free library' image" were needed in his library. Faster production of notices and methods for identifying delinquents at charging points were seen as the best ways of achieving some of these policy goals. Again, online circulation control systems were seen as the most likely ways to provide these capabilities. Others felt, however, that exemption from fines offered no motivation to faculty to return materials and that slow production of notices did not elicit a very good return rate. Perhaps related to the general problem of controlling delinquency, two librarians wanted to change the policy on nonaffiliates; nevertheless, a third said the library wanted policy changes to extend borrowing privileges to additional groups of nonaffiliated users.

Simplification or streamlining of procedures to make them more businesslike and efficient was named as a desired policy change by five librarians. One of these said that "policies [should] reflect more accountability and to demonstrate standard business practices (e.g., using 'inventory control' rather than 'circulation')." The philosophy may stem not only from pressure to save money, but also from the belief that libraries can emulate business management techniques successfully, achieving more effective as well as more efficient services that way. Some librarians expressed relief that collection of fines had been turned over to college or university financial offices, not so much because it removed an unwelcome task from the circulation department, but because financial offices *succeeded in collecting the fees* while the libraries had not. One librarian sought a policy change to eliminate overdue fines altogether. No doubt she believed overdue charges did not motivate prompt returns and cost more to collect than they produced in revenue. Nonetheless, most libraries continue to maintain relatively innocuous daily fine charges for overdue materials and to complain about their ineffectuality in promoting returns.

Introduction of stricter limits—on the number of items a client could borrow, the number of items a faculty member could place on a reserve list, and the number of times an item could be renewed—were named in five replies. As discussed in Chapter 2, several libraries have already imposed limits on reserves and renewals; however, none mentioned limits on the number of items that could be borrowed by college or university affiliates, although they were often imposed on guests or other non-affiliates. The tone of the majority of survey responses leaned toward greater restrictiveness in general, summed up dramatically by the librarian who did not want to promote the image of free services. Yet the notion of free library service is implicit in the array of curricular and research activities to which the payment of tuition entitles students. For faculty, it must be an attraction of no little import; otherwise, why would so many institutions provide their faculty members with all the extra privileges, particularly the exemption from overdue charges? One librarian implied faculty were not charged for lost books, either, though in most places some responsibility for return of materials is demanded.

Another policy change being actively sought in three libraries was to bring variations in regulations in different areas of the library or in different departmental libraries into harmony so that all areas/departments followed the same procedures. Individual interpretations of a single rule may cause unavoidable confusion, but different rules in different departments are another story. The trend toward consolidating groups of libraries in college or university systems, as well as within a single institution, to facilitate automation or purchasing, processing, and/or general administration is making it more difficult to continue maintaining divergent circulation practices. Although sharing automated systems does not require conformity, it certainly furnishes an opportunity to avoid more complications than absolutely necessary and a reason to simplify procedures making programming, training, and operation of the new system easier. The key word here is *necessary*. Sometimes complicated rules and procedures are necessary to accomplish needed services, particularly since collections differ widely in the number of items, range of topics, level of materials, and so forth as well as in the manner in which faculty may want to use them, student interests, and more. Circulation staff, particularly the department managers, have to ask themselves, their colleagues, and their counterparts in other departments, branches, and/or related institutions, whether it is serving a purpose to have different fine schedules, loan periods, eligibility requirements, or other procedural variations. If one library allows 30-day loans and another has monthly loans (i.e., an item taken out on the 25th of one month is due on the 25th of the next), are the two really too far apart to compromise? If, however, one library has four-week loans and the other has two-week loans for the same type of materials, it might be much harder to get them to agree on a single loan period. The philosophy or policy principle the rules are designed to serve need to be similar, if not identical, in order to arrive at mutually agreeable decisions.

OBSERVATIONS ABOUT POLICY CHANGES

Very little empirical research seems to have been done to provide any theoretical underpinnings for circulation rules, although individual libraries may do information studies of their own. Some changes seem to stem from a series of complaints, while others are the result of having to make do with fewer staff-hours, or of changing department heads or directors. Coherent rules with proposed changes that have been pretested or based on some experiential data are not usually the rule. If no one complains too much and the department is operating fairly well, most people are willing to let it go at that.

Tradition seems to play a significant role in all of this, too, despite efforts to make far-reaching technical changes. Librarians purchasing automated systems are warned against duplicating manual operations and are encouraged to use new systems in new ways, taking advantage of these capabilities to change the goals and objectives of their department. Nevertheless, this advice is often ignored and librarians use the computers to do what they have been doing for years, albeit more rapidly, more efficiently, and more accurately. Few institutions' circulation systems appear to be fundamentally user-oriented, even toward that special portion of the academic population comprising faculty and staff. Most seem to be concerned primarily with materials—possibly because users give little encouragement to circulation librarians by abusing the privileges accorded them, or, perhaps because these departments are judged on the basis of their success in maintaining a high level of material returns not on increasing the number of checkouts. For one thing, academic libraries purchase far fewer duplicates of titles than do public libraries; thus, each item is likely to represent the only copy of a title that will be made available to the entire community. If it is lost or is deliberately not returned, it frequently is gone forever, never to be replaced. Deliberate misshelving of books that cannot be borrowed or renewed keeps them hidden from everyone but the self-serving perpetrator. This ploy was encountered during my library school days, much to my distress, when a bibliography I needed desperately was always missing from the shelf. One day I observed someone retrieving it from another stack and "rescued" it later from its secret location. Good shelf-reading controls this sort of antisocial behavior as well as accidental misshelving. Recent trends in coping with tighter library acquisition budgets make replacement of titles previously purchased more unattractive than ever, and more rapid obsolescence of publishers' backlists make it more difficult, too. All of these factors contribute to making the focus of document delivery, of which borrowing is still the primary service option, the *document* rather than the *delivery*.

SUMMARY

The circulation survey asked questions of librarians working in libraries serving all kinds of two- and four-year college programs as well as graduate and professional degree programs in academic institutions of all sizes. They were asked questions about the circulation system itself, about any new systems or policies that were planned, about policy formulation, and about current problems.

The most striking response to the inquiry about current systems was the large number of libraries still operating manual instead of computerized systems. The McBee keysort system was the most popular of those named, with Gaylord's charging machines close behind. Many employed signed book cards, sometimes in duplicate. Of those libraries with computerized systems, four were online and three were offline, batch-processing systems. Even in these seven libraries, not all chargeouts were necessarily online since reserve materials and branch/departmental operations often were not included in the main system.

All but three of the circulation departments using manual systems, all of those using offline automated systems, and one library with an online system that did not include its reserve circulation intended to change to an online, all-inclusive, library-controlled, computerized circulation system. Several were well along in the planning, negotiating, purchasing, or implementing phase of the automation process. Some had done a great deal of planning, but were limited by budgetary restrictions from executing them. Several indicated they were moving forward in their plans as part of a group or consortium without specific timetables. Many were pursuing circulation modules only as a part of larger systems in which all technical service functions (acquisitions, cataloging, public catalog display, serials control, ILL, *and* circulation) were integrated. The circulation module was seen as central to some and peripheral to others when describing the proposed integrated system. (This may have been influenced more by the role of the respondent, the library director or circulation manager, than by the actual importance attached to any part of the proposed system.)

Of the three libraries planning no changes to their manual systems, only one librarian indicated that it was because they were satisfied that their current one met all of their needs. One hoped the bibliographic utility with which the library was affiliated would develop an online circulation system; the other was part of a larger university system which controlled development of automation for all its constituents. In both of these cases, the librarians wanted automated circulation, but they were unable to obtain it on their own.

Libraries with online systems were generally satisfied with them and were interested primarily in extending them to more materials or in adding more modules to produce an integrated system.

Policy formulation varied widely in this sample of academic libraries. In a few places, many people within and without the library contributed to circulation policy. In the majority of libraries, however, policy formulation was limited to circulation departments and/or library administrators. Exactly which administrator participates (director, deputy director, head of public services, etc.) seems to depend on the size and organizational structure of each library. Most circulation department heads were responsible, though rarely alone, for some part of the policy formulation process. In some libraries, committees with representation from various library departments, faculty, and other university staff also advised upon or reviewed policy changes.

Regular policy review was conducted in only seven libraries, one of which claimed to review policy continuously. The others conducted reviews annually, sometimes as part of a year-end annual review of all departments and services. Most policy reviews were irregular or were done "as needed," when initiated by problems, complaints, or other indications of dissatisfaction with the status quo. Five librarians said they had no policy reviews whatever.

Major circulation problems experienced in several of the libraries included (1) lack of needed information, (2) abuse of their privileges by faculty, (3) frustration with the tedious work for both staff and clients in using manual charging systems, (4) materials missing from the shelf, (5) inability to identify delinquents at the chargeout desk, (6) inaccurate recordkeeping, and (7) failure to secure timely return of materials. There is no way to determine whether this last-named problem is as severe as one might believe from the replies, since the survey did not ask for data on the proportion of materials returned promptly, late, and not at all. Furthermore, there are no standards against which to judge performance either in general or within one specific library. A nonreturn rate of, say, eight percent might appear enormous to one librarian and insignificant to another. Increases or decreases over time may indicate the effectiveness of the rules and their enforcement in a library. Raising or lowering the daily charge for overdues may be less significant than applying whatever charges are currently mandated in a consistent manner, even for items thrown into book drops or accompanied by tearful excuses. Even eliminating daily charges altogether and establishing different penalties for delinquents might prove more successful in the long run, and such are the plans of one survey respondent.

Interestingly, clients' complaints overlap those of the staff, with lack of needed information heading the list. This complaint is followed by missing materials and tedious manual checkout procedures. Clients also chafe at reserve room limits and lack of permission for renewals, especially telephone renewals. There were few client complaints about the size of fines, though one librarian reported clients were annoyed by the strict adherence to the letter of the rules by staff. In spite of it, nonreturns were still considered a problem in this library.

Future plans for many libraries involve computers. Yet, comments from some librarians indicate recognition that, by themselves, computers will not end their problems: "While automation will not solve all circulation problems, we are looking forward to its benefits in accuracy, time saving, and the stopped borrowing by repeat delinquents." Another said, "We find that we must hire intelligent, hard-working people (since they are often the main contact for the library user) and they spend most of their time filing slips and tallying checklists. We hope that automation—or semi-automation as the case may be, will reduce some of the tedium & free the staff for somewhat more creative projects."

A librarian who enjoyed an automated system commented, "Automation has allowed us to cope with an increase in circulation. This increase may, itself, be as a result of automation because patrons use terminals for . . . access to our collection as well as the collections of some 20-24 other academic libraries . . . who also use [the same circulation system.]"

Policy changes being planned usually involve providing clients with more information or the imposition of new restrictions on clients, loans, and/or materials. Only two replies suggested liberalizing policies or regulations. If, as is indicated above, automation tends to increase circulation, these more restrictive policies may serve to dampen the effect or eliminate it altogether. It may not do clients much good to find the titles they want are available in the library if they no longer have access to them, or if they can use them only for a few hours, or if they can use them only in-house. The desire to catch the worst culprits and prevent repeated offenses in borrowing may result in limiting everyone in the system to the detriment of satisfying overall library goals. The dilemma over conflicting goals and objectives is clearly evident in one library director's comment: "Circulation policies have, historically, been highly complex and tailored to the real and imagined needs of various user groups. . . . Some would say that the Library was highly service-oriented; others would say that it was careless and permissive." This director's response is "to simplify and standardize as much as possible."

Everyone sees the capabilities of online systems as an aid to solving their problems. The desire to respond in kind seems clear throughout the survey. Libraries where problems frequently involve faculty abuses, nonaffiliated delinquencies, or even student violations look forward to automated systems that will help find and mark these people and force them to obey circulation rules. Those who are told by clients that desired materials are never available want to limit loan periods or renewals, remove categories of materials from circulation, or at least improve their ability to locate and recall materials. In this effort, computers are seen as the best available means of succeeding. Circulation departments struggling to keep up with paperwork look to the computer to eliminate it. Service-oriented librarians want remote access or self-service searching and charging for clients via their own terminals. Thus, automated systems—online, integrated systems—are eagerly awaited in the great majority of these academic libraries so that the librarians can perform whatever tasks are necessary to enable each one to achieve its own particular goals.

Public libraries have the most diverse clientele from toddlers attending play sessions with their parents and school children with "library" assignments to college students; teachers; adults seeking best sellers, escape reading, or self-help books and do-it-yourself aides; and post-doctoral researchers seeking material for biographies, histories, novels, or other complex studies. They also have enormously eclectic collections. When I worked as a public librarian, I was approached on the same day by a composer seeking recordings of Nazi music that he hoped would provide background themes while he worked on the music for a television drama about the Holocaust and by an ice-skating instructor looking for instrumental music to use in choreographing competition routines for her figure-skating students. Naturally, both of these clients expected to take their selections home, and so they did.

Circulation policy documents from seventeen public libraries are described in this chapter. These libraries are located in cities in the South, Northeast, Northwest, and Far West, in small towns in the Midwest and Northeast, and in suburbs of cities; two are county and two are regional networks. They are geographically distributed and represent different types of governmental jurisdictions. They also provide examples of different community sizes and styles.

In public libraries, the circulation desk is the most visible service point, and borrowing materials is the most highly prized service. Unlike academic libraries, where many of the most heavily used materials are in reference collections (including many periodicals and serials) or put on reserve for classes to share in-house, the most popular items on public library shelves usually circulate, and the proportion of circulating to noncirculating materials is much higher.

Many libraries sent staff manuals rather than documents intended for distribution to clients. Some of these manuals displayed sophisticated formatting—boldfaced headings, page headers and footers, and centered titles. Some of them were hundreds of pages long, describing each routine in detail with examples and illustrations. Client documents ranged from small sheets and flyers to larger foldouts and multipage brochures. All were relatively professional looking. Some were printed on slick paper in several colors with attractive graphic designs. If one adjective were applied to the group of documents, *neat* would be the one I would choose, applicable equally to the staff-only manuals and those intended for client distribution.

The policies are divided into three groups. Documents from libraries that serve the larger cities are described first. These are followed by a second group of suburban and smaller city and town library policies. The final group include the regional and county library policies and those of their constituents.

ATLANTA-FULTON PUBLIC LIBRARY

A draft circulation policy dated February, 1984, spells out borrowing rules for the Atlanta-Fulton (Georgia) Public Library (A-FPL).[1] A comment on the accompanying survey form explains that, "All documents to be publicly distributed are in the process of being revised, rewritten, newly developed, etc. However, the information on [them] is taken directly from the policy."[2]

The policy begins with an overall mission statement in which the library's primary public is identified as "permanent residents of Fulton County and Atlanta in DeKalb."[3] The geographic locality may sound somewhat peculiar, but Atlantans know that their municipality extends wholly or partly into more than one county, unlike other cities where municipal boundaries coincide with county lines. That part of DeKalb County located outside the City of Atlanta is served by a separate library system, DeKalb County Library, which has its own policies and regulations.

Beyond the service commitment to permanent residents of the city (actually, subsequent statements redefine this primary clientele more specifically to mean the adult residents),[4] the policy defines nine other client categories: (1) fee-paying nonresidents; (2) business firms, including domestic and foreign government offices, located within Atlanta proper—a "corporate body" rather than a personal type of client; (3) preschool institutions not affiliated with a public or private school (here, too, the schools, not their students, are the clients); (4) post-secondary school students with nonresident permanent home addresses but with Atlanta-Fulton County local school addresses; (5) patients of any of the city's health care facilities; (6) members of the press; (7) nonresident library staff members; (8) residents under the age of twelve; and (9) visitors. Qualifications for inclusion in one of these nine categories is spelled out in detail as well as the proof that must be submitted before service is rendered. Interestingly, nonresident students in elementary and secondary schools located within the city are excluded from service. They are not mentioned in any of the client categories named, nor are they covered anywhere else in the document. Children under the age of twelve, though residents, are not furnished with a permanent library card without the signature of an adult.

Fees for nonresident service are $75 for persons under sixty-five and $50 for persons over sixty-five. Proof of age must be shown before the lower fee is accepted. Nonresident taxpayers make up an even more complicated category-within-a-category; the fee for these people is waived upon submitting proof of current taxpaying status.

Accountability for borrowed materials is implied in the requirements that businesses and schools name an officer on their applications and that adults countersign for children. A passage cautions clients "to safeguard their library card because financial responsibility lies with the person . . . to whom the card was issued"[5] and reiterates personal responsibility for overdue fines and the cost of lost or damaged materials.[6] These passages (and others relating to the confidentiality of circulation records and protection of client privacy) indicate that library policymakers believe that circulation documentation has legal implications and that they tried to anticipate instances of legally binding financial liability. It may be that legal expertise was sought in the preparation of these statements hopefully to reduce the number of delinquents by being explicit about legal implications for clients. (User accountability to libraries and of administrators to government authorities occurs in some academic library policies, too—notably, those of the University of North Florida.)'

Business and school clients must have their library cards in hand to borrow materials; residents can be served upon presentation of another (unspecified) identification. Some latitude is accorded to librarians in charge of circulation in permitting such loans free of charge or applying a $3 penalty when library cards are forgotten or lost repeatedly. The choice is left to the staff member's discretion.

The initial mission statement also defines what kinds of materials are borrowable: "In addition to books, the library lends films, audio and video-cassettes, recordings, art prints, and pamphlets."[7] This wording expresses a traditionally bibliocentric approach, namely that the lending of things other than books is remarkable and must be specially mentioned.

In contrast to the complicated list of client categories and a similarly intricate schedule of fines and fees to be discussed later in this section, there are only four loan periods: (1) twenty-four hours for films and videocassettes, (2) ten days for reserved materials (materials requested by another client), (3) two months for art prints, and (4) twenty-eight days for everything else. The only materials for which renewals are specified are the 24-hour film and video loans, and these need only be requested for the loan to be extended.

Four pages of text in the eleven-page policy are devoted to fines and fees. The section on overdue fines begins with a statement of purpose that is refreshing in its directness: "The purpose of the library's overdue fine and retrieval policy is to encourage return of the library's materials. Persons will be given every opportunity to return materials; however, legal action will be taken against those who violate the law by not returning library materials."[8] It is not stated whether policymakers refer to a specific law or whether general laws against stealing or defacing public property were interpreted to include library materials. Clearly, the notion that delinquents might get away with abuses was being dispelled.

The process of fine and retrieval is also detailed:

Overdue fines are charged at the rate of 5 cents per day, per item, with the following exceptions: films and videocassettes are charged at the rate of $3.00 per day, per item; art prints are charged at 25 cents per day, per item.

If materials are not returned within 40 days after the due date, the account will be referred to a collection agency, at which time fines will double, retroactive to the first day overdue to a maximum of $5.00 per item. Pamphlets and mass market paperbacks have a $1.00 maximum; films, videocassettes and art prints have a $10.00 maximum.

Accounts referred to the collection agency will have a $5.00 service fee added to the account.

If materials are not returned within 120 days after the due date, the account will be referred to the Fulton County Sheriff for retrieval of the library's materials, with any additional costs added to the account.[9]

Charges for materials lost or "terminally damaged" are essentially replacement costs, determined by finding listings in bibliographies, by application of Bowker's price averages, or by a designated specialist staff member's judgment. Items that can be repaired are also subject to fines: $3 for hardcover books, $1 for paperbound books and pamphlets, whatever figure deemed appropriate by a specialist staff member for visual materials, and the price of replacing the whole set for missing parts of sound recordings.

A schedule of other fees identifies some kinds of services that are not free. A-FPL charges for any service that "incurs extra costs not absorbed by the library annual budget."[10] These include reserving items,[11] interlibrary loans, and computer searches. Specific fees are not named, but they are geared to cost recovery, e.g., postage charges are levied for reserves, whereas interlibrary loans and computer searches vary depending on the charges imposed by the lending library or the length and kind of online search conducted.

Though these rather mild attempts to recover costs seem innocuous enough, the precedent they set raises hackles in many quarters. One particular target of opponents to public library service charges is online searching because it could remove access to this important source of information from the reach of just those less affluent clients whose only possible route to it is through the public library. It is hard to fault the library, whose only alternative may be total inability to provide online searching for anyone without recovering costs. Critics of public library fees for service (and also, sometimes, of service fees in academic libraries) argue that the costs of online searching should be absorbed by the institution, if not through budget increases, then by eliminating other, less vital services. The debate continues and will not be resolved here; however, A-FPL opted to differentiate between information in materials it owns and information in materials it does not, offering the former free and the latter for a fee.

TACOMA PUBLIC LIBRARY

Tacoma Public Library in Tacoma, Washington, sent excerpts from its "Administrative Policy,"[12] as well as a small flyer intended for clients, which explains the loans and overdues for eighteen kinds of materials (Figure 4-1).[13]

Tacoma's answer to the question of who may borrow is linked to state law which is quoted in the policy document: "Every library established or maintained under this act shall be free for the use of the inhabitants of the governmental unit in which it is located, subject to such reasonable rules and regulations as the Trustees find necessary to assure the greatest benefit to the greatest number."[14] Before discussing clients at all, the responsibility attached to having a library card was stated:

The Library assumes anyone having a card has permission to use it unless the card has been reported lost. If someone other than the registrant desires to charge Library materials, the card itself must be presented.

Responsibility for all lost or damaged materials charged to a card rests with the registered patron, unless the card has been reported lost prior to the date when the materials were charged out.

The responsible person in the case of Business cards is the signer of the application and, in the case of cards issued to juveniles, the registered patron and the parent or guardian whose signature is on the application.[15]

Figure 4-1
Tacoma Public Library Circulation Flyer

Loan Periods and Limits

To insure that the Library has an adequate
supply of materials for all patrons, the
maximum number of items allowed out on one
card at any given time is ninety-nine (99)

ITEM	LOAN PERIOD	LIMIT	MAX. FINE
New Fiction	7 days	none	$ 6
New Non-Fiction	7 days	none	$ 6
Most Other Books	28 days	none	$ 6
Pamphlets	28 days	none	$ 6
Magazines	7 days	none	$ 6
Art Prints	28 days	2	$ 6
Posters	28 days	6	$ 6
Records	7 days	6	$ 6
Cassette Tapes	7 days	3	$ 6
Video Discs	2 days	2	$10
Video Tapes	2 days	2	$10
8mm Films	7 days	6 reels	$ 6
16mm Films	2 days	4 reels	$10
Projectors	1 day	1	$10
Screens	1 day	1	$10
Slide Sets	28 days	3	$ 6
Toys and Games	7 days	3	$ 6
Comic Books	28 days	none	$ 6

Overdue Fines

The fine for most items is 5¢ per day, up
to a maximum of $6 per item. Some fines
are $1 per day, up to a maximum of $10 per
item. Overdue notices will be sent when
items are approximately one week overdue.
After six weeks, the cost of the item will
be added to the fine and the current total
will be billed. When items become sixteen
weeks overdue, the account will be referred
to a collection agency.

Tacoma Public Library System

MAIN LIBRARY
1102 Tacoma Avenue South
591-5666

FERN HILL BRANCH
765 South 84th Street
591-5620

KOBETICH BRANCH
212 Brown's Point Blvd.
591-5630

MCCORMICK BRANCH
3722 North 26th Street
591-5640

MOORE BRANCH
215 South 56th Street
591-5650

MOTTET BRANCH
3523 East G Street
591-5660

SOUTH TACOMA BRANCH
3411 South 56th Street
591-5670

SWASEY BRANCH
7001 6th Avenue
591-5680

Operating Hours

Monday - Thursday
9:00 - 9:00

Friday - Saturday
9:00 - 6:00

Six categories of client are entitled to free library cards based on interpretation of the state law: (1) city residents, (2) people who prove they pay taxes on city property, (3) people who pay other business-related taxes to the city, (4) library staff members including "active volunteers," (5) people specially designated by the library (for example, consultants employed by the library), and (6) city employees regardless of where they live. Everyone else pays a nonrefundable fee for service unless a contract specifies otherwise. (One such contract refers to Fircrest residents.)

Fees charged to other clients are low, $20 or less, though they are subject to change. Temporary residents are charged $10 for a 90-day card, and members of a nonresident family receive a discount after the purchase of the initial card.

Special cards are issued free to certified staff members of Tacoma's schools, both public and private, as well as to clients teaching outside of Tacoma but who hold a nonresident card. A teacher's card enables the holder to take fifty items at once, to keep all but the seven-day items for six weeks, and to be exempted from overdue fines, though not from charges for damage or loss. Materials taken out on a teacher's card are specified *"for classroom use only"*;[16] the card will be cancelled if abused. Videorecordings cannot be borrowed with a teacher's card because of possible copyright infringement.

Two specially designated cards are described for corporate body clients: the business teacher's card—essentially the same as the teacher's card but intended for licensed day care centers and preschools—and the business card, which carries no special privileges intended for other organizations, e.g., business, government agencies, associations, or charitable and nonprofit organizations.

Other pages detail registration procedures. Documents used to establish a prospective client's identity and eligibility include driver's licenses; passports and visas; state identification cards; military, employment, immigration, or school identification cards; and Indian tribal identification cards. A firm statement that nothing else can be substituted is included.[17] When it is not possible to verify an address, cards are mailed to the address given to insure the validity of the residence. The description of registration policy closes with a final admonition that, *"No materials whatsoever may be taken until an address is verified."*[18]

Juveniles under fourteen years of age are required to have a parent or guardian's signature in addition to establishing their identity and residence. They *and* the responsible adults are liable for obligations attached to their cards.

Registration for a library card is not a one-time act, although the length of a card's validity is not specified. Re-registration policies for clients with less than $5 in outstanding fines involves presentation of the expired card and verbal verification of identity and residence as well as full payment of any outstanding fines. An additional requirement for clients owing more than $5, obviously designed to screen out undesirables at the point of re-registration, is that they must also reestablish identity and residence by presenting one of the acceptable forms of identification instead of merely giving their word. Lost cards require payment of a $1 fee before renewing registration. Also, lost cards cannot be replaced unless any fines against the original have been paid in full.

Several restrictions are placed on videorecordings other than not being loaned to teachers for classroom use. They are kept behind the circulation desk; they can be returned only to the location where they were checked out; they cannot be taken to other parts of the library or viewed within the building without first being checked out; no more than two recordings can be borrowed at any time; they can be checked out only on an adult card; and clients between fifteen and eighteen are required to register for a "media responsibility card" before being permitted to borrow them. In addition to accepting full responsibility for the cost of damaged or lost videorecordings, borrowers are responsible for their use, absolving the library of any complicity in the viewing of R-rated films. (X-rated films are not even mentioned.) Film industry audience ratings are noted on videorecordings of current motion pictures.

Other materials, though their circulation treatment varies, do not warrant so much attention. Formats listed on the patron flyer run the gamut of book and nonbook materials. Noteworthy because they do not always circulate if they are part of the holdings are video discs, projectors, screens, toys, games, and comic books. There are no special limits on the numbers of printed items that can be borrowed, including the comic books. Nonbook formats are limited from a minimum of one each for the hardware items to a maximum of six posters, sound discs, and/or 8 mm films. The rationale is "to insure that the Library has an adequate supply of materials for all patrons"[19] and a total maximum of ninety-nine items of all kinds is imposed, across the board.

Books are divided into new and old collections but not into hardcovers and paperbacks. New items are lent for seven days; older books can be kept for twenty-eight days. The 28-day loan also applies to pamphlets, art prints, posters, and slide sets. Seven-day loans apply to magazines, sound recordings, 8 mm films, toys, and games. Videorecordings have two-day loans. Renewals are not mentioned.

Overdue fine policies and procedures are noted on the patron document. Most items cost five cents daily up to a maximum of $6, although videorecordings cost $1 per day with a ceiling of $10. The higher limit also applies to films and hardware.

Overdue notices are sent after an item is one week overdue, and the cost of the item is added to accumulated fines after six weeks, when the total is billed to the client. After sixteen weeks, the library refers open accounts to a collection agency. These practices are part of a general methodology that appears to be gaining acceptance among public librarians. It is an assertive posture that not only is a more positive response to delinquency, but also should insure that a problem client's abuses cannot continue to grow. Clearly, it depends on a perception of the public library as an agency whose free services are limited and which expects a large measure of client accountability in return.

LOS ANGELES PUBLIC LIBRARY

An attractive brochure entitled "Your Library" (Figure 4-2)[20] and excerpts from a staff document covering circulation and registration policies were sent to explain the who, what, and how of circulation in the Los Angeles Public Library (LAPL).[21] A large urban system consisting of a main library, sixty-two branches, and five bookmobiles, LAPL describes itself as "one of the major cultural resources of the City . . . a resource shared by millions of people throughout Southern California and the West."[22] Unlike some urban library systems in which there is one extremely large central library and many, much smaller branches, LAPL has seven geographic regions, each with a headquarters library serving its region as a central resource plus the central library located downtown. Together, branch and regional headquarters libraries have more than half of the total holdings of the system.

"The Los Angeles Public Library issues free library cards to all borrowers who meet identification requirements."[23] This cryptic statement on the client brochure is reiterated, without explanation, in the pages of the staff policy. "Residents of Los Angeles are also eligible for borrower's cards at most other libraries in Los Angeles County" continues the client brochure, enabling one to deduce that these are the "borrowers" named previously.[24] Details in the pages of the "Registration Policy" do not explain the requirements. LAPL classifies its clients by age and special privilege, with three age groups designated adult, intermediate, and juvenile. Age specifications are not defined further. Members of LAPL's youngest group of clients must print or write their names to qualify for a library card. Special privilege groups include organizations, the handicapped, clients with "authentic research need," teachers, and vacationers. The handicapped can borrow materials without having to go in person to the library.

Clearly worded statements indicate a cardholder's obligations: "Until the Library is notified of a lost or stolen card, a Library Card is valid and its owner is responsible for any lost or overdue materials and fines an illegal user may incur."[25] Organizations are required to submit a letter on their official stationery "accepting responsibility."[26] LAPL reserves the right to

Figure 4-2
Portion of Illustrated Brochure

LOS ANGELES PUBLIC LIBRARY

The Los Angeles Public Library is one of the major cultural resources of the City of Los Angeles; a resource shared by millions of people throughout Southern California and the West. Funded through the City budget and governed by an appointed Board of Library Commissioners, it provides a wealth of information and a continuous flow of recreational reading.

As the City has grown and changed, so has the Library system and its services. Traditional library materials and services have been joined by many new programs, audio-visual materials and innovative ways to better serve all the citizens of Los Angeles.

The Los Angeles Public Library is recognized throughout the country for the high quality service and assistance it provides the public through its Central Library, network of branches, bookmobiles and special programs.

Today's library is more than books and buildings; it is information of all kinds. It is answers to simple and complex questions, and materials to meet the needs and interests of the multi-cultured, broadly diverse population of Los Angeles.

The Library has long pioneered in creating programs to reach and serve the public. These efforts have made Los Angeles Public Library agencies vital components of their communities and providers of extensive resources and information for the cultural, educational, business, personal and leisure needs of City residents.

CENTRAL LIBRARY

The Rufus B. von KleinSmid Central Library, 630 W. 5th St., is the heart of the Los Angeles Public Library System. It is headquarters for the entire operation and holds more than two million of the system's five million items.

Through its subject departments and special services, Central Library assists all the agencies in the system and is a major public reference and information center for Southern California and several Western states.

It is a depository for government documents and has the only complete U.S. patents collection west of the Mississippi. In addition, specially trained librarians provide information and reference service to patrons in the library and by telephone.

To better serve the many agencies and functions of local government, municipal reference libraries and staff are located in the City Hall complex, Water and Power Department headquarters and the Police Department's Parker Center.

The Southern California Answering Network (SCAN) and Southern California Inter-Library Loan (SCILL) are headquartered in Central Library because of the depth of the Central Library collection. (See Special Services.)

Subject departments and specialized resources at Central Library include:

Art, Music, Recreation	History
Audio-Visual	Literature and Philology
Business and Economics	Map Room
California History	Newspapers and Periodicals
Children's Literature	Patents
Fiction	Philosophy and Religion
Foreign Languages	Science and Technology
Genealogy	Social Sciences

BRANCHES

With its 62 branches and five bookmobiles, the Los Angeles Public Library has long pioneered in creating community involvement programs designed to reach residents all over this far-flung city. The branch operation is divided into seven geographic regions: Central, East Valley, Hollywood, Northeast, Southern, West Valley and Western. Each region includes a headquarters library which serves the area much the same as Central serves the entire system.

For many communities, the fact that the library can be entertaining as well as informational is a delightful new discovery.

Branches gear their collections and activities to meet the needs and interests of their particular neighborhood. Activities are as varied as the subjects in their book collections and the patrons they serve. Branches provide special outreach programs, hold language classes, serve as referral centers for job and career information, as well as provide reading skill development classes, how-to training in crafts, gardening, cooking and home repair. The wide range of projects, programs and services is all free of charge.

For more information, call a nearby branch library. (See Directory, other side)

CHILDREN'S SERVICES

Children's Services provides books and guidance for the individual child from pre-school age through seventh grade. Central Library, all branches and bookmobiles maintain collections of books for children, as well as magazines, records, cassettes, filmstrips and study prints. Children's librarians are on hand to guide and encourage youngsters in their reading, and to plan programs, projects and activities designed to stimulate a child's interest in reading. These librarians also visit schools to discuss and demonstrate the fun and value of books and libraries.

revoke a card "for infringement of the rules."[27] While these statements are not elaborated, they demand client accountability and demonstrate intolerance of borrowing abuse. Reasons for suspending a card include "abuse of library privileges; misconduct in an agency; violation of State and/or Municipal Codes; excessive fines and/or delinquent book charges; submission of forged or fictitious information."[28] Reinstatement is permitted if the problems are resolved. Cards are revoked if they are reported lost or stolen, if they are voluntarily returned, if they are requested by parents or guardians, or if a client is reported dead. Clients who forget their cards can be served provided they do not owe the library anything. Client records are stored in a municipal computer with reports available in microfiche or online, depending on the presence of hardware in an individual branch. Privacy of client records is not guaranteed.

Library cards are valid for three years with automatic renewal so long as the person remains in good standing and wants it. If a card expires, another application must be made. Information obtained from the automated system makes it relatively easy for LAPL to monitor re-registration and to determine the status of clients. Computer-generated reports to all LAPL units are used to flag clients who need "immediate action [to] be taken on [their] record."[29] In this way, the library minimizes abuses.

Circulating materials include books, periodicals, pamphlets, pictures, clippings, maps, orchestrations, recordings, tapes, films, microfilm, microcards, and more (reference materials can also circulate as a special loan with permission from a librarian-in-charge). The policy states that "the majority of library materials are purchased for circulation and are lent for a period of fourteen days, with the privilege of reissue, except under certain conditions, to the patron who presents a valid Library Card."[30] The total number of items a cardholder can borrow at once is limited to thirty—ten books, ten recordings (although it is not specified, this probably means sound recordings, not videorecordings), and ten other items. If, as a new registrant, one has a temporary card, the limit is reduced to a total of six items—three recordings and three books or other printed materials. Limits can be waived for teachers who qualify for special privilege status and so can the 14-day loan period. Similarly, loan periods can be extended for vacationers, and the length of extended loans is left to the discretion of the librarian-in-charge. (No additional details define this librarian as a branch or unit head, circulation department head, or director of the entire system.) Indeed, the librarian-in-charge has wide discretionary powers over circulation privileges, enabling normally noncirculating materials to be borrowed, revoking or imposing item limits, and extending or limiting loan periods. Ordinary renewals, not just special extensions, are also decided by the librarian-in-charge, and these cannot be done by mail, telephone, or by presenting only the transaction card.

Most materials can be returned to any LAPL unit, or they can be sent to the home library by mail or put in a book drop. The date of postmark or receipt at other agencies and bookdrops is taken to be the date of an item's return, giving clients the benefit of any time lag until the items are received in their home unit. Films, filmstrips, art works, posters, orchestrations, and special loans are excepted from this and must be brought back to the unit from which they are borrowed. Some branches participating in a Universal Borrowing Program permit all holdings to be returned anywhere in the system.

One paragraph of the circulation policy absolves clients from responsibility for library materials that are quarantined or destroyed by the City Health Department. Smallpox and polio are named as diseases that might require such action.

No list of fines or charges is included either in the client brochure or the pages of policy sent by the library. Whether this is intended to accentuate the positive or is only a coincidence could not be determined. There are two mentions of fines: One refers to special materials for which 50 cents an hour is charged; the other refers to materials confiscated by the City Health Department (for which the client is not fined). Charges for reserving materials are levied whether the item is owned by the client's home library but is not on the shelf or is interloaned from another source.

THE FREE LIBRARY OF PHILADELPHIA

Two sets of staff policy documents—one for automated and one for nonautomated units—and two illustrated client brochures were sent to explain circulation policies at the Free Library of Philadelphia (FLP).[31] The more complete informational booklet titled "A Guide, The Free Libraries of Philadelphia" (Figure 4-3) opens with a brief description of its primary clientele: "Do you work, live, pay taxes, or go to school in Philadelphia? Are you a senior citizen living anywhere in the Philadelphia metropolitan area? If so, your library card, good at the Central Library, branch or regional libraries is issued without charge. Others are invited to use the library but pay a $15.00 annual fee."[32]

The policy manuals elaborate further, dividing potential registrants into four basic categories: adults entitled to full-term cards, adults entitled to a one-year card, children entitled to the full-term card, and children entitled to a one-year card. Each of these groups is divided into subgroups. The cutoff age between adults and children is fourteen. According to the policy document: "Patron registration remains in effect indefinitely if the card is used actively and the patron information does not change."[33]

The first-named group comprises, as might be expected, Philadelphia residents. Proof of residency must be established by showing two items of identification containing full name and home address. A list of acceptable documents includes, in addition to the usual driver's license, credit,

Figure 4-3
Illustrated Booklet

A
Guide
THE FREE LIBRARIES OF PHILADELPHIA

Where They Are

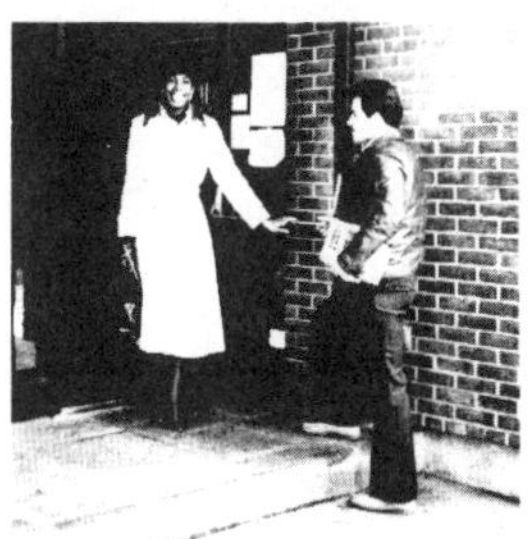

What They Do For You

How To Use Them

employment, or health service cards, utility and tax bills, informal identification (letters from employers, teachers or other school officials, or rental managers), telephone listings that can be checked on the spot, or identification by a staff member. The old-fashioned personalized kind of service, "I know you, therefore you qualify," which might be thought applicable only in small towns, is still valid in this great urban system.

Other adults eligible for free full-term library cards include nonresidents paying Philadelphia taxes, agents representing homebound clients, agents of corporate bodies located in the city, and nonresident senior citizens. Children entitled to free, full-term cards include residents, families of nonresident taxpayers, and foster children.

Though a responsible adult's verbal or written permission is required for all children's cards, an elaborate procedure is followed to persuade cooperation from adults. Strategies include phoning the party, offering to monitor use of the card, and contacting the agency in the case of a foster child. Children registering for library cards are told not to permit anyone else, even siblings, to use their cards, and it is emphasized to them that they are responsible for everything taken out with the card. A choice is offered to parents or guardians of restricted children's cards with special limits or unrestricted library cards. The latter requires the adult's written signature, not merely verbal assent. Children also must sign their names to apply for a card; adults who cannot write are permitted to make an "X" instead.

One-year library cards are issued to nonresidents who pay a nominal fee—$15 in 1983—and they are issued free to Friends of the Free Library, students of any age attending a Philadelphia school, members of the military and their immediate families stationed near the city, and temporary residents of Philadelphia. The library cards themselves carry a statement of personal responsibility over the recipient's signature (Figure 4-4).

Many material formats are mentioned in the client guide, but the policy statements and flyer describing the automated circulation control system mention only books, filmstrips, and records. A note says that films are to be added. Other circulating nonbook materials include pamphlets, pictures, chamber music, choral music, orchestra scores and parts, phonograph records, materials for the blind, and cuneiform tablets from the Rare Book Department!

Books are loaned for 21 days, as are most nonbook materials. Overnight or weekend loans are made for films; 28-day loans are made for embossed books for the visually handicapped; and six-month loans are made for choral music. Cuneiform tablets and orchestra scores are loaned by special arrangement.

Policies for the automated system, referring mainly to books, include several special loan periods determined by individual librarians, i.e., interlibrary loans, official library use loans, and bindery loans (the choice here is between regular and rush status). Paperback books have their own

Figure 4-4
Responsibility Statement on Library Card

procedures, depending on whether they are fully cataloged. Paperbacks cataloged and classified like hardcover books are circulated the same way. Uncataloged paperbacks are charged for twenty-one days, but different overdue procedures are followed. The third kind of paperback includes those given subject headings and shelved in the vertical files. These are treated like pamphlets. Renewals are not extended automatically but are permitted or refused by appropriate staff members in each agency depending on whether the materials are in demand.

Typically, adults can borrow twelve books at once, and children are limited to five, regardless of the type of checkout system. An individual librarian can impose stricter limits than these. Nonbook material limits are not mentioned.

Overdue charges are modest: five cents a day for adult materials, pamphlets, and periodicals and one cent a day for children's materials. Overdues for children's materials, pamphlets, and periodicals accumulate to a ceiling of $1; adult charges accumulate to a maximum of $5. Reimbursement fees for lost or destroyed materials include the following standard charges: $10.00 for hardcover books, cassettes, or filmstrips; $41.25 for filmstrip viewers; $10.00 per disk for sound recording albums; $3.00 per disk for those that accompany books in kits; and $3.00 for paperback books, pamphlets, or periodicals. Actual retail prices, if available, can be charged instead of the standard fees. Defacing, but not destroying printed materials, cost $1.00 an item; losing the protective plastic book or record covers cost clients $1.50 each. Other fees govern nonreturn of materials for the visually handicapped, items from the special music collections, and other visual media. A charge of 25 cents is levied for reserving an item, refundable "for credit" if the reserve was not filled.

Clients have a total of ninety days to return overdue materials during which two overdue notices and two bills are sent. Materials charged out by computer appear on a Shelf Clearance Report used to insure they are not reshelved without being checked in. At the end of ninety days, selected open accounts are sent to a collection agency or credit bureau. If this is done, no additional fee is charged to the client. If the account continues to remain unresolved, the policy states: "Litigation is the final step in the overdues cycle and may be initiated only by the division chief for cases referred from the collection agency."[34] This wording indicates that lawsuits are neither automatic nor commonly instituted, though the library clearly wishes to retain the right to sue.

PASADENA PUBLIC LIBRARY

A variety of colorfully illustrated handouts for the public gives some of the details about circulation at the Pasadena Public Library (PPL) in Pasadena, California. One foldout brochure titled "Get Acquainted With

Your Pasadena Public Library"[35] (Figure 4-5) offers basic information about registration for a library card; another titled "28 Libraries Are Better than One"[36] enumerates and describes the services of the Metropolitan Cooperative Library System (MCLS), organized in 1965, to which PPL clients are entitled. Bilingual bookmarks in Spanish and English furnish a list of fines and fees (Figure 4-6), and bilingual registration forms accommodate a diverse client group. A special edition issue of PPL's newspaper, *In-the-Know*, is devoted to describing a construction project to expand the stacks and improve access for the handicapped.[37]

California, like several other states across the country, has a program of universal borrowing for all residents. A prospective client has to establish proof of current residence in the state but does not have to be a Pasadena resident to apply for a free card. This makes for much simpler registration rules and many fewer categories of clients. The MCLS brochure states: "Equal access . . . means that if you live in any MCLS community, you can use and borrow materials from the collections of all MCLS member libraries. When borrowing materials, you should be prepared to show proof of residence. You may be issued more than one library card, depending on local policies and circulation systems."[38]

PPL distinguishes between adults and children, with fourteen years of age as the minimum necessary for an adult card. Juvenile registration forms have a line for a parent's signature. All registration forms ask clients to volunteer personal data which the library promises to keep confidential and use only for planning services and selecting materials. The adult application requests a great deal more information than does the juvenile form, including one's educational level, income, occupation, hobbies and reading interests, and the preferred time for using the library.

The PPL brochure lists as circulating materials books, records and cassettes (sound recordings), pamphlets, magazines, and films.[39] The MCLS brochure adds many more specialized formats including maps, newspapers, technical materials of various kinds, patents, scores and sheet music, orchestrations, microforms, framed art prints, and special materials for the visually or hearing impaired.[40] Most PPL materials circulate for 21 days. Fifty items can be checked out to any one card number, and the computerized circulation system is programmed to block loans for any more than that.

A relatively simple fine structure is outlined, with a daily charge of ten cents per day for adult materials and five cents per day for children's materials. Ceilings for accumulation of charges are $5.00 for adult materials and $2.50 for children's. A $2.00 penalty is imposed for replacing a lost or stolen library card, and a $5.00 processing fee is added to replacement charges for lost materials. Clients are alerted that the computer "prints notices for overdue materials . . . and automatically cancels borrowing privileges when serious abuses occur."[41] An overdue notice is sent when

Figure 4-5
Introductory Brochure

Get
Acquainted
with your
Pasadena
Public
Library

Figure 4-6
Pasadena Public Library
Bookmarks Containing Circulation Information

CHECK it out...

WE WOULD LIKE TO FAMILIARIZE
YOU WITH OUR POLICIES...

Fines on most adult materials - 10c/day; maximum
fine: $5.00

Fines on children's materials - 5c/day; maximum
fine: $2.50

Overdue notices will be
sent when items are 14
days overdue.

Fine notices will be sent
as needed.

A $2.00 replacement fee is
charged for lost or stolen
library cards.

A bill for replacement
of item is printed when
item is 21 days overdue;
processing fee of $5 is
added to cost of item.

Patron will not be allowed
to check out or renew items
for following reasons:
a) any item overdue 21 days
b) total fines in excess of
   $5 adults; $2 children
c) number of items checked
   out exceeds 50
d) expired library card

Two renewals are allowed
on most items.

SU BIBLIOTECA!

MIENTRAS QUE COMENZAMOS A USAR
NUESTRA SISTEMA DE COMPUTADORA,
QUEREMOS FAMIARIZARLOS CON
NUESTRAS POLIZÁS ...

Cuotas en la mayor parte de
materiales para adultos - 10¢/por
día; máximo debido: $5

Cuota en materiales para niños -
5¢/por día; máximo debido: $2.50

Avisos de materiales que no re-
gresan a tiempo se mandaran quando materiales estan 10 días pasa-
das del día de regreso

Los avisos se mandaran quando
cuotas suben hasta $5 o mas

Una cuenta de restitución de
material sera imprimida quando el
material no se haya regresado
despues de 45 días del día de regreso; se cobrara $5 ademas del
costo del material

El patrón no tiene permiso de
sacar o prorrogar materiales por

a) cualquier material que no re-
   grese 45 días despues del día
   indicado
b) deudas totales en exceso do
   $5 para adultos: $2 para niños
c) quando el numero de material
   sacados este en exceso de 50
d) una fecha expirada en la tar-
   jeta de prestámo

SOLAMENTE UNA PRORROGA SE PERMITE
EN CUALQUIER MATERIAL

ESPERAMOS SERVIR LE MEJOR CON
NUESTRA COMPUTADORA

RECUERDEN, TODO LAS SERVICAS IE
LA BIBLIOTECA SON GRATIS, MIENTRAS
QUE ESTAS POLIZAS SEAN SEQUIDAS!

items are fourteen days overdue, and a bill is sent seven days later; it is assumed that an item remaining unreturned after an overdue notice is sent must be lost. If materials are returned but fines are not paid, a fine notice is generated. The computer blocks loan privileges for clients owing "total fines in excess of $5 adults; $2 children" or holding "any item overdue 21 days."[42]

PPL's client-oriented spirit is clearly coupled with expectations that rules will be obeyed. The computer system is the key to enforcement. The cooperative borrowing system can open valuable opportunities to Pasadena's clients given the general availability of automobile transportation in the area.

HAYS PUBLIC LIBRARY

The following description of circulation policies at the Hays Public Library (HPL) in Hays, Kansas, is based on a staff document titled "The Policies of the Hays Public Library,"[43] a description of checkout procedures and preparation of circulation statistics, a sample "Dear Client" letter for a delinquent patron,[44] and two papers from the state librarian's office describing the Kansas Library Card and state resource sharing plans.[45]

A paragraph of the policy describes eligibility for service:

The library shall serve the citizens of Hays. Patrons residing in the area encompassed by the Central Kansas Library System are served by Hays Public Library through contractual arrangement with CKLS, as a member library of that system. The rights of an individual to the use of the library shall not be denied or abridged because of age, sex, race, religion, national origins or social or political views. The library . . . will lend materials requested by other libraries through interlibrary loan. Students of Fort Hays State University are permitted to use the library's services. An Adult Library Card will be issued to persons age 12 and over.[46]

The library also accepts a Kansas library card—an identification of a client in good standing in his or her home library—as if it were a local one. No mention is made of fee-paying clients or temporary service arrangements, but the broad client group outlined above appears to cover everyone who might conceivably approach the circulation desk for service.

No details are given for verifying identity, but, with a much smaller potential for ineligible applicants than in large cities, establishing one's identity might not be so great a concern. The library card is of great importance, however, for at HPL nothing can be borrowed without a card.

Materials listed as available for circulation include hardcover and paperback books, magazines, (sound) records and tapes, and paintings. Films from the state film service, large print books for the visually handicapped, vertical file materials (usually pamphlets and clippings), telephone directories, and a projector and screen are also listed. Films are designated specifically as being lent to groups and organizations but not to schools.[47] The process for circulating films is not described nor is there any indication that the projector and screen are related to the lending of films and/or are intended for use outside the library.

Loan periods are relatively short, and there are limits on all forms of materials. The average loan is for two weeks, and it applies to all books except best sellers and to magazines, sound recordings, and interlibrary loans. Best sellers go out for one week; art works are loaned for four. Ten items is the limit for sound recordings and magazines, though an additional limit on magazines states that no more than five issues of the same title can be borrowed at once. Adult art works require a $5 deposit, refundable upon the safe return of the painting, and only one picture can be borrowed for one deposit. Children's pictures do not require any deposit, but the limit still appears to be one to a customer. The limit on books—as many as can be carried out in a Bonanza food box—is considered "no limit—within reason."[48] Its applicability to best sellers as well as ordinary books is not stated. Renewals are limited, too. The two-week books, sound recordings, and art works can be renewed for another loan period but not more. Best sellers, magazines, and interlibrary loan books are not renewable.

HPL had enough delinquents to warrant the following admonition to the checkout staff: "STOP! Check the Rolodex before checking out anything. . . . If the patron's name does appear there . . . (t)he problem must be resolved before the patron is allowed to use the library."[49] The policy document echoes this sentiment: "The use of the library's services may be denied for due cause. Such cause may include failure to return library materials, failure to pay penalties, destruction of library property, disturbance of other patrons, or any other objectionable conduct on library premises."[50]

Clients are notified if they keep materials overdue for a week, a follow up contact by a staff member occurs after two more weeks, and a letter from the director is sent after another two weeks. The letter, while worded courteously and positively, is firm about client responsibility and is clear about the withdrawal of privileges saying, in part:

When your library card was issued, you made an agreement to obey the library rules and regulations, which include returning your books on time, paying fines for overdue books when it is impossible for you to return them on time, and paying for lost or damaged books. . . . If you do not do so, your right to use the library may be withdrawn so that others may have a fair chance to use the library.[51]

Overdue fines are five cents a day for most adult materials and two cents a day for all magazines and children's materials. Best sellers cost more—ten cents a day—and art works are charged at the rate of 25 cents per day. Children have a ceiling on accumulated fines of 50 cents a month or a total of $2.50 per item; adults can pay a maximum of $1.25 per month or a total of $5.00 for most materials. Maximum penalties are doubled for best-selling seven-day books. Any lost or damaged items costs the borrower either replacement or repair charges.

Circulation policies at HPL seem to combine an expansive view of mission with a fairly strict sense of propriety. The director participates directly in efforts to get clients to cooperate in contrast to other libraries where an amorphous "library" sends overdue notices and bills. It reflects the more personal environment of a smaller city where the library staff know their clients.

GREAT NECK LIBRARY

The Great Neck Library (GNL) in Great Neck, New York, provides its clients with a small printed brochure titled "Great Neck Library, Information for Borrowers,"[52] which outlines basic policies in three sections: obtaining cards, borrowing materials, and paying fines (Figure 4-7).

Great Neck Library gives free library cards with full privileges to "any resident or taxpayer of the Great Neck Union Free School District."[53] Children's cards are furnished to those from age five to the sixth grade, thus linking library perceptions of adulthood to achievement of a certain educational level rather than a minimum age. Children below the age of five must be registered for library service by their parents.

Proof of residency must be furnished with adult applications for library cards, and a current driver's license, lease, tax bill, utility bill, or community pool card are suggested to satisfy the requirement. Children in Great Neck's public schools and two of its parochial schools are explicitly excused from providing proof of eligibility for library service because their school registration records are used instead. Children attending other private schools and nonresident students of Great Neck schools have to show a letter from a teacher on school stationery.

Nonresident cards are provided free to people who work, but do not live, in Great Neck. These cards have to be renewed annually and are not included in county-wide borrowing services. Except for these two limitations, nonresident service seems identical to resident service. Employees must present an official letter from their Great Neck employer to qualify for a free card. Other nonresidents can purchase cards for a fee of $45 a year.

Cardholders who forget their library cards are given temporary borrowing privileges without charge if they have "valid identification."[54] Special arrangements for handicapped clients are noted too: extended loans, especially of Library of Congress' talking books; service by mail and/or lending to a client's agent; and indefinite loans of tape recorders, lighted magnifiers, and other equipment for people with impaired sight.

GREAT NECK LIBRARY
INFORMATION FOR
BORROWERS

LIBRARY CARDS

Any resident or taxpayer of the Great Neck Union Free School District may obtain a free resident's library card. Youngsters in the sixth grade or below are given a special children's library card.

Residents' library cards may be obtained at the main library or any branch by filling out an application form and presenting proof of residency, such as a current driver's license, lease, tax bill, utility bill or Parkwood Pool card. Students attending the Great Neck Public Schools, North Shore Hebrew Academy or St. Aloysius School do not need identification since school registration records will be used for verification. Children under five years of age must be registered by their parents.

Non-residents employed or attending school in Great Neck may obtain a free non-resident's library card. Other non-residents may obtain this library card by paying a $45 annual fee. Non-resident library cards must be renewed after August 31st of every year.

Non-residents' library cards may be obtained at the main library or any branch by filling out an appropriate application form. Students and employees must present identification and proof of their status, such as a current paycheck stub or letter from their employer or teacher on business or school stationery.

The brochure states that cardholders are responsible for materials charged out on their cards unless they have reported a card lost or stolen. This admonition is reinforced by a statement that "the Library must be notified immediately if a library card is lost or stolen. . . . There is a replacement fee of 25 cents for all library cards."[55]

Types of materials identified in the brochure include ordinary adult books, "[n]ew books and current editions of selected annual publications," and books with a limited use classification, those books kept behind the circulation desk, children's books, uncataloged paperback books, magazines, pamphlets, and (sound) recordings.[56] Ordinary adult books and all of the children's books can be borrowed for twenty-eight days; the special classes of adult books, magazines, pamphlets, and recordings are limited to 14-day loans. Twelve pamphlets, recordings, and magazines can be borrowed at once; but, no more than six issues of one magazine or six 45 rpm sound recordings can be included in that total. No maximum number is imposed on adult books, but clients are asked to limit themselves to "that which can be reasonably used and which does not unduly affect other borrowers."[57] Renewals are permitted for materials that are not requested by another client, but the brochure states that they should be *limited* to maintain an adequate supply of materials for all clients.[58]

The section on overdues and fines is headed "Returning Materials." All materials can be returned to any branch or the main library. This privilege extends to items borrowed from other public libraries in the county as well as local materials. Overdue fines for most materials are five cents per day with a maximum charge of $3 per item or half of its retail price, whichever is less. Overdue children's materials cost the borrower two cents a day with a maximum charge of $1 or half the retail price, whichever is less. Overdue notices are sent when materials are three weeks overdue, followed three weeks later by a bill for replacement costs, assuming that anything not returned by that time is lost.

Certain materials are treated differently, and fees depend on an item's cost and format. According to the brochure:

Periodicals which cost $2 or less, pamphlets, and 45 r.p.m. records, are loaned in bags containing one to six items. The overdue fine on these materials is five cents per bag per day, with a maximum of $3 per bag/50 cents per item. The overdue fine on children's periodicals which cost $2 or less and children's pamphlets is two cents per bag per day, with a maximum of $1.50 per bag/25 cents per item. These materials should be returned together in the same bag in which they were charged out.[59]

When materials are lost or are damaged beyond repair, a fee approximating the cost of their replacement is charged, as described in the brochure: "For books published in 1975 and later this is the retail listed price of the book; for books published prior to 1975 this is the retail listed price plus $3 to cover the increased replacement cost of the book."[60] A standard fee of $1 is charged for periodicals which cost less than $2 an issue (those over $2 cost the retail price), pamphlets, 45 rpm records, and adult uncataloged paperbacks; children's paperbacks are 50 cents. Damaged items which could be rebound cost their borrowers a $4.50 bindery fee. Clients are warned that borrowing privileges will be rescinded if more than $25 is owed to the library.

ELMHURST PUBLIC LIBRARY

Two attractive brochures introduce clients to the circulation policies of the Elmhurst (Illinois) Public Library (EPL) in Elmhurst, Illinois (Figure 4-8). One, titled "Welcome to the Elmhurst Public Library,"[61] is a general guide to the collections and services of the library; the other, titled "About Your Library Card,"[62] briefly spells out circulation rules and lists the libraries participating in the Suburban Library System network.

The general guide states that free library cards are available to "[c]itizens who live or own property within the corporate limits of Elmhurst . . . (and) persons working within Elmhurst corporate limits."[63] Proof of residence or current employment within the boundaries of the service area must be furnished by applicants when they fill out their application. Residents receive cards entitling them to services both at EPL and other libraries in the network. Persons who only work within the service area are given business cards.[64]

Nonresidents can pay $35 a year for a library card good only at EPL, or, for twice that amount, they can obtain a card that enables them to use the services of the network. A special rate for nonresident senior citizens—$5 a year—purchases a card valid only at Elmhurst.

Cards for residents expire after an unspecified period of time, and business cards are good for two years. Revalidation requires that a person "present your card at the circulation desk during the expiration month with proof of residence, and a new expiration date will be issued. Please do not throw away your expired card."[65]

No special requirements for children's cards are described in either brochure. The guide states that "the Library allows patrons of all ages access to all library materials. If parents prefer, they may request a special card which restricts their child to materials in the Young People's collection."[66] Leaving the choice up to parents is a refreshing change from policies that cast the library into the role of decision maker or gatekeeper. EPL uses the terms *young people* and *Young People's Collection* in their documents. This seemed more ingratiating to young clients than *juvenile*, the most familiar term. Elmhurst's young clients do not seem to have run amok as a result of the freer policies.

Cardholders' responsibilities are clear:

Figure 4-8
Client Brochures

When accepting a card from the Elmhurst Public Library, we ask that you notify us of any change of address, and that you pay promptly all charges for damage, loss or delay in returning all library materials. You will be responsible for all materials you have borrowed from the Library, and your privileges will be revoked for lack of payment of bills.[67]

A variety of material forms are described in some detail in the guide including books, newspapers, magazines, films, slides, videotapes, sound recordings, pamphlets, pictures, music materials, toys, art works, college catalogs (on microfiche), and telephone directories. Most of them can be borrowed, but current issues of magazines cannot be borrowed, and no mention of loans is made for college catalogs or telephone directories.

Three weeks is the usual loan for noncurrent or nonseasonal books, music, pictures, and toys. A three-day grace period extends the time during which these materials can be returned without overdue fines. Current and seasonal books, cassette players, videotapes, 8 mm films, slides, magazines, pamphlets, and sound recordings can be borrowed for one week, and 16 mm film projectors and slide projectors are limited to three days or overnight. Loan periods range from four weeks for art works to six weeks for special vacation loans. Two art works can be borrowed at a time, but no other limits are mentioned.

To borrow a videotape, clients must sign each time a Videotape Responsibility Statement, assuring that special loan rules are understood (Figure 4-9). Videotapes have higher overdue fines—$2 per day—and a $100 fee (or less, if the actual retail price was less) if they are lost or damaged.

Most materials cost five cents a day when overdue. Projectors are rented for $1 and, like videotapes, cost $2 per day when overdue. Art prints held overdue are $1 a month. If materials are returned in a book drop after hours, they are checked in as if they had been returned the following day. At least ten cents per day is charged for overdue materials returned somewhere other than where they had been borrowed. A fine of 50 cents is charged for the loss of one's library card.

Operating in a network environment results in some adjustments, such as charging double overdue fines for handling overdue materials belonging to other libraries. A long list of network participants, with reciprocal borrowing privileges, however, offers large benefits to Elmhurst's clients in return.

PENINSULA LIBRARY SYSTEM

The Peninsula Library System (PLS) in northern California comprises seven city libraries (San Mateo, Burlingame, Daly City, Menlo Park, Redwood City, San Bruno, and South San Francisco) as well as the San

Figure 4-9
Video Responsibility Statement

ELMHURST PUBLIC LIBRARY
VIDEOTAPE RESPONSIBILITY STATEMENT

Z No. of item   Condition of item   Due Date

I assume responsibility for the BETA / VHS videocassette titled:

This item is due back in the library on the date indicated on this card and on the item. I agree to pay a fine of <u>$2 per day for each day overdue.</u> The videotape will be returned to the Circulation Desk. <u>IT MAY NOT BE RETURNED IN THE BOOK DROP.</u> I also agree to pay a charge of $100 should the item be lost or damaged, or the replacement cost of the tape whichever is less. I understand that the use of this video-tape is at my own risk and that the library is not responsible for any damage that may be incurred through its use.

Date of Checkout   Signature of Borrower

Z No. of Borrower   Telephone No. of Borrower

Mateo County library system. A brochure describes the Peninsula Libraries Automated Network (PLAN) along with a bookmark-sized information piece.[68]

PLAN is a shared computer system in which cardholders in any one library unit automatically are eligible for service in all of them. Eligibility for service is determined by member libraries, but PLS requires a library card with a computer-readable label. Implementation of an automated system within each individual library is not a prerequisite for system-wide borrowing services. Books checked out from any library can be returned anywhere else. The system is affiliated with other cooperatives in the San Francisco Bay area as well as the California State Library, and clients can be served with the resources of this larger network of institutions through interlibrary loan. The policies of the four member libraries whose documents were sent, Burlingame, Menlo Park, San Bruno, and San Mateo, are described.

Burlingame Public Library

Burlingame sent several documents intended for public distribution as well as a typed summary of circulation policies which appears to be intended for its staff. A general guide titled "Welcome to the Burlingame Public Library" answered most circulation questions.[69] The guide begins,

A library card is free to anyone who lives in Burlingame or Hillsborough. You need only fill out an application and show proof of your residence. Children and young adults are asked to have a parent sign their application. . . . If you are a resident of California, and hold a valid library card from your home library, you may make application to use the Burlingame Public Library as a 'Universal Borrower'. You may borrow materials from the Burlingame Library using your own home library card. Burlingame Library honors the library cards of all San Mateo County residents without a special registration.[70]

Burlingame's informational bookmark[71] lists seven categories of materials that can be borrowed for twenty-one days and renewed once: older adult fiction, adult nonfiction, juvenile fiction and nonfiction, juvenile bound magazines, most pamphlets, paperback books, and sound recordings (records and cassettes). Four more categories of materials are allowed seven-day loans with no renewals: new adult fiction, unbound adult and juvenile magazines, study guides and selected college catalogs, and hardware for the sound recordings. Slide projectors, 8 mm motion picture projectors, 16 mm motion pictures, and videocassettes can all be borrowed for twenty-four hours without renewals. Art prints can be taken for the longest loan—six weeks—but cannot be renewed. Burlingame has a rental collection, for which they charge 50 cents for the first three days and ten cents a day thereafter. The general guide mentions maps with three-week loan periods and 8 mm films with one-week loan periods. No limit is imposed on the number of books that can be borrowed at one time unless they are "in demand."[72]

Circulating encyclopedias, both children's and adult, have seven-day loan periods in a separate category in Burlingame's typed summary of circulation policies.[73] Like other seven-day materials, these cannot be renewed. It also lists adult bound periodicals and newspapers as noncirculating. Two categories of college catalogs are listed here, one with three-week loan periods and the other with seven-day loan periods. Librettos are accorded a separate category with a 21-day loan with a single renewal. Burlingame permits renewals to be made by telephone as well as in person. Overdue materials are not renewable, nor are items requested by other clients. Vacation loans and teacher's collections are special kinds of loans described in some detail:

All materials that circulate for 21 days may be checked out for a vacation loan. Vacation loans are available all year round for a period of 6 (six) weeks. Vacation loans *may not* be renewed. To be eligible for a vacation loan, a patron must be outside the local calling area for 3 or more weeks. Vacation loans are granted on the honor basis.

All material that circulates for 21 days may be checked out for the purpose of a teachers collection. Adult and juvenile materials may be part of a teachers collection and will be filed in juvenile circulation. The Children's Department staff will be responsible for overdues. Teachers from Burlingame Schools, which have school cards, may use the school card to borrow a teachers collection.[74]

Clients are alerted that audiovisual materials must be returned to the desk from which they were checked out. A penalty of $1 is levied if such materials are found in book drops or if they are damaged before reaching their correct destination.

Overdue fines at Burlingame are five cents per day for children's materials, ten cents per day for most adult materials (except $1 per day for art prints), and $1 per hour for equipment. The accumulation of overdue fines is limited to $1.50 for children's material and $3.00 for adult material. Art prints and equipment have a maximum fine of $10.

Overdue notices are sent to clients as a "courtesy reminder," not as an obligation, and overdue accounts are considered delinquent "within 60 days from the due date" and are turned over to a credit bureau for collection.[75] Parents are held responsible for overdues checked out by minor children. People are also warned that, "If you have not notified the Library of a lost or stolen Card, you will be held responsible if someone uses it to check out materials."[76]

Other fees include 25 cents for placing a hold on a title, 50 cents for library card replacements, and rental collection charges, as already noted.

Menlo Park Public Library

Menlo Park Public Library's materials did not include information about how free cards can be obtained or who is eligible to receive one. However, listed among its charges is $24 per year for a nonresident card or $6 for a card for a period of three months. Whether these charges are applied only to non-Californians or to people from anywhere outside of Menlo Park is not specified.

Menlo Park's two brochures both list a variety of materials that can be borrowed. The more complete guide states:

Books, cassettes, records, and pamphlets circulate for three weeks; magazines and 8mm films for one week; 16mm films for one day; and art prints for one or three months. Borrowing limits: 5 books on the same subject (no limit on the total number), 10 records, 3 cassettes, and 2 art prints at one time.

Books, records, and cassettes may be renewed once per household if not previously requested by another borrower; up to 5 items may be renewed. SORRY, NO PHONE RENEWALS, AND NO RENEWALS OF INTERLIBRARY LOANS.[77]

The other brochure, giving more up-to-date loan periods and other circulation regulations adds:

(1) children's periodicals can circulate for twenty-one days instead of seven;

(2) art prints require a $1 fee for one-month loans or a $2 fee for three-month loans;

(3) videocassettes are available for overnight loans as well as 16 mm films, all from the Peninsula Library System collection, not the library's own holdings;

(4) limits on the numbers of materials borrowable at once include four 16 mm films, two videocassettes, two of one kind of magazine and a total of six, and ten pamphlets.[78]

The overdue fine schedule for Menlo Park materials (i.e., not PLS 16 mm films and videocassettes) is identical to Burlingame's as are the maximum accumulations. PLS materials are charged at $2 a day per reel, though the maximum accumulation is also $10.

Higher prices prevail for other services—card replacement cost $1, and 50 cents is charged for checking out materials without a card. Menlo Park adds a $5 processing fee to the replacement cost of a lost or damaged item.

San Bruno Public Library

San Bruno Public Library sent a circulation manual intended for use by its pages, those younger, part-time staff members who typically do much of the shelving, checking in and out of materials, and covering the desk in public libraries.[79] One section covers the issuing of library cards to "people with permanent San Bruno addresses . . . [and] people who work or pay property taxes in San Bruno but do not live here."[80] When faced with a nonresident, the manual directs the staff member to "refer those applications to the adult desk staff."[81]

Residents, taxpayers, and people employed within San Bruno are immediately divided into those who already have received plastic cards and those who have not; the former group is charged 25 cents for a new one. Identification must be supplied by applicants with their names and addresses printed on (not handwritten), in order of preference, a California driver's license, a preprinted check, a credit card containing an address, a utility bill, a food stamp or Medi-cal mail, other official printed government mail, a renter's agreement or apartment ID card. Doubtful identification is referred to the adult staff.

Fourteen years of age is the demarcation between adult and children's cards, and children must have parents fill out and sign their application before they can take out books. The manual states: "A child should at least be in kindergarten and should be able to write at least their name before they get a card. We prefer to wait until a child is in first grade, but if the parent insists, we will issue a card to a kindergartener."[82] Parents are expected to vouch for the child's address, though if the child attends a San Bruno school that is sufficient.

Regarding children's applications, young desk staff are warned: "BE SURE (IF A PARENT IS NOT PRESENT) THAT THE APP[LICATION] LOOKS LIKE IT HAS BEEN SIGNED BY AN ADULT. SOMETIMES THE KIDS SIGN THEM AND YOU CAN TELL."[83] For all applicants, an important step in the process is determining whether an applicant has ever had a library card. The manual cautions accepting a person's recollection:

AT SOME POINT DURING THE APPLICATION PROCESS—PREFERABLY *BEFORE* YOU TYPE THE CARD—PLEASE CHECK TO SEE IF THE PATRON ALREADY HAS AN APPLICATION ON FILE, EVEN IF HE/SHE SAYS THEY DO NOT. SOMETIMES PATRONS FORGET THEY EVER HAD A CARD (ESPECIALLY KIDS) AND SOMETIMES THEY HAVE OUTSTANDING CHARGES AGAINST THEM THAT THEY'RE HOPING YOU WON'T CATCH.[84]

San Bruno has seven- and 21-day loans. Seven-day materials include 8 mm films, periodicals, new fiction, nonfiction books of fewer than 500 pages, and seasonal materials. Gift paperbacks are circulated on the honor system without being checked out, and they can be kept as long as the client desires.

Twenty-one day loans apply to sound recordings on discs or cassettes. They and the 8 mm films are never to be returned in book drops; an automatic fine is levied if they are. Part of the return process is supposed to be an inspection of the physical condition of the recording or film. A reference is also made to audiovisual equipment being returned, though the length of time these items could circulate is not noted. Overnight loans of PLS films and videorecordings are probably identical to those described for Burlingame and Menlo Park, but they are not included in this manual.

The rules for magazines include the following information:

Some magazines are kept at the desk because they tend to disappear. If a patron wants to see the most current issue of one of these 'desk' magazines (in plastic covers), please have him/her sign the magazine card and keep the card at the desk until the patron brings the magazine back. . . . In the case of PLAYBOY, *patrons must be 18 years of age,* so if you have any doubts about their age, ask to see their driver's license or refer the problem to the adult desk staff.[85]

Handling *Playboy* must have presented problems to these circulation assistants, since the assistants might be under eighteen. (One cannot help but wonder if any of them snuck a look through the pages upon their return.)

San Bruno permits telephone renewals. If there are any limits on the number of renewals, they are not mentioned. San Bruno's own clients can check out two items without their cards. Marks are made on the applications and book cards so that if such forgetfulness persists beyond three incidents, the client is asked to purchase a new card. The cards of clients from other PLS libraries are not used in San Bruno's checkout machines. The checkout system depends on how often they are likely to return. The desk manual states:

To circulate books to patrons of other PLS libraries, first check the blacklist rollodex near the calendar for the patron's name. . . . If the patron is clear, stamp the due date on the book card and write the patron's name and address on the book card. . . . A patron from another PLS library must have their library card with them to check out books here. . . . If you know the patron is a frequent or heavy user of our library, you may have the patron fill out an application and issue him a San Bruno Library card to be kept on file here. Both the card and the application in such a case should be stamped "FOR USE IN SAN BRUNO ONLY."[86]

Information on overdue fines or other fees was not given.

San Mateo City Libraries

Like Menlo Park, San Mateo City Libraries sent a brochure listing its new loan periods, renewal policies, and fine/fee schedules, effective as of May 3, 1984.[87] Most materials can be checked out for twenty-one days; three types of material are available for only seven days and one type, art prints, for forty-two days. The mix at San Mateo is slightly different than at San Bruno or Menlo Park, however. Seven-day loans apply to new adult fiction books and periodicals and 8 mm films. Twenty-one day loans without renewals apply to new adult nonfiction, sound recordings on disc and cassette, slides, picture file materials, all pamphlets, and juvenile periodicals. The same loan period with a single renewal is applicable to all juvenile books and older adult books. San Mateo's renewals must be done in person.

Sound cassettes and slides are available only at San Mateo's central library, whereas the other nonbook materials are also part of branch collections. PLS 16 mm films and videocassettes are available from the central library for overnight loan.

San Mateo's overdue fine and fee schedule matches Menlo Park's in every respect but one—borrowing materials without a card costs 25 cents.

In most respects, the four PLS libraries have very similar circulation policies.

LIBRARY EXCHANGE AIDS PATRONS (LEAP)

The evolution of this multilibrary circulation system in Connecticut is succinctly described in the LEAP *Procedures Manual* 1983 (Figure 4-10)[88]:

The bibliographic data base in the CLSI installation in the LEAP libraries was originally designed to support circulation. It has since developed into a union list of LEAP titles, and is on the verge of becoming a fully automated catalogue.[89]

Six libraries share the LEAP system: Hamden Library houses the computer, and North Haven, Cheshire, West Haven, North Branford, and Northford are connected to it by means of a telecommunications link. LEAP maintains statistics on circulation services to cardholders from approximately 300 public, school, academic, and special libraries throughout the State of Connecticut. They include such institutional libraries as the West Haven Veterans Administration Hospital and the Enfield Inmate Library; such corporation libraries as Xerox Educational Publications; such diverse universities as Wesleyan, the University of Connecticut, and Yale; private and public schools; and, of course, public libraries all over the state as well as one in Massachusetts.

Policies practiced in all LEAP libraries include the following:

(1) Materials can be renewed in any LEAP library even if they are not locally owned. This is done by reassigning the terminal to the owning library and checking its hold files.

(2) Renewals of overdue materials, typically prohibited, are made if the overdue fine is paid.

(3) Borrowing by nonresidents without their cards, or by clients of another town with delinquency status or specially flagged identification in the LEAP database, is forbidden.

(4) If the home library approves, bills can be paid anywhere.

(5) One LEAP library can place holds on materials owned by others. Agency-specific holds take precedence over system-wide holds, however, so local taxpayers are not forced to wait while outsiders use their materials.

(6) Electronic mail is used for speedy ILL service. Computer communications are cheaper and less disruptive than answering the telephone.

(7) A list of default replacement charges for materials in the database indicates a strong consensus on this issue.

Figure 4-10
Staff Manual, Library Exchange Aids Patrons (LEAP)

Hamden Library

Two policy documents from the Hamden Library (HL) were sent: a general guide intended for clients (Figure 4-11)[90] and an excerpt from the HL board's manual.[91] The board document begins with a resolution to provide access to library materials and information *free of charge* for "individuals residing in the public library's tax supporting political subdivision."[92]

Important provisions of Hamden's policy coincided with those of the statewide borrowing system concerning the definition of a resident: "a person is a resident of a town if that person is principally domiciled in that town. A borrower who holds dual residency or who owns property in more than one town is considered a resident only in the town in which he/she is principally-domiciled. In all other towns, that borrower is considered a non-resident."[93] Under the heading "Registration," the client guide states, "To apply for a library card all you need is proof of your Hamden address; a card will be issued immediately,"[94] and Connecticard information adds, "Your Hamden library card may be used in any public library in the state."[95]

The board manual states that adult library cards can be obtained by persons aged sixteen or older on presentation of a driver's license with a current Hamden address. Children's cards, available to anyone under sixteen, require "a reference signature from a parent or *legal* guardian. The parent who represents the child's ID must have identification which meets the [adult] specification . . . , and must sign as a reference for the child in our presence."[96] Applicants who cannot show acceptable identification are registered and are permitted to borrow one item on faith, while the cards were sent by mail to the addresses they gave in an envelope marked "DO NOT FORWARD, RETURN TO SENDER." A similar registration procedure is described for nonresidents with local library cards who wish to register for a Hamden card. Proof of name and address is required, but it can be waived the first time. Identification has to be presented in person the next time the person wishes to borrow Hamden materials.

A wide variety of circulating materials is listed in the manual including books, records (sound recordings), pamphlets, magazines, filmstrips, toys, super-8 films, encyclopedias, 16 mm films, super-8 and 16 mm projectors, slide projectors, screens, Polaroid cameras, and videocassettes. The books and cameras circulate for twenty-eight days, and most of the other items circulate for fourteen, although encyclopedias and video materials can be taken only for three days, and 16 mm films and equipment have more limited loans. A grace period of four days covers all materials except 16 mm films. On the fifth day, however, the charge begins with five times the daily charge.

Renewals, in person or by telephone, are allowed once for 14- or 28-day materials if no one has requested them. They must be made at the branch

Figure 4-11
Library Guide

HAMDEN
LIBRARY

Policies and Procedures

from which the materials have been borrowed. Extended loans can be approved by the town librarian for a maximum of twelve weeks if needed.

Audiovisual equipment, except for cameras, and 16 mm films can circulate only to persons eighteen years old or over. Equipment has to be used in the library building, but the films themselves can be taken out for twenty-four hours, without renewal privileges. People borrowing equipment sign a "responsibility slip,"[97] assuring that the cost of any damages resulting from improper handling do not have to be absorbed by the library.

Video materials are lent only to Hamden residents with a valid library card who are willing to pay the full replacement cost plus a $5 processing fee if anything should happen to the tape including theft, loss, or damage (even if repair was possible). A maximum of two cassettes can be borrowed for a three-day period, and they are not renewable. The policy clearly states that the library denies responsibility for notifying clients that their videotapes are overdue, for any damage to the client's equipment caused by using library tapes, or for infringements of copyright by the client.[98]

Loans of Polaroid cameras are restricted to Hamden residents. Cameras can be reserved, just like books, although the client must be free from outstanding fines of any kind in order to enter a reserve request. Cameras cannot be returned in bookdrops, and borrowers must declare themselves responsible for any fines, damages, or replacement charges. The policy includes a denial of library responsibility for damage to the client's film while using borrowed cameras.

In the Connecticard system of universal borrowing, books and magazines may be returned to any public library participating in Connecticard, but nonprint materials must be returned to the library from which they are borrowed.

The daily fine for most materials is five cents a day with a maximum accumulation of $5.00 for adult materials and $2.50 for children's materials. The fines for 16 mm films and equipment (except cameras, which are included with the bulk of circulating materials) are 25 cents per reel or piece of equipment per hour during hours the library is open and $2 per day for videorecordings.

Overdue notices are considered a courtesy, and the policy states that they *may* be sent after materials are two weeks overdue.[99] No bills for accumulated fines are sent. Replacement charges for lost or "severely" damaged materials are augmented by a $5 processing fee, but clients have the option of supplying the library with identical items and paying only half the processing fee. A page of the manual explains the cost of the processing operation.[100]

Uncataloged paperback books, pamphlets, and magazines circulate generically and have a separate policy governing replacement. These cost an average of $2.50, plus $1 processing fee. One can purchase a library-approved paperback instead, but the processing fee has to be paid. A lost library card costs $1; replacing a lost or damaged camera costs $110; lost camera cases cost $20; and lost instruction booklets cost $1.

Hamden Library's fines and fees are modest, and loan periods are longer than in many other public libraries. The materials with the highest replacement costs—films, videocassettes, and most equipment—are loaned only to residents. The fact that Polaroid cameras circulate for the longest loan periods and are treated like ordinary material is unique.

WASHOE COUNTY LIBRARY

The Washoe County Library (WCL) in Reno, Nevada, sent most of a computer-processed circulation manual intended for staff members.[101] One section covers registration policy and another interlibrary loans. Sections covering policies for materials, services, and special patrons were not sent, leaving many unanswered questions.

Free library cards are given to adult residents who can show "acceptable identification and a reference,"[102] provided they have lived in the county for three months or have proof of property ownership, a business, or employment within the county. Family members of cardholders are also entitled to free cards, and no children's age cutoff is named. New or temporary residents can obtain a card good for three months upon payment of a $25 refundable fee. A person using this type of card is not allowed to borrow audiovisual materials and is limited to four items at a time. The library promises to refund the fee within 30 days after receiving a formal request.

Reciprocal borrowing is extended to people with valid cards from other Nevada public libraries as well as from seven California counties and three local academic institutions. WCL cards are honored at the University of Nevada, Reno, if cardholders are over eighteen and in good standing. University borrowing requires obtaining a sticker, renewing it annually, and returning all materials to the university libraries.

Two special categories of borrower are mentioned: (1) Churchill County borrowers, who can obtain Western Nevada Rural Bookmobile Library Cards from any of Washoe's branches upon request by their home library and (2) temporary residents of Incline Village, who can borrow two items with valid Visa or Master Charge credit cards. (Other residents of Incline Village have to have a post office box to apply for a regular library card.)

Documents accepted as proof of residence include a valid state driver's license or nondriver's card, imprinted checks, escrow papers, utility bills, leases, passports, out-of-state licenses, convicted person's cards, automobile registrations, social security, and alien registration cards. Local high school student identification cards are also acceptable.

Unacceptable documents include rent receipts, police cards, food stamp cards, unemployment benefit cards, VA hospital cards, imprinted business cards, Job Corps cards, and certain college identifications. A reference, which has to be given in addition, was defined as "a relative living anywhere in the USA at a different address."[103] Close friends could sponsor a person without living relatives. (One might question the value of out-of-state references, but clients residing in Reno in connection with divorce proceedings or other business of a short term nature might be expected to have a high mobility rate, and the reference could be the library's only future point of contact with them.)

Borrowable materials named in the manual include books, sound recordings, and films. Since items WCL loans to other libraries on interlibrary loan have 28-day loan periods, this probably is the loan period for locally circulated materials as well. Renewals are permitted once for items not requested by another client and must be made in person. ILL items circulated to WCL clients are allowed two weeks or less, though renewals are permitted. The manual indicates that nonbook media materials are interloaned as well as books and that WCL also provides film service on contract to members of the state's media cooperative. A limit of two items is imposed on new cards during the first two weeks. The manual states, "This is to provide time for *computer* data entry . . . also a safeguard for those few patrons who are one time borrowers with no intention of returning their materials."[104] Otherwise, there are no limits on the number of items a person can take out unless division heads choose to impose one—for holiday materials, school assignments, or "Nevada books."

Fines at WCL are slightly higher than at many other public libraries in the survey. Overdues for adult materials including sound recordings are 15 cents per day; children's materials are 10 cents per day. The maximum accumulation for adults is $7.50; for children $1. Films cost $10 per film per working day. A grace period of five days is given to senior citizens, but, on the sixth day, the full charge is levied. Fines are not to exceed the actual cost of an item.

Overdue notices are sent after twenty-one days and bills after forty-two days. WCL division heads have the power to adjust bills in response to clients' requests. Replacement charges are rounded off to the nearest $5, and a schedule of standard charges includes $20 for hardcover books and all sound discs, $15 for "quality" paperbacks and cassettes, and $5 for mass market paperbacks. A $5 processing fee is added. If the price in the bibliographic record is higher than these allowances, the fine is to be adjusted to the nearest $5. Collection notices are printed after seventy-two days and are sent to the various divisions for disposition. Eventually, outstanding bills for more than $20 are put in for collection, after which adjustments can no longer be made.

WCL strikes a balance between the extremely legalistic language and procedures of some larger city libraries and the freer, less complicated regulations of smaller libraries. The structure is heavily dependent on information provided by the computer database.

BALTIMORE COUNTY PUBLIC LIBRARY

Baltimore County Public Library (BCPL) in Towson, Maryland, sent three documents intended for client distribution: a guide to branches,[105] a schedule of fines and fees,[106] and a flyer addressed to parents whose children are applying for a library card (see Figure 4-12).[107]

The guide states: "Anyone who lives, pays taxes or attends school in Baltimore County is entitled to a free library card, which may be used for borrowing and returning materials in any Maryland public library."[108] Responsibility for materials is politely, but carefully, spelled out: "Once materials are checked out on your card and on cards you have signed for a child, they become your responsibility."[109] Children under fourteen have to have the signature of a parent or guardian in order to get their cards. The flyer for parents also indicates that the parent's signature allows children unrestricted access to the collections.[110] If they prefer to restrict the child to the children's collection, they must bring the application to the library and discuss it with a librarian who has the authority to issue a restricted card.

Under "Materials," the guide lists books, magazines, pamphlets, maps, Maryland materials, sound recordings, large-type books, 16 mm films, and filmstrips.[111] The fine and fee schedule adds toys and games, videocassettes, and art prints to this list.[112] The guide states that most materials can be borrowed for twenty-one to twenty-seven days and that there are usually no limits on the total number of items; however, no renewals are permitted.[113] BCPL allows clients to borrow materials once without their cards for a fee of 25 cents with identification.

The fine schedule had been updated with new numbers typed in over the older ones. The daily charge for ordinary overdues is 11 cents per day. Filmstrips, art prints, 16 mm films, and videocassettes cost more: 25 cents, 50 cents, $1, and $2.50, respectively. Maximum accumulations, never to exceed an item's cost, range from 20 cents for a comic book to $50 for a videocassette. Charges for most ordinary materials can accumulate to $4.00; paperbacks, pamphlets, and magazines have a ceiling of $1.50; art prints are $15.00. Lost materials are billed at their purchase prices plus 50 cents, except for unclassified paperbacks, $2.50; pamphlets and magazines, $2.00; comic books, 30 cents; and cassette carriers, $4.50 for sound and 60 cents for video materials. Clients have the option of replacing an item instead of paying for it. Replacements for a library card are $1 for the first and $1.50 for each subsequent loss. BCPL charges the same overdue fees for adult, young adult, and children's items within each category of material. Both the daily charges and the maximum accumulations are the same.

Figure 4-12
Client Guide

branches
HOURS & SERVICES

BALTIMORE COUNTY PUBLIC LIBRARY

SUMMARY OF PUBLIC LIBRARY POLICIES

In answer to the question "Who may borrow?", most public libraries participating in this survey answered: first, residents and taxpayers. Several in California, Connecticut, and Kansas added to the list of primary clients the cardholders from any other public library in that state. All of them have a prescribed registration procedure requiring the prospective client show proof of identity and eligibility and sign an application. One library permits borrowing before establishing these proofs; some mail the library card to verify residence after the client has satisfactorily proved identity. Most listed the documents they accept as proof; some are quite strict in what is and is not considered acceptable. In almost every library, residents and taxpayers are treated identically; however, in one library some materials are reserved only for residents.

Children cannot obtain a library card without the signature of an adult, although one library goes to great lengths to help a child fulfill the requirement if the responsible adults are unwilling to provide it. Usually, the age of adulthood is fourteen. In one library, it is sixteen. In another, three age groups are defined but not specified, and one uses grade level rather than age.

Policies also describe service to nonresident users. In several libraries, students at local colleges and universities are served free, as are people who work but do not live within the library's boundaries. One library serves senior citizens without charge, even if they are not residents. Several libraries have contractual arrangements with other jurisdictions to serve their users free of charge. Many libraries charge fees to nonresidents, but most of them are relatively low. Some larger city libraries have significantly higher fees for nonresident service.

Regarding the question "What can be borrowed?", books are the chief material collected by the public libraries surveyed. Sound recordings, magazines, pamphlets, and films are held in most collections. Some also have circulating slides, photographs, videorecordings, and hardware of various kinds. Quite often, county, regional, or state libraries have collections of 16 mm films and videorecordings that can be borrowed by clients of local libraries, but the transactions are done at the local level.

Children's and adult materials are usually separated for circulation purposes. New and older books, cataloged and uncataloged items (especially paperbacks), and fiction and nonfiction titles are other divisions often encountered. These divisions define the particular loan period, overdue charge, and other circulation rules for the materials. Encyclopedias and other reference materials often form a separate category. Materials that are new, cataloged, intended for adults, fiction, and popular tend to circulate for shorter periods; materials that are older, uncataloged, intended for children, and nonfiction tend to circulate for longer periods and be renewable. Uncataloged materials sometimes can be borrowed for indefinite periods but more often are circulated generically for a specific loan period. Nonbook materials—audiovisuals, art prints, pamphlets, music, maps, toys, newspapers, and magazines—usually qualify for special treatment, with newspapers, videorecordings, and 16 mm films having the shortest loan periods and the strictest regulations. Hardware also has strict limitations on use. Only art prints are generally given longer loans, usually six weeks, and are often renewable as well.

Longer loan periods are most often twenty-one days, although twenty-eight days is also found; shorter loans are usually seven days, although overnight loans are common for special kinds of material. Renewals, usually only one, are often denied for the seven-day items. Some libraries allow telephone renewals; others require that the materials be brought to the library. Most insist that renewals be done at the owning library, not at other branches. Extended loans for vacationers, teachers, or the handicapped are often made but sometimes require a librarian's permission.

Overdue charges are nominal, ranging from five to ten cents per day for adult materials and from two to five cents per day for children's materials. Fines for special materials are often much higher, from twice the ordinary charge to $1 or more, and sometimes they are charged by the hour rather than by the day. However, ceilings on the accumulation of overdue charges are usually so low that daily fees become meaningless. Rarely is the ceiling higher than $10 (usually for a relatively expensive item such as a 16 mm film or a videorecording), and ceilings of $3.00 for adult materials and $1.50 for children's materials are more typical. Replacement fees are sometimes augmented by a processing fee, and a number of libraries set a time limit on overdues, after which the materials are considered lost and bills are issued.

A few libraries have step-by-step procedures for collecting fees and obtaining the return of materials, ending with litigation. Most send the bills to a collection agency as a last resort. All of them make efforts to insure that such offenders do not continue to borrow or to obtain new cards. The withdrawal of borrowing privileges as punishment for neglect or abuse of circulation rules appears in several client documents. Statements of client responsibility for library materials charged out on their cards are universal. Some also have a separate statement of parental responsibility for children's borrowing and warnings to all clients not to lend their cards unless they are willing to be responsible for these loans, too. Loss of a card is usually penalized by a replacement fee. A few libraries claim to charge clients for materials borrowed on lost or stolen cards if they have not been reported.

Most libraries send overdue notices and bills to clients on a regular schedule, but a few claim that such notification is a courtesy and that notices cannot always be expected.

COMPARISON WITH ACADEMIC LIBRARY POLICY ISSUES

In comparison with the issues of concern reflected in academic library policies, these public libraries are far less worried about keeping outsiders out of their buildings. Fees to outsiders for borrowing are low, and some states have universal borrowing programs which make fees irrelevant. No special privilege category compares with that accorded to faculty, although sometimes library board and staff members have extraordinary privileges that go unmentioned in any documents.[114]

Stack books, the older books, appear to be the primary fodder for the circulation mill in public libraries, too. Most materials circulate, however, with the exception of reference works (*some* of which do) unlike academic libraries where periodicals and other special materials often do not. Public libraries make an important distinction between fiction and nonfiction.

Fines and fees are lower in these public libraries, and usually one overdue notice and one bill are sent to clients. The higher, hourly fees charged by academic libraries for reserve collection materials approximate the scale of fees charged for special or interlibrary loans of films and video or equipment. The range of equipment available in public libraries is much broader.

The philosophy and tone of the public library policies are divided between those who maintain a legalistic approach, quoting statutes and wording responsibility statements very carefully, and those who take a wholly positive view of their service group and mission. Client documents, however, even in the public libraries that have grave warnings about the nonreturn of materials, tend to deemphasize penalties and presume cooperation. Several libraries have separate lists of fines and fees and do not dwell on them in their general guides. "We hope you won't need this," was the heading on one list of penalties.[115] That seems to be the tone of many staff-only manuals as well, except for the legalists who keep an eye toward the courts as their last resort in reclaiming materials and obtaining cooperation.

Chapter 5 examines the policy-making process in public libraries. Understanding it will help put these policies into perspective.

NOTES

1. Altanta-Fulton Public Library, "Circulation Policy," draft ed. (Atlanta, Ga.: the Library, 1984), 11 p.

2. Comment on "Survey of Circulation Policies and Practices," [p. 4].

3. "Circulation Policy," [p. 1].

4. Although the initial definition of resident does not mention age ("Circulation Policy," p. 2) there is a separate category for "Residents under 12 Years of Age" ("Circulation Policy," p. 5).

5. "Circulation Policy," p. 5.

6. "Circulation Policy," p. 11.

7. "Circulation Policy," [p. 1].

8. "Circulation Policy," p. 7.

9. "Circulation Policy," p. 7.

10. "Circulation Policy," p. 10.

11. The term *reserves* in public libraries has a different meaning than it does in academic libraries. Public library *reserves* are equivalent to academic library *holds*, and both refer to items out in circulation that are requested by another person.

12. Pages from Tacoma Public Library policies include the following: "Administrative Policy Number 10.20, Problem Patrons" (1981); "Administrative Policy Number 10.17, Registration Policy" (1980-1983), 3 p.; "Administrative Policy Number 10.17.1, Item F—Definition" (n.d.); "Registration Policy Procedures" (1983); "Patron Re-registration Policy" (1983); "Administrative Policy Number 10.29, Video Materials Procedures"(1983); "Administrative Policy Number 10.29.1, Media Responsibility Card Procedures" (1983).

13. "Loan Periods and Limits," (Tacoma, Wash.: Tacoma Public Library, n.d.).

14. The law to which the policy refers is the Revised Code of Washington 27.12.270, quoted in "Registration Policy," p. 1.

15. "Registration Policy," p. 1.

16. "Registration Policy," p. 3.

17. "Registration Policy," p. 3.

18. "Registration Policy Procedures," p. 1. Emphasis is in the original.

19. "Loan Periods and Limits," [p. 1].

20. "Your Library," (Los Angeles: Los Angeles Public Library, n.d.), 7 p.

21. Pages from the Los Angeles Public Library policies include the following: "Registration Policy," (1982); and "Circulation Policy," (1982).

22. "Your Library," p. 1.

23. "Your Library," p. 7.

24. "Your Library," p. 7.

25. "Registration Policy," [p. 1].

26. "Registration Policy," [p. 1].

27. "Registration Policy," [p. 1].

28. "Registration Policy," [p. 2].

29. "Circulation Policy," [p. 3].

30. "Circulation Policy," [p. 1].

31. The following documents apply to automated libraries: "Registration: Automated Procedure," (Philadelphia: Free Library of Philadelphia, 1983), 24 p.; and "Materials Circulation: Automated Procedure," (Philadelphia: Free Library of Philadelphia, 1983), 30 p. In addition, two memoranda from the director, Keith Doms, cover implementation of the policies cited above.

The following documents apply to nonautomated libraries: "Registration: Photocharging Procedure," (Philadelphia: Free Library of Philadelphia, 1983), 27 p.; and "Loan Procedures," (Philadelphia: Free Library of Philadelphia, 1970), 42 p. (Many pages were revisions of a 1964 version, with dates ranging from 1966 to 1976; some examples contained dates as late as 1984.)

A memorandum dated 1968 from the chiefs of FLP's extension division and central public departments covers reserve requests and applies to all units, automated or not.

The following documents are distributed to the public: "A Guide: The Free Libraries of Philadelphia: Where They Are; What They Do For You; How To Use Them," (Philadelphia: Free Library of Philadelphia, 1983), 13 pages of foldout; and "Automation Is Coming To Your Library," (Philadelphia: Free Library of Philadelphia, n.d.), 2 p.

32. "A Guide," p. 1.

33. "Registration: Photocharging Procedure," p. 4; "Registration: Automated Procedure," p. 3.

34. "Materials Circulation: Automated Procedure," p. 15.

35. "Get Acquainted with Your Pasadena Public Library," (Pasadena: the Library, n.d.), 5 p.

36. "28 Libraries Are Better than One," (Metropolitan Cooperative Library System, n.d.), 6 p.

37. "Library Launches Million $ Remodeling Project; Special Edition," *In the Know* (July/August 1984), 4 p.

38. "28 Libraries," p. 2.

39. "Get Acquainted," pp. 2-4.

40. "28 Libraries," p. 3.

41. "Get Acquainted," p. 1.

42. This information is from the English-language bookmark, titled "Check it out . . . ," and is repeated on the Spanish-language bookmark, titled "Su Biblioteca!"

43. "The Policies of the Hays Public Library," (Hays, Kans.: the Library, 1978-1983). (The pages are numbered in several sequences.) Includes, as appendices, the "Library Bill of Rights" and "Freedom to Read" statements of the American Library Association, as well as job descriptions for principal positions.

44. The sample letter, undated, was signed by the director, Melanie Miller.

45. Duane F. Johnson, "Kansas State Library, Position Paper: An Interlibrary Loan Development Plan: Better Information Service and Education through Sharing of Improved Resource Library Collections," (Topeka: Kansas State Library, 1983), 10 p. plus addenda; and "We Would Like to Introduce You to the Kansas Library Card," (Topeka: Kansas State Library, 1983), 5 p.

46. "The Policies," [p. 5].

47. This kind of discrimination against the use of films by schools occurs elsewhere in the country and is usually attributed to the fact that schools have their own film services available, while other organizations and individuals do not. Therefore, schools are specifically eliminated from eligibility for public library film services. It may even be mandated by state law or rulings of state education agencies.

48. "Checking Out Materials," (Hays, Kans.: Hays Public Library, n.d.), p. 2.

49. "Checking Out Materials," p. 1.

50. "The Policies," [p. 5].

51. "The Policies," [p. 19].

52. "Great Neck Library: Information for Borrowers," (Great Neck, N.Y.: the Library, n.d.), 4 p.

53. "Great Neck Library," p. 1.

54. "Great Neck Library," p. 2.

55. "Great Neck Library," p. 2.

56. "Great Neck Library," pp. 2-3.

57. "Great Neck Library," p. 2.

58. "Great Neck Library," p. 3.

59. "Great Neck Library," pp. 3-4.

60. "Great Neck Library," p. 4.

61. "Welcome to the Elmhurst Public Library," (Elmhurst, Ill.: the Library, n.d.), 5 p.

62. ". . . . About Your Library Card," (Elmhurst, Ill.: Elmurst Public Library, 1983), 2 p.

63. "Welcome," p. 4.

64. "Welcome," p. 4.

65. "Welcome," p. 5.

66. "Welcome," p. 4.

67. "Welcome," p. 4.

68. "Computer Checkout; You'll Notice the Difference," (Belmont, Calif.: Peninsula Libraries Automated Network, n.d.), 3 p.

69. "Welcome to the Burlingame Public Library," (Burlingame, Calif.: the Library, n.d.), 3 p.

70. "Welcome to the Burlingame Public Library," p. 1.

71. "Burlingame Public Library: Circulation Policies," (Burlingame, Calif.: the Library, n.d.), 2 p.

72. "Welcome to the Burlingame Public Library," p. 1.

73. "Return of Library Materials . . . ," (Burlingame, Calif.: Burlingame Public Library, 1983), 1 p.

74. "Circulation by Time Period," (Burlingame, Calif.: Burlingame Public Library, 1981?), p. 5.

75. "Return of Library Materials. . . ," p. 1.

76. "Return of Library Materials. . . ," p. 1.

77. "Menlo Park Public Library," (Menlo Park, Calif.: the Library, n.d.), p. 8.

78. "Menlo Park Public Library Hours," (Menlo Park, Calif.: the Library, 1984), pp. 1-2.

79. "Shelving," (San Bruno, Calif.: San Bruno Public Library, 1982?), 25 p. (unnumbered).

80. "Shelving," [p. 19].

81. "Shelving," [p. 19].

82. "Shelving," [p. 20].

83. "Shelving," [p. 20]. Emphasis is in the original.

84. "Shelving," [p. 19]. Emphasis is in the original.

85. "Shelving," [p. 13]. Emphasis is added.

86. "Shelving," [p. 15].

87. "San Mateo City Libraries: New Loan Periods, Renewal Policy, and Fine/Fee Schedule," (San Mateo, Calif.: the Libraries, 1984), 3 p.

88. Louise Brundage, *Procedures Manual,* rev. by the LEAP Procedures Committee (Hamden, Conn.: LEAP, 1983), 173 p. (The pages are in several numbered sequences: 95, 38, and 32 p. plus 8 p. of index.)

89. *Procedures Manual,* p. I-1.

90. "Hamden Library: Policies and Procedures," (Hamden, Conn.: the Library n.d.), 5 p.

91. "Free Access to Library Materials and Information," (Hamden, Conn.: Hamden Library Board, 1983), 10 p. (Excerpts from the board's policy manual; pages are mostly unnumbered.)

92. "Free Access," p. 1.

93. *Connecticut General Statutes,* Chapter 190, Sections 11-24b and 11-31a.

94. "Hamden Library," p. 5.

95. "Hamden Library," p. 1.

96. "Free Access," [p. 3].

97. "Free Access," [p. 7].

98. "Free Access," [p. 7].

99. "Hamden Library," p. 2.

100. "Free Access," [p. 11].

101. *WCL System Circulation Manual,* (Reno, Nev.: Washoe County Library, 1984), ca. 36 p. (Pages are numbered in several sequences.)

102. *WCL System Circulation Manual,* p. III-1.

103. *WCL System Circulation Manual,* p. III-4.

104. *WCL System Circulation Manual,* p. I-16.

105. "BCPL Branches: Hours & Services," (Towson, Md.: Baltimore County Public Library, 1983), 5 p.

106. "Schedule of Fines & Fees," (Towson, Md.: Baltimore County Public Library, 1984), 2 p.

107. "Baltimore County Public Library," (Towson, Md.: Baltimore County Public Library, 1982), 2 p.

108. "BCPL Branches," p. 4.

109. "BCPL Branches," p. 4.

110. "Baltimore County Public Library," p. 1.

111. "BCPL Branches," p. 5.

112. "Schedule of Fines & Fees," p. 1.

113. "BCPL Branches," p. 4.

114. In my own experience, this was the case. I suspect few libraries publicize that such privileges are a perquisite of office for board members or of employment for staff members.

115. "San Mateo City Libraries," p. 2.

5   *PUBLIC LIBRARY RESPONSES TO THE CIRCULATION QUESTIONNAIRE*

The same questionnaire answered by librarians in the academic institutions was submitted to the public library participants. Seventeen libraries responded. In addition to the libraries whose circulation policies were described in Chapter 4, five more public librarians responded only to the questionnaire, sending no policy documents. The two network systems, LEAP and the Peninsula Library System, returned only one questionnaire but policy documents are from both the network and some of the individual libraries.

This chapter is divided into four main sections focusing on the circulation system, institutional policy-making, problems that circulation departments are currently facing, and future plans for circulation. A fifth section provides a summary. The replies given to the survey were accurate in spring 1984, but the information may have changed to some degree in each institution.

THE CIRCULATION SYSTEM

Of the seventeen libraries surveyed, twelve had computer-based circulation systems and five did not. Three of those with automated systems also used manual charging systems for some portion of the materials circulated—one had three systems in use simultaneously. In all, twenty-one systems were being used.

All of the computerized systems reported were minicomputer-based stand-alone turnkey systems. All were online. Not one of the twelve libraries had a self-developed system. None shared their computer with nonlibrary entities, though several of the computers were shared by multiunit library systems or several independent libraries. None relied on batch-mode or offline processing for primary circulation functions, although secondary functions in some systems are performed in those modes.

Eight libraries had CLSI circulation control systems, two had GEAC, and two had DataPhase systems. Two of the libraries running more than one system simultaneously used CLSI for the larger portion of their transactions, and the third had a DataPhase system termed "underconfigured" by the responding librarian.

The manual charging systems used included five photocharging systems, three of which were Recordak, three Gaylord systems, and one McBee keysort system. The library using the McBee keysort was in the process of automating fully and expected to phase out both this and its photocharging systems within two years. The other two libraries combining automated and manual systems did not comment on when they expected to dispense with their manual operations. The librarian from one of the Gaylord libraries commented, "[The Gaylord Model C] serves the needs of our current circulation level, apart from the routine mechanical shortcomings of the machinery." Mechanical failures are, perhaps, more dramatic and traumatic with computer-based systems than with their simpler noncomputerized cousins. Although vendors of automated systems claim to approach perfection in their performance, every computer user can tell at least one horror story about "crashes" and "downtime" (sudden system failures and periods when the computer does not operate) usually caused by simple mechanical failures, programming bugs, or sudden loss of power due to storms.

Only one library indicated having separate reserve book room procedures, presumably the special hourly loan book and journal collections of academic libraries, not the requests for titles not currently available of most public libraries. This procedure was reported to be operated with a manual system. Two others reported having hourly loans for films and reference books, but they indicated that these functions were performed using their computerized systems.

Since fewer public libraries had manual circulation systems than academic libraries, it was expected that answers to a question about plans for changing the systems would be negative for the most part. Among the respondents who were using only manual systems, one said there were no plans to change. The others indicated that changes were being planned, one in the near term, one within ten years, and the third without any stated timetable.

Of those libraries with computer-based systems, the three partially computerized libraries intended to complete the implementation of their systems, making changes that had been anticipated in their original automation plans. The two GEAC libraries and five of the CLSI libraries reported there were no plans to make changes in their systems other than those associated with new "releases," i.e., ongoing enhancements to the software. Librarians from one of the DataPhase libraries said they intended to make changes because the system was not adequate for their needs. However, the response from the other DataPhase user said changes were contemplated to "install one of the next generation 'integrated' systems, which will allow us to support public access terminals and potentially share other functions such as acquisitions on the same machine or machines." One CLSI user concurred in the latter type of projection saying, "We will stay with CLSI and will continue to expand the system with such things as Datalink, Search helper and the on-line catalog."

Thus, excluding the libraries planning changes to which they were previously committed and those intending to enhance existing systems as new possibilities emerged, only one library with an automated system was actively planning to change its system; three with manual systems expected to implement computer-based systems.

Librarians with computer-based systems were asked to describe the changes to policies caused by the introduction of automation. Three of the twelve librarians mentioned changes in sending notices and bills. Two of these said overdue notices were sent earlier and/or for more types of materials; the third said all notices were now centralized where previously each unit had sent its own. Two librarians said they had introduced grace periods during which overdue materials could be returned without charge. Three more said that loan periods had been adjusted in some way to accommodate automation. One general comment was, "There was a concerted effort by the eight participating jurisdictions to have common policies. Each policy to be manipulated by the automated system was reviewed."

In some instances, policies were changed to extend service, but in others the changes limited service more than before. One library introduced telephone renewals. Another library restricted borrowing without a card if the client had forgotten it. Many mentioned changes in registration procedures:

Increased identification required.

Registrations are non-expiring.

Patrons were required to have a borrower's card before circulating materials when automated procedures were issued.

Policies for patron identification have been tightened to identify those with outstanding fines and materials. . . . We now also require re-verification ("re-registration," but without issuing a new physical card) of all patron data annually. New patron types and categories have been added due to the convenience of the automated system, with specific special privileges or responsibilities.

In general, the changeover in public library circulation operations from traditional manual or older mechanical methods to computer-based systems seems to be much greater than in academic libraries. Many more of the public libraries in the survey had turnkey automated systems handling most of their circulation transactions. Most of the replies from computerized libraries indicated satisfaction with their systems, except for those still in the process of implementing computers in all their units, or those who found they still had to perform some tasks manually, e.g., placing holds on ordered materials not yet part of the database.

The number of instances in which photocharging was used was higher in the smaller group of public libraries than among the academic libraries. Photocharging furnishes less accessible information about materials out in circulation than charging systems that result in files of book cards. Once an item is charged out with a photocharging system, the record will not be consulted merely to locate that item, say, in order to recall it for another client. Usually, the transaction record will be accessed only to type an overdue notice, often not until the item has been overdue for four or more weeks. The longer a library waits to type its overdue notices, the fewer of them will have to be done, thereby saving time and money. The public libraries in this survey were not interested in recalling materials and, thus, were able to survive without information about materials that were out in circulation, but not long overdue.

Only one public library uses the McBee keysort system—so much more popular in manual-mode academic libraries—in which clients must write out their names and addresses. Both Gaylord stampers and photocharging systems dispense with that need. The tradeoff is that the McBee keysort system makes it possible to locate overdue items in a file arranged by call number, main entry, or title. Using the Gaylord system requires keeping the book cards in chronological order.

Libraries still using manual-mode circulation systems generally want to change to computer-based systems as soon as possible. Nevertheless, only one of the five libraries using manual methods of circulation is already in the process of acquiring a computer system. Two more indicate the time for computers is still far off. The other two, though they plan to make the change, offer no timetable for automating. This is a sharp contrast to the academic library group, where a large proportion of institutions with manual-mode circulation systems are in the process of acquiring a computer-based circulation system. Admittedly, more of the public libraries than academic libraries already have computers, leaving fewer with both the need and wherewithal to plan for them.

POLICY-MAKING IN THE INSTITUTION

Questions asking who contributed to the formulation of circulation policies drew replies that were almost evenly divided between those indicating that administrators made policy decisions, many requiring formal approval by library boards, and those indicating that policy-making committees made the decisions. The following comments illustrate the former:

All policy decisions are made at the administrative level and in certain instances by the Library Board (particularly those policies involving charges).

The Library Board, Director, Circulation Supervisors, and patron suggestions affect Circulation policy.

All suggestions are reviewed by Library Administration and may or may not be forwarded to the Board of Library Commissioners for adoption.

Administrators and managers, as part of the Management Team, line supervisors of circulation points. Suggestions often grow from line staff of all levels, but policy formulation proceeds at the Management Team level.

Administrators review and approve or disapprove recommendations from system's Circulation Control Department.

In all, seven respondents indicated that administrators formulated policy, with or without the approval of their library boards or input from other sources.

Six responses indicated that the committee method of policy-making was followed. The following comments illustrate instances in which the policy-making role was assumed by committees. Here, too, references are made to final approval by library boards.

A Project Managers Committee with one representative from each of the eight member jurisdictions discusses and recommends circulation policy to the Governing Board, comprised of our Library Directors.

Policies are periodically reviewed and a designated committee is formulated to make recommendations to the Administrative Council regarding revisions to, and/or additions to, existing policies. The most recent designated committee contained both professional and clerical personnel representing small, medium and central circulating libraries as well as central support and administrative services. The group was formulated in this manner in order to ensure that the varying viewpoints and experiences that arise from working with diverse constituencies would be adequately represented.

We formed a Circulation "Task force" which met to review circulation policies, recording of statistics, and potential computerized operations. The group was comprised of the Director, the Head of Library Services, all department heads . . . and an Adult Dept. staff member. . . . All circulation policies must be approved by the Board of Trustees. Although they rarely dispute our suggestions, they do take an active interest in Library operations.

Our circulation policies are drafted by a committee that includes administration and circulation staffs. We also work with the regional staffs as our policies are also state-wide in nature.

Circulation policies are written and revised by a committee composed of: Asst. Chief, Central Public Services Division; Asst. Chief, Extension Division; senior coordinators from the Offices of Work with Adults and Children, and the Information Systems Manager.

A staff committee was formed a year ago to review all of our circulation policies and make recommendations for changes. These recommendations were reviewed by the administrative staff. After all recommendations were finalized, the new policies were presented to the Board of Trustees for approval.

From the comments, one might question the classification of policy-making into *administrator* or *committee* modes. The lines between them are, indeed, blurred. Some of the committees were made up entirely of administrators (assistant division chiefs, coordinators, etc.); some of the administrator/policy-makers operated in quasi-committee mode (the "Management Team.)" If the respondent emphasized the administrators' role, it was classified as administrative policy-making; if the committee was emphasized, it was classified the other way.

Two librarians described pluralistic styles of policy formulation. One said that "All staff who work at circulation/reference desk and administrators" contribute to policy. The other explained a two-step process: "Circulation staff then the Department Heads will discuss to formulate a policy. It will then go to the Public Relations Committee." Although a committee was involved, it appeared that a fully designed policy was sent by the circulation staff and department heads to the committee for approval in much the same way that approval was sought from library boards for policies that were already determined.

The last librarian wrote: "Policy is made by the Board of Directors for the . . . library." Then she added, "Suggestions as to changes may be offered by staff, administration, public, or the . . . Procedures Committee. . . . Circulation staff and administration are always consulted by the Board of Directors about proposed changes."

Periodic review of circulation policies was conducted in eight of the libraries surveyed, although five of these did not specify how much time lapsed between successive reviews. Two replied that policies were reviewed annually, and one more said it was done monthly. The other eight responses to this question indicated irregular or continuous review procedures. Two were rather vague, identifying the frequency of review as "on a routine basis," and "no formal reviewing." Three others said reviews were done *as the need arose* and two more, on an *ongoing basis.* The final reply, from a circulation department head, stated: "Policies [are] reviewed by me each time I use a policy." The answer might be taken to mean that changes were made all the time (i.e., ongoing review) or only on an as-needed basis. In any case, all sixteen respondents said that their policies were reviewed at some time during the normal course of events, even the library without a formal review procedure.

Asked who conducted policy reviews (and, thus, who might be expected to initiate changes), respondents gave many different answers. Review by committees, cited in six replies, was most popular; a seventh said, "Circulation policies are reviewed, individually, by members of the original committee who [formulate policy; they] also collect comments of Extension Division staff."

Heads of circulation departments were named as policy reviewers in two libraries. Another librarian said, "The Director and Circulation Supervisors are involved"; a fourth said that the entire circulation staff reviewed departmental policies.

The library board reviewed policies for one library, but procedures were evaluated by that library's Data Management Services Department, and changes they recommended were referred to the Director of Technical Services. Traditionally, circulation departments are considered public service functions, despite the fact that many operations are performed out of public view and without public contact. As far back as the 1950s, Tauber identified the *technical* aspects of both circulation and reference services. It is interesting, therefore, to note that circulation is under the authority of the *technical services* director in this library.

One librarian reported that policy review was a pluralistic endeavor in which members of the library board, administration, and staff performed periodic reviews; however, a second respondent for that library added, "[Review is] usually on the division head level."

Other respondents did not specify *who* conducted policy reviews in their libraries.

A survey question asked if existing policies were in the process of being revised. Nine librarians said "Yes," six said "No," and two left the answer blank. One of those responding negatively added, "Policies were completely revised to complement the installation of the automated circulation system."

The nine people responding affirmatively were asked to describe the purpose of their revisions in progress. In three libraries, current or impending automation projects had motivated the revisions. One described efforts to harmonize policies for different libraries contemplating a shared computer system: "Representatives will soon be working cooperatively, as part of the citywide automated circulation system implementation effort, to standardize or make increasingly compatible, the circulation policies of the three City library systems thereby simplifying local and inter-library use for City residents." The other two, unhappily, were attempting to minimize confusion caused by the simultaneous use of automated and manual systems in different units of their library systems. One said they were trying to "keep procedures as parallel as possible for public using two different circulation systems, e.g. off-line and on-line registration procedures differ, leading to public confusion for borrower's card renewals—possible at either type agency." The other echoed this need from the staff members' viewpoint, "At present the manuals (which include existing policies and procedures) for photo-charging and online operation are being revised and consolidated."

Five of the six remaining libraries were accommodating internal needs of different kinds including writing and/or rewriting circulation manuals and statistical and data management procedures, re-registering patrons (for the first time in many years), and examining methods of encouraging a higher rate of returns, or, conversely, preventing continued abuses. In connection with encouraging returns and preventing abuse, one library was considering raising fines and another was looking at stricter identification requirements for transients in the community. The re-registration, too, was said to be part of an overall effort to identify and maintain data on clients with serious records of abuse. That same librarian, however, was also examining the possibility of lowering the age at which an adult library card could be obtained, from sixteen to twelve, and increasing the maximum numbers of nonbook and periodical items that could be borrowed at one time. Only this librarian and one other who said that "we are in the process of revision to make the policies more liberal" expressed a desire to expand or otherwise extend services. The second of those two librarians (and the sixth who said that policy revision was in progress) was attempting to achieve compatibility with statewide borrowing procedures.

Seven libraries of the nine revising policies had automated systems; two did not. Five libraries of the eight who were not revising policies had automated systems; two did not. The presence or absence of an automated system did not seem to have any specific impact on the process.

CIRCULATION PROBLEMS

Survey participants were asked to name their worst circulation problem as well as their clients' biggest complaint. The replies were analyzed not only to identify specific problems and complaints and the frequency with which they occurred, but also to identify the relationship of both to the presence or absence of automation in the library and to determine whether the staff and client problems matched.

One librarian replied to the query about the biggest circulation problem:

No major problems, other than the problems of success—circulation is up sharply, in some cases growing 20 percent, with an overall growth of 15 percent in 1983. Notices are computer generated and get out on time. We have cut our loss rate to 0.5 percent by judicious use of required identification and verification, system-wide blocking of patrons with outstanding materials, calling and reminding/urging people with overdue materials to return them, and using the City Attorney and/or a collection agency to enforce ultimate recovery. Fine revenue is up and loss rates are down sharply, making more materials available to the public.

No other institutions seemed to fare as well as this library did, although one other reply said that the library's automated system was too new for problems to be identified. The problems affecting circulation departments were numerous. The following problems were specifically mentioned as circulation's biggest headaches; the numbers in parentheses indicate the number of libraries making the complaint:

- high rate of nonreturns (5)
- inaccurate information (4)
- inability to trap delinquent clients (4)
- inability to handle overdues in timely fashion (3)
- missing materials that clients claim were returned (2)
- lack of funds for needed staff/supplies, etc. (2)
- automated system cannot satisfy needed functions (2)
- theft of materials (2)
- materials put on hold but never picked up (1)
- maintenance of dual circulation systems, part manual and part automated (1)
- demand for best sellers too high (1)
- high cost of a labor-intensive system (1)
- inability to provide desired titles to clients (1)
- poor statistical reporting/management information (1)
- client anger over the use of collection agencies (1)
- malfunctions in systems (1)
- amount of time spent on routine clerical tasks (1)
- *new* materials often not returned (1)

Two of the five librarians naming the high rate of nonreturns as their worst problem had automated circulation systems, but not all their units were online. For these libraries, nonreturns overshadowed the inconvenience of operating dual systems, since neither of them complained about that.

The top four of all eighteen problems identified (nonreturns, inaccurate information, the inability to trap delinquent clients, and the inability to provide timely overdue notices) accounted for 43 percent of the complaints. All but nonreturns should be resolvable with the implementation of automated systems and, indeed, only two of the automated libraries complained of any of these four problems. However, automated systems cannot eliminate nonreturns by one-time borrowers or produce missing materials that clients claimed had been returned. The only completely satisfied librarian used a combination of tactics (or policies) to achieve a trouble-free operation.

Careful examination of the problems themselves is revealing, too. By dividing them into three groups relating to clients, operations, and materials, it can be seen that four of the problems primarily concern client services (inaccurate information, demand for best sellers, lack of desired titles, and anger over collections), four primarily concern materials (nonreturns, thefts, claimed returned, and new materials not returned), and nine concern staff or system operations (trapping delinquents, providing timely overdues, funding, insufficient system capabilities, malfunctions in systems, dual systems, statistical reports, clerical tasks, and high cost of operations). One wonders whether concentration on operations rather than on either client services or protection of materials is characteristic of this function.

Few problems were related solely to computer-based circulation operations, but those that did included insufficient system capabilities, the operation of dual systems, and lack of funds for needed terminals and staff. (This last problem is endemic to computer operations of other kinds as well, and lack of funds for other purposes is universal in nonautomated operations, too.)

The librarian who said there was too much demand for best-selling titles that had to be reserved may have pinpointed a problem pervading many public libraries. One would imagine that high demand is a positive factor for public libraries. However, if budgets and purchasing policies cannot or do not respond, clients may blame the circulation staff for their unsatisfied requests. Another librarian complained of nonreturn problems only for new materials which are usually the highest demand items. Loan policies typically restrict the length of time clients can borrow new materials and never permit renewal of items other clients have requested. Thus, the only alternative available to someone who borrows a high-demand title and does not finish it within the limited loan period is to keep it overdue and bear the penalties. If a library combines selection and acquisition policies that restrict the number of copies of popular titles they purchase with circulation policies that limit the use of the ones that are purchased, a problem is bound to arise that defies solution.

Together, complaints about nonreturns, missing materials that clients claimed had been returned, and outright thefts accounted for nearly one-third of all circulation problems. It is unfortunate that circulation librarians operate in an environment in which clients' good intentions are suspect, but the replies to this survey indicate quite clearly that such is the reality. One librarian commented, "Probably our biggest circulation problem concerns patrons who receive overdue notices and swear they have returned the book(s). Occasionally they have. Usually they haven't, but in the interest of public relations we believe them."

What do clients complain about? Circulation librarians offered the following list:

- lack of notification about overdues or fines (4)
- not enough titles available (4)
- fines (3)
- loan periods too short (2)
- renewal restrictions (2)
- use (or threat) of collection agency (2)
- waiting for popular titles (2)
- incorrect records (2)
- library service area does not coincide with city boundaries (1)
- receipt of overdue notices for items already returned (1)
- lack of information (1)
- confusion about procedures (1)
- waiting for library cards (1)
- keeping track of borrowed materials (1)

Fourteen client complaints were identified, just four fewer than the staff problems named. The top three complaints in the client list (lack of notification, not enough titles, and fines) accounted for 41 percent of the total. If waiting for requested titles, which could be interpreted as not enough *desired* titles, was added to these, the proportion of complaints accounted for rises to nearly 50 percent.

Clients did not complain often about fines—only three mentioned them—but two resented the use of collection agencies for outstanding bills. One librarian was amused by this posture, writing the following comment: "We enjoy a high rate of return via the agency. The problem lies in the irate patrons who just cannot understand why they have been sent to a collection agency because they have not returned or paid for materials." Client complaints appeared to focus most on circulation information, with eight instances of complaints related to insufficient or inaccurate information (lack of notification of overdues, incorrect overdue notices, and lack of information). Next to this issue, the lack of materials and distress over restrictions were each mentioned six times.

One complaint did not seem to involve the library at all—trouble keeping track of what was borrowed—although the large number who complained about overdue notifications might also have had this in mind.

Comparison of the top four staff problems with the top three client complaints, both of which accounted for approximately 40 percent of the totals, produced the following list:

Staff Problems	**Client Complaints**
Nonreturns	Lack of notification about overdues and fines
Inaccurate information	Waiting for materials
Inability to trap delinquents	Fines
Inability to produce timely overdues	

Only one of the issues matched—both librarians and clients were aggravated by a lack of timely overdue and fine notices. This was clients' primary complaint, the librarians' fourth. Only two librarians mentioned their inability to satisfy demand as a big problem, but clients listed not getting what they wanted one of their three main complaints. Librarians were more concerned about getting back borrowed materials, something ignored altogether by clients. The different perspectives of client and librarian undoubtedly influenced these priorities.

This survey would lead one to believe that providing notification about overdues and fines is a critical service important to clients and librarians alike. Yet, a few of the public libraries and more of the academic libraries stated that notifying clients of their overdue materials was a *courtesy*, not an obligation on the part of the library. One of the public libraries no longer sent notification of fines owed for materials returned overdue. Although these institutions had computerized systems that produce notices automatically, they did not appear to welcome the opportunity to send *more* of them. Instead, they seemed ready to eliminate notices previously part of their regular routines. Why this should be so may have less to do with the work of producing notices than with the cost of sending them. As long as the production of overdues lagged, postage and handling were also lower. This is not true once a computerized circulation system is in place. Even in a small public library, thousands of notices may be produced each week, and the cost of mailing them is much higher. In a medium to large city library system, the cost differential could be significant.

Looking only at the problems and complaints in libraries with computerized circulation systems, there is almost no shift in priorities. The following lists tabulate the replies from the twelve automated libraries:

Staff Problems	**Client Complaints**
Nonreturns (3)	Notification of overdues (4)
System capabilities (2)	Fines (3)
Lack of adequate funding (2)	Anger over collection agency (2)
System malfunctions (1)	Waiting for popular titles (2)
Dual systems (1)	Not enough titles (2)
Theft/nonreturn of new materials (1)	Renewals (1)
	Waiting for cards (1)

Missing materials claimed
   returned (1)

Anger over collection agency (1)

Materials on hold not
   picked up (1)

High demand for best sellers (1)

Errors in overdues (1)

Loan period too short (1)

Confusion about procedures (1)

Keeping track of borrowed
   materials (1)

The biggest circulation problem is still nonreturns, and the biggest patron complaint is still lack of notification about overdues. Problems related to the automated systems and those involved with operating dual systems show up here, too, as expected. Nine different staff problems and twelve client complaints were identified—just the reverse of those determined for the group as a whole. This means that clients using libraries with automated systems continue to have their complaints, but the staff tend to perceive fewer problems.

FUTURE PLANS FOR CIRCULATION

The final topic with which the survey dealt was future plans for circulation. As has already been discussed, librarians with manual circulation systems said they want to have computer-based systems. Three of the five librarians with manual systems said they were planning to move to computer-based systems. Of these three responses, one indicated that they had progressed to the point where responses to a Request for Proposal were being evaluated; the other two gave no specific timetable for the acquisition of computers. The fourth reply said, "Would love to have a computerized system *asap*. Realistically—many years off." The director of the fifth library, who said there were no plans to change systems, described the situation as follows, "We have no plans to change our current circulation system. 1989 would be the earliest date at which such a change would be financially feasible."

Librarians with computer-based circulation systems were largely satisfied with them. Ten of the replies to the question about plans to change systems were negative though three qualified their replies, indicating that they meant to expand existing systems but not change to entirely new systems. One librarian left this answer blank. Thus, only one librarian out of twelve using automated systems planned to make changes of a fundamental nature. This librarian said, "Our objective would be to obtain some form of 'non-stop' or 'fault-tolerant' system to avoid the problems of down time, and to obtain enough computer power to handle more public access and to widely share knowledge of what is on the system, out in circulation, and on order, for both staff and public."

Integrated systems were high on everyone's priority list, even the libraries without computers. One librarian said the library wanted to acquire "an automated total library system that would include all circulation operations and an online catalog in order to: eliminate routine clerical procedures; provide access to records system-wide; and be able to track material from the time it is ordered." Another said, "The Library plans to implement an integrated automation system," and a third echoed, "We want an integrated system including an on-line public access catalog." One director of an already automated library, however, added this caveat about integrated systems: "I am not a believer in the integrated system and am still adopting a doubting Thomas posture. Most of the working integrated systems are mainframe based [i.e., use larger computers], and even those that are mini-computer based have a very small number of terminals."

Asked to identify services not currently offered that they wished to furnish to the public, one librarian with an automated circulation system focused primarily on remote access, saying clients wished to "select material at home via cable TV," and that self-charging and the ability to renew materials or place holds from home or office were also accorded high priorities in the library. Another indicated the desire to reach the public outside of the building, too, but without sophisticated technology. This respondent opted for establishing kiosks in mass transit stations and expanding services for the homebound. Five more replies said either that there were no additional services they wished to provide or left the answer blank. An eighth reply said that future planning might include all of the suggestions on a list that included self-charging by clients, materials by mail, and selective dissemination of information.

Four more public librarians with automated circulation systems gave replies which centered on relatively prosaic services not currently available from their systems, e.g., automatically printed receipts for each item loaned and/or all fine payments by clients; the ability to place holds on materials still on order (this suggestion came from a DataPhase library—CLSI users could do it provided they entered on-order titles into their database); the ability to generate automatically overdue notices for materials with short loan periods sooner than for materials with longer loan periods; a film booking system that was integrated with the rest of the circulation module; notices that were printed on mailing forms (this is available but costs more than using standard sheets that are inserted into envelopes); and, finally, improved management information including statistical reports.

Identical requests were made by some librarians from nonautomated libraries. They wanted to furnish the following services to the public: film booking, a variety of loan periods, the ability to send overdue notices one week after the due date, the ability to renew material at any location in the system, automated reserves and interlibrary loans, the ability to charge materials to nonlocal clients, and the ability to provide materials by mail.

Two librarians with manual systems replied that they wanted to provide circulation information for clients—to tell them what materials were outstanding or what they owed in fines—and to determine shelf status and location of wanted materials immediately without physically inspecting the catalog and/or the shelves.

Automation, in the form of standardized, turnkey, minicomputer-based systems, cannot supply all of the above services, but virtually all systems support a variety of loan periods and provide status information for materials. Film-booking modules are not unusual and were offered by all the systems used by the libraries participating in this study, although they were not necessarily part of the vendor's basic package. The schedule for automatically generating overdue notices can be set by the library in most turnkey systems, but they do not always accommodate different options for different materials. Indeed, even though multiple loan periods are available, a standard loan period—the one most frequently used—is usually selected as a default value, while all other loan periods must be manually set by the computer operator (by keying in a new date, pressing a different function key, or scanning a special indicator). If the operator forgets to switch to the variant due date, no beeps indicate the failure. Instead, a best seller intended to circulate for, say, seven days, will be given the longer loan, say, twenty-one days. Even when the incorrect due date flashes on a video display terminal, a tired, inexperienced, or careless operator may not notice it is not the one that should have been assigned to the item just charged.

Interestingly, although the ability to renew materials at any location in a system (checking at the same time to see if any requests were made for the titles) is not only possible but is easily done with shared automated systems, libraries that have them do not all permit it, whereas libraries with manual systems, who cannot automatically check the status of titles, sometimes do. In some places, renewals are discouraged because there are limited supplies of borrowable materials—something automation does not affect—but in others the reason given for not renewing materials except at the home library is that only there can reserve or hold lists be checked. Libraries with manual systems who allow renewals anywhere rely on telephone calls to the owning library or prepared lists of requested titles to determine whether candidates for renewal are free of outstanding requests. This could be done by any library, with or without an automated circulation system.

Equally interesting is the fact that so few (only two) librarians claimed to want to offer self-service charging for clients. Aside from the preparation of overdue notices, charging materials is probably the most tedious and repetitious task performed by circulation staff members. Nonetheless, few respondents saw their automated systems as a way to dispense with this task. Only two librarians specified wanting status information on materials—a capability furnished by most automated systems—and desired by many more of their academic library colleagues. This may reflect a different priority assigned by public librarians to locating materials for recall (if they think of recalls as a desirable service at all), although it is an important service for academic library clients.

Examination of answers about current policies thought to be in need of change revealed that most librarians were satisfied with the status quo. Eight people replied that none of their library's policies needed change or that recently implemented changes would address all problem areas successfully. A ninth said, "Policies are OK," but added a wish for better identification for prospective cardholders. Four more named registration procedures and/or policies relating to library cards as the area in greatest need of change. Of these, some wanted more liberalized procedures, for example, "In our future planning is the hope that we will have a single statewide card." Others wanted stricter rules such as better identification or clarification of client categories and privileges.

Two respondents said that fine policies needed attention. One wanted to raise the maximum fine while the other wanted to lower it. One of these librarians also wanted to have a fine notice sent to clients when the total amount owed reached a certain figure. Other answers about future policy changes mentioned once included increasing the length of loan periods, codifying legal actions for nonreturn of materials, and revising the entire policy as part of automating circulation.

SUMMARY

In public libraries, the most striking reply to questions about current circulation systems was the large number of libraries operating fully online, minicomputer-based systems. Twelve out of the seventeen libraries responding to the survey had such systems. Only five still had completely traditional manual-mode systems, and three of their automated fellows also had some portion of their operations performed manually. The manual-mode systems included five photocharging systems, with Recordak named in three instances, three Gaylord systems, and one McBee keysort.

Like their academic counterparts, possessors of online automated systems were satisfied with them, looking primarily to extend them to all units and/or all materials or to enhance them in time as their vendors developed new capabilities. Only one librarian mentioned connecting other external systems to the CLSI system she had, but others wanted additional modules to create integrated systems for their libraries. Provision of online catalogs to clients was a priority for two librarians.

Circulation policies were formulated either by administrators or committees in most of these public libraries. Only two libraries reported a more free-wheeling style of policy formulation in which clients, administrators, circulation staff, and library boards all participated. One librarian said that only the library board formulated policy, but circulation staff and administrators were always consulted. Periodic policy review was widespread, too; all respondents claimed to review their circulation policies at some time during the normal course of events. A few claimed to review policies continuously or whenever a question arose; several named different periods of time for reviews (annually, monthly, weekly), but most did not specify when or how frequently they reviewed their policies.

Unlike their academic library colleagues, none of these librarians expressed frustration over their charging systems—absent, particularly, was the need for clients to write their names and addresses with the attendant ills of illegibility, length of time needed to make out forms, and so on. However, many of public librarians' problems were already familiar, having appeared on academic library lists too. Public librarians were distressed primarily by the high rate of nonreturns, inaccurate information, the inability to trap delinquent clients, and their inability to send overdues in a timely manner.

Clients, on the other hand, were concerned about not being notified about overdues and fines, about the lack of enough materials or desired materials, and fine charges. Though timely notification about overdues was a headache for both staff and clients that should have been resolved with automatic notice generation in computerized systems, a comparison of problems and complaints reported only by automated libraries found the same complaint at the top of the clients' list. The staff members, however, made no mention of it. Clearly, there are differences about what constitutes "timely notification."

No shift in emphasis was found in the group of staff problems in automated libraries. Nonreturns still led all the others, and thefts or nonreturns of new materials and missing materials claimed returned were included further down on the list. The fact that lack of information did not figure on either the staff or client list is interesting, too. Clients still focused on the lack of wanted materials, with waiting for popular titles, not enough titles, and high demand for best sellers together outweighing the leading complaint.

What did these librarians anticipate for the future? All but one of those with manual systems sought a computer to replace their existing system. They anticipated integrating other functions with their circulation module—something that their colleagues with more computer experience did not universally emphasize. Instead, librarians with computer systems had narrower, more practical goals. One said, "Further analysis of special privilege categories of patron . . . to more closely define the primary clientele we serve, and to lessen confusion in who gets what kind of card." Another wanted better registration identification. Several indicated a desire to simplify, clarify, or otherwise streamline procedures, including one reply which described a single, statewide borrowing card as a future goal. Few were interested in greatly expanding services, although access to circulation services from remote sites was named by one respondent. Four people gave no reply to the question about what new services they would like to provide. Five others wanted additional modules or added enhancements to their computer systems including production of receipts, additional notices, different kinds of notices, or more loan periods. Most of these requests seemed to focus on types of service still being handled in a manual mode despite the implementation of the computer system. Future systems were expected to deal with these services as well, preferably in one integrated system.

Public access to information, either bibliographic or circulation, was a high priority for the future for one of the automated libraries and two of the manual libraries—not a very large total. Doing the traditional circulation job well seemed to be everyone's primary concern. The librarian whose institution was evaluating responses to an RFP said,

[We] see the acquisition of an automated circulation system as a major component in *improving* the quality of its services. In particular, we anticipate that the system would permit patrons to access the composite resources of [all participants] from any given site, provide a more timely and accurate response to individual patron requests for specific materials; provide more materials to patrons by reducing the amount of the collection lost in circulation and in the process obviate the need to expend a significant amount of our budget to replace such "high casualty items" on an annual basis.

Perhaps this quotation best expresses public librarians' hopes for the future and explains why librarians who have begun achieving these goals appear to be so satisfied.

Librarians in library media centers (learning resource centers, media resource centers, or just plain libraries) located in elementary and secondary schools proved to be the most difficult group of professionals from whom to obtain information about circulation policies and practices. Librarians from only six institutions sent documents describing their circulation policies. A seventh person noted "Not Applicable" in the margin next to the request for policy documents, indicating the possibility that many schools do not have any written policies, either for staff or for the public. Such a situation may well be the case in small schools where there is only one staff member and controls do not have to be formalized. The distribution of responses is not as broad geographically or in any other factor that might have been desired, e.g., size of schools or school districts, grade levels, and so on.

For the most part, documents intended for library staff were supplied; only a few items appeared to be intended for use by the public. Most of the documents were short, simple, typed and duplicated sheets, with very little added in the way of special formatting or illustration. One difference between school policies and many public and academic library policies was found in their choice of terms for materials and procedures, for example, *magazine* instead of *periodical*. In general, the schools use simpler, more familiar terms—*keep a daily count*, instead of *maintain statistics*.

The circulation policies of four high schools are described, followed by the policies of two elementary school districts. One of these school district libraries is primarily a professional library, although it lends, indirectly, to students as well as teachers.

MORRISTOWN HIGH SCHOOL LIBRARY

Three pages of a staff manual covering the circulation policies of the Morristown, New Jersey, High School Library furnished the information included here.[1] Listed under the heading "Daily Routines" were the library's hours of service—7:30 A.M. to 2:40 P.M. every school day. Although the hours of service are not strictly a circulation issue, activities in school library media centers are surely limited by them. Whenever possible, this information is given along with specifics about who may borrow, what may be borrowed, and how it may be borrowed.

Students of Morristown High are required to show their identification cards and to write down the name of their attendance teacher.[2] Students are not permitted to borrow materials for other classmates or friends.

Rules for outsiders are discussed next. The policy states: "Even though this is a public school library *and theoretically has a closed membership,* anyone who comes in and requests help is welcome. The faculty of neighboring schools may enjoy the same borrowing privileges as members of our own school community."[3] Nothing more is said about whether students from other schools, parents, or other categories of outsiders might also be extended loan privileges. The policy continues, "We have an excellent relationship with the Morristown-Morris Township Public Library from whom we may borrow materials and through whom we initiate interlibrary loan procedures."[4] No mention was made about lending school library materials *to* the public library, but interlibrary loans normally go in both directions.

Morristown High teachers had broad privileges, on the order of postsecondary school faculties: "If a staff member needs library materials for professional reasons he may sign them out for an extended period of time or on permanent loan; otherwise, materials are signed out in accord with the standard circulation and overdue policies."[5] Pencilled in the margin is the additional note, "and returns." The policy makes no mention of teachers producing identification; perhaps the school is small enough to permit such lack of control. Either everyone on the staff is immediately recognizable, or no other adults are assumed capable of trying to assume the role of a teacher from this or another school to obtain illegal loans.

Four types of circulating materials are identified in the policy: books, magazines, vertical file materials, and recordings (probably sound recordings). Any of these can be placed by teachers on closed reserve; however, closed reserve is not defined—whether the materials can be used only for one hour, one day, or overnight; whether students must prove they are taking a particular class to use them; and so on. Another mystery is "overdue reference circulation"[6] (*reference* is pencilled in), which might be circulating reference materials. A sentence in the "Opening Procedures" section states that personal visits are made when these materials are one week overdue.[7] Newspapers are mentioned in several places, but these probably do not circulate since no overdue penalties or procedures are given for them.

There is only one standard loan period, but it fluctuates from two to three weeks depending on the day of the week when materials are borrowed. "The circulation date is advanced one week every Wednesday morning,"[8] means that materials borrowed on Tuesday are due fifteen days later, but materials borrowed on the next day are due twenty-one days later. Faculty loans are filed separately from student loans.

The most lenient rules govern materials held overdue. No overdue charges are levied by the library at all, but several measures are used to obtain return of the materials. Three overdue notices are sent, two weeks apart, beginning when an item becomes overdue for a week. If none of the notices brings back the materials, librarians have three alternatives: to send a form letter to the student's home, to speak to the student personally, or to suspend borrowing privileges. No indication is given as to which punishment is to be applied in which cases. It must be assumed that the librarian can use his or her judgment.

If materials are lost, the purchase price is charged for books and recordings and the cost of a single issue for a magazine. Vertical file materials cost 25 cents each, regardless of the actual purchase price, if any. No additional assessments are made for processing or handling. End-of-the-year overdue procedures include withholding graduation invitations (but not necessarily diplomas or transcripts) from seniors with outstanding books, magazines, or recordings. Vertical file materials do not count. Students from other classes have their report cards withheld. In order to secure release of invitations or report cards, students must return the materials or settle their debts.

Morristown High School Library's policies appeared to be far less formal than any of their academic or public library counterparts. The need to identify its primary client group—Morristown High students—is eliminated by the use of student identification cards. Teachers are accorded great privileges. Librarians are willing to admit and serve outsiders despite their expressed perception that this is contrary to mainstream practice.

Almost all of Morristown High School Library's borrowing rules differ from any of the academic or public libraries described in earlier chapters. All circulating materials are treated identically. No mention is made of renewals or requested materials. Closed reserve is not described, but it probably involves only in-house use of materials. The complete lack of overdue fees and minimal charges for lost materials indicates no desire to penalize people for infringing on the rules and little attempt to recover costs. (This may be the result of state or local legislation or education department regulations and is found in others of the policies reviewed in this chapter.) Here, indeed, is a circulation operation aimed almost entirely at client service.

MONTGOMERY BLAIR HIGH SCHOOL LIBRARY MEDIA CENTER

The section of Blair High School's Faculty Handbook devoted to library policy and procedure,[9] a circulation policy document from Maryland's Montgomery County Public School system,[10] and two circulation forms, one for magazines and one for vertical file materials,[11] were sent to describe the circulation policies of Blair High School in Silver Spring, Maryland. The county document outlines a philosophical framework within which individual schools formulate their own specific policies. Although it is helpful in understanding the objectives of such practices as maintaining statistics and dividing materials into categories, it does not contribute any details specifically applicable to the operation at Blair High School. It does suggest several policy components that show up in Blair High's documents, such as the division of circulation into categories by form and provision for the creation of reserve collections at the request of faculty members.

Blair High School Library Media Center is open on "all regularly scheduled school days" at 7:15 A.M. and remains open until 3:45 P.M.[12] The opening paragraphs of the Faculty Handbook state "The library collection includes more than 20,000 print items and 10,000 nonprint items (records, tapes, slides, film loops, filmstrips, kits, transparencies, microforms, etc.) and more than 280 pieces of audiovisual equipment."[13] Videos and microcomputer software—formats thought of as popular in school library media centers—are not specifically mentioned anywhere. All library materials circulate to faculty members, but the documents do not indicate whether students have equal access.

The two printed forms, yellow for vertical file materials and green for magazines (Figure 6-1), indicate a one-week student loan period for both types of material. Unfortunately, none of the documents give student loan periods for any other materials including books, the most likely type of material to have a longer loan period. The county policy indicates that reference books are to be made available for overnight loans—whether to all clients or only teaching staff is not specified.

The circulation forms have places for students to sign their names and give their grades and homeroom sections. Seven vertical file titles can be listed on one yellow slip, but only one issue of a magazine can be entered on the green slip. One line in the Faculty Handbook hints that students can borrow equipment: "Both student and faculty must assume financial

Figure 6-1
Montgomery Blair High School Circulation Forms

MONTGOMERY BLAIR LIBRARY

**VERTICAL FILE
CIRCULATION SLIP**

Subject _______________________

Number Of Items _______________________

*Vertical file material may be borrowed
for one (1) week.*

Item titles or numbers:

1. _______________________
2. _______________________
3. _______________________
4. _______________________
5. _______________________
6. _______________________
7. _______________________

Due Date _______________________

Name _______________________

Grade and Homeroom Sec. _______________________

**MONTGOMERY BLAIR
LIBRARY MEDIA CENTER**

MAGAZINE REQUEST

Title of magazine _______________________

Date of magazine _______________________

Page numbers _______________________

Magazines may be borrowed for one (1) week.

☐ In circulation, request again
☐ Lost
☐ Not received
☐ Do not subscribe
☐ Available on microform

Date due _______________________

Name _______________________

Grade _______________________

Homeroom section _______________________

Today's date _______________________

responsibility for equipment taken out of the school building."[14] There is no further discussion of student use of nonbook materials or equipment. This regulation may be interpreted as referring to students' borrowing equipment on behalf of teachers, except that the county policy includes overnight loans of equipment to students as well as teachers and outlines procedures for insuring that they will be handled responsibly (requiring parents' and/or principals' signatures). Thus, it is likely that Blair High students are able to borrow equipment. Textbooks handed out by teachers for use in their classes by students are sometimes administered through the library, too, and treated as a special kind of loan.

The Faculty Handbook outlines sweeping borrowing privileges for teachers:

Faculty members may borrow any print or non-print materials housed in the library for an indefinite period by signing a circulation card. A notice will be sent to you each nine weeks to verify our records. Students may sign materials out for you if you send a note authorizing them to do so. Faculty members are expected to return these materials at the end of the school year.[15]

Teachers who borrow pieces of equipment can keep them until they are finished, but it is expected that use will be confined to the school building. If teachers want to take equipment outside the school, approval of an administrator is required.

In addition to locally held materials, a collection of films owned by Montgomery County school district is available for loan by Blair High's faculty. Titles in this collection are listed in catalogs kept in the library and in all departmental offices. Although requests are supposed to be made in advance so that orders can be placed twice a week, "emergency requests" are accommodated, too. Films arrive in the school each day by 10:30 A.M. and must be returned by 9:00 A.M. the day they are due. The length of film loans, however, is not specified. Free films (from organizations) and rental films (from dealers or distributors) can also be obtained for teachers provided approval (from whom was not specified) is given for each title requested. If fees are required, the requestor must also have administrative approval. Other external resources to which Blair High teachers have access through the school's library include the Educational Services Center's Professional Library located in Rockville, Maryland, and the Montgomery County Public Library, as well as statewide interlibrary loans. Catalogs for both the professional collection and the public library are kept in the school library, and the school library staff calls in teachers' requests.

Any materials can be put on reserve at faculty request; how reserve circulation differs from ordinary circulation is not explained.

Only the county circulation policy offers any description of procedures followed when materials are not returned. It mentions both overdue and lost book files in a general context. Although individual schools are not required to follow every provision, guidelines are clearly presented. The obligation of the library staff to send notices to students for their overdue materials is emphasized, and a variety of methods are enumerated. The county policy makes it clear that overdue fines are not expected to be charged, but that replacement costs for lost or damaged materials must be paid. It permits report cards to be withheld, if principals wish, until all debts are settled.

Montgomery Blair High School and/or its county school district follow many of the same policies as Morristown High. Neither school charges overdue fines (the Montgomery County Public Schools' policy does not recommend overdue fine charges); both emphasize sending notices regularly. Both give teachers enormous latitude in borrowing and returning materials and equipment. Although Blair's hours are a little longer, they are still confined to regular school days. Relationships with the public library are important to both institutions. Blair, however, does not discuss willingness to serve the general public. Montgomery County Public Schools furnish collections of films and professional literature to teachers in addition to general guidelines for service. If Morristown High's school district or county provide similar services, they are not mentioned. On the whole, there are many more similarities than differences between the circulation policies of these two schools.

J. M. WRIGHT TECHNICAL SCHOOL

Thirteen brief rules govern circulation policies applicable to students using the library at J. M. Wright Technical School in Stamford, Connecticut. A typed sheet containing the thirteen rules, dated 1984-1985, was sent by the library director.[16]

Materials available for circulation include only books and magazines—both current and back issues—as well as reserve collections comprising these materials. If nonbook materials and associated equipment are part of the library's holdings as is common throughout schools, they either do not circulate to students or they are administered by a different unit of the school, e.g., a separate media center.

Two types of borrowing periods are described: two-week loans, also described as loans for ten school days, and overnight loans, due at 9:00 A.M. the following morning. Books and back issues of magazines circulate for the longer loan period, and books are renewable for a second two-week/ten-school-day period. Reserve collection materials and current issues of magazines circulate for the shorter period. There are limits on the numbers of each type of material that can be borrowed: five regular, non-reserve books, five magazines, and one reserve book (or magazine) can be taken on any one day. It is not specified whether the five magazines had to be back issues or could be current issues.

Rule number ten emphasizes that no fines are charged for overdue materials, but rule number eight states that notices will be sent to students who keep materials overdue. Wright's students are responsible, however, for lost or damaged materials. Although exactly what fees are involved, the repair or replacement costs, the original purchase prices, and/or the additional processing fees, is not specified, students are expected to pay for whatever they do not return in good condition.

No information is given about circulation to faculty members and people from outside the school, interlibrary loan arrangements with other schools in the district and county or with the local public library, hours of service, or other policy issues of interest. On the whole, Wright's students have privileges and restrictions similar to those of students in larger institutions. They do not pay fines, though they are held responsible for materials they do not return or damage while they are on loan. There are regular circulating collections with loans as long as several other schools and reserve collections with overnight loans. Current issues of periodicals, often excluded from any circulation in many libraries, can be borrowed overnight, too. Limitation of materials to books and periodicals, while unusual, may be the result of separate media centers for nonbook materials. Renewals, not mentioned in many other schools, are permitted at Wright.

The thirteen rules of circulation for J. M. Wright Technical School represent the sort of simplified service policy that would be adequate to handle the needs of a small student body using a limited collection of materials.

HIGH SCHOOL OF GRAPHIC COMMUNICATION ARTS

The librarian in charge of the library of the High School of Graphic Communication Arts (GCA), located in New York City, described some of the circulation regulations followed by the school in answering the survey questionnaire.[17] She also sent a document from the Board of Education of the City of New York's Division of Educational Planning and Support (DEPS) titled "Standards for Unified Media Programs," which offer general guidelines for all school library media programs.[18] Like the Montgomery County Public Schools' circulation policy document described in connection with Montgomery Blair High School, however, the DEPS "Standards" is an advisory document, not an established policy from which individual schools are expected not to depart. Its provisions probably help shape the policies of individual schools and also shed light on objectives the individual schools are trying to achieve.

All the information in both documents (the survey questionnaire and DEPS "Standards") relate only to students. Rules and regulations applying to faculty or any other groups were not given. Only books are mentioned, although one would expect that periodicals and, possibly, other nonbook materials and equipment might also be available for circulation.

Interestingly, one of the "Standards" recommendations is to locate the library media center near a building's outside exits in order to permit access when the school is closed.[19] This policy rarely is implemented according to the small sample of schools in this study. Yet, school collections contain a variety of book and nonbook materials not usually duplicated in public library collections. These constitute a valuable resource from which students are cut off completely when schools are closed, especially during those vacations during the school term when students try to catch up with time-consuming projects like reading and writing papers and also during the summer, as well as on weekends and the late afternoon/early evening hours. Hours of service at GCA are not included in the director's description, but so few schools report activity other than on the regular school schedule that it is probable this one does not depart from tradition.

GCA's students register for a free borrower's card when they enter the school. The card is to be used for the entire time they remain there, provided no outstanding debts are left unsatisfied at the end of each term. According to the director:

Cards expire uniformly at the end of each school semester but are renewed for subsequent terms only if the student has a clear record in the library. Lost cards are replaced for a small fee only if there are no outstanding books or fines. Students must return all books and/or pay any fines due before borrower's card is renewed or replaced.[20]

GCA's policies about outstanding fines—although no fine schedule or list of daily charges was given—indicates that this school library media center does, indeed, charge something for books that are not returned on time. Generous renewal provisions should obviate overdue fines altogether: "All loans are renewable indefinitely as long as no request is made for the material(s)."[21]

Loans are for two weeks, and students are restricted to taking two items at a time. All materials are due two weeks before the end of each term so that there is time to distribute overdue notices before students disperse for vacation. A great deal of attention is paid to overdue notices. Each month, students receive notices for their overdue materials. Teachers receive notices for anything still overdue one week before a term ended (Figure 6-2), and, at the end of the term, a list of all students with outstanding materials or fines is compiled and distributed to all teachers in the school. No mention

Figure 6-2
High School of Graphic Communication Arts
Overdue Notice

HIGH SCHOOL OF GRAPHIC COMMUNICATION ARTS
Pat DeMeo, Principal

____
Date

M _______________________   _________
   E.R. Teacher   E.R.

The following student(s) has(have) uncleared library records. Please
send to library today. On this sheet, mark next to each name

        notified
        absent
        truant
        discharged
        wrong E.R.

and return to library. Thank you for your cooperation.

is made of withholding report cards, diplomas, or graduation invitations, perhaps because beyond the preparation of the notices and lists and the nonrenewal of expired library cards, further actions are the responsibility of school administrators, not librarians.

Circulation policies described here for GCA's library media center resemble those of other schools in the amount of attention paid to notices and the short loan period for books, but its fine policies are more like those of public libraries, and denial of borrowing privileges results from nonreturn of materials or nonpayment of fines after the end of a term. Interestingly, the rather strict limit of borrowing only two books at a time is not in accord with the DEPS "Standards," which recommends that "students are permitted to choose books for circulation freely *without restrictions as to number or type.*"[22] However, most schools limit the number and type of materials students can borrow at once; accumulations of many items could be amassed by students who keep borrowing but do not return items already on loan.

The DEPS "Standards" also states that "reference, non-print and periodical materials are available for home loans and loans to classrooms."[23] GCA's library media center may well have these materials available for loan, but the librarian's description did not mention them. If so, it is likely that all materials are circulated in basically the same fashion, with the same loan periods and maximum limits, or there might have been a hint about the existence of other regulations for nonbook materials. This is conjecture, however, because no indication was given that materials other than books are being circulated.

Another interesting provision of the DEPS "Standards" is that "students are trained to help in circulation routines, equipment operations, and distribution."[24] This may be included merely to permit or encourage the use of student aides to help librarians with circulation operations. It could be construed, however, as a recommendation encouraging self-charging by students—a novel idea in schools as well as everywhere else. While it is not surprising that the "Standards" outline facilities, collections, and services that seem more idealistic than prescriptive or operational, it is too bad that these kinds of provisions appear to be so far beyond the reality, particularly in a special high school located in a great city, where innovation might be expected to flourish.

WICHITA LIBRARY MEDIA SERVICES

The single most attractive brochure from any of the schools was sent by the Library Media Services Department of Wichita (Kansas) Public Schools' Division of Curriculum Services (Figure 6-3).[25] It describes departmental services to its school community. A separate typed sheet[26] also included in the Wichita packet describes the department's philosophy: "The Library Media Services Department promotes the sharing of ideas on a system-wide basis for motivation and optimum use of library media through inservice meetings and workshops. Library media specialists and teachers use a team approach as they plan for maximum usage of materials."[27]

The department maintains a System Media Center that contains a wide variety of circulating materials. The center's hours are from 7:45 A.M. to 4:45 P.M.; it remains open through lunch hours and, more important, serves its clients all year long, providing daily deliveries to schools as well as a walk-in service.

The center's offerings include books in single and multiple copies, pamphlets, clippings, book jackets (presumably for review and selection), sound recordings on discs and tape, filmstrips, study prints of art works, current and back issues of magazines, 8 mm loop films, slides, and realia (i.e., three-dimensional objects), as well as an AECI (not explained) traveling museum of materials—some of which must be hand carried to their destination—and a "Community Coordinated Child Care Collection" (also not explained).[28] These materials cover all parts of the curriculum and all grade levels from pre-kindergarten to adult. In addition to the System Media Center, two other centers, the Murdock Teacher Center and the Hillside Grove Resource Center, serve special needs. The professional collection at Murdock is aimed at teacher education; Hillside concentrates on special education materials, particularly those "for the visually impaired and blind, including large print, tactile objects, and Braille,"[29] available to all citizens of the state with need for them.

Telephone orders are publicized in both documents, but personal selection of materials is also encouraged.[30] The typed sheet states that the System Media Center includes teachers, library media specialists, and patrons in the community among its clients. They can borrow its materials for a two-week loan period and renew them by telephone for another loan period.[31]

Students are not mentioned directly as clients, but they can obtain System Media Center materials on loan through their own individual school libraries or by the individual school library purchasing the titles for their own collection. The sheet explains,

The school mail truck delivers every day to all of the public schools. . . . Large quantities are shipped in boxes by supply trucks. The System Media Center serves every school in much the same way that each Library Media Center provides for the needs of the building. The Center supplies recommended resources as suggestions for purchase.[32]

None of the information about any of the media centers discusses nonreturns, fines, overdue notices, bills, limits of any kind, or penalties of

Figure 6-3
Client Brochure

any kind. Perhaps even though the two documents examined do not cover these problems, the policies do exist. Answers to questions on the survey questionnaire indicated that no fines are charged, which parallels policies in many other schools. However, since the media centers deal directly with the general public (even if they are probably a small group of self-selected clients) and may have had multiple requests for the same materials from their public school clients, policies should have been (and probably were) developed to handle instances in which materials are not returned promptly.

No mention is made of videorecordings or microcomputer software in the collections of the Wichita Library Media Centers. These newer media may have been purchased and integrated into the collection by the time of this writing, or these materials, present in the collection, might be excluded from circulation. Should Wichita have circulation experience with videos and microcomputer software that is as successful as it is for its other nonbook media (and as circulation of newer media already has been in a nucleus of public libraries), it could serve as a model for other innovative programs.

Including the general public in the client groups being served and keeping the System Media Center (which seems to be the department's main unit) open throughout the year are two of the most unique features of Wichita's Library Media Services circulation policies. Delivery of documents to clients and the encouragement of telephone requests (and renewals) are also unusual, though not so much so when one considers that the end users in most cases are probably not individual members of student bodies or the general public, but school libraries and classrooms. The emphasis on rapid service to users and deemphasis on protection of the materials and the accountability of users was refreshing, at the very least.

FAIRFAX ELEMENTARY SCHOOL MEDIA CENTER

The report of an automation pilot project involving the Fairfax Elementary School Media Center in University Heights, Ohio, dated October, 1983, provided a little information about its circulation policies, too.[33] As part of the Cleveland Heights-University Heights City School District, approval and encouragement for the project had to come from the administration of the school district as well as from the school's own administration. The pilot project linked Fairfax's media center with a much larger network including the Cleveland Public Library and the Cleveland Heights-University Heights Public Library. Technical and administrative problems had to be resolved, and all of the bibliographic data for Fairfax's materials had to be entered into the database in order to get the project up and running.

The objective of the project was "to find a relatively inexpensive way to computerize clerical procedures (circulation control, inventory, and rapid processing of new books) in order to make better use of the library/media specialists' time with the students (there is no clerk)."[34] Fairfax used 12,000 machine-readable book labels to enter its holdings into the database.[35] In contrast, the existing database against which these titles were matched in the entry process contained over 1,000,000 titles.

One of the first steps in the successful pilot project was "to establish Fairfax as virtually a branch of [the Cleveland Heights-University Heights Public Library] system."[36] Interlibrary loans are expedited by having, through the school's terminal, instant access to the holdings of all the titles in the database. Students are registered in the automated system by applying for special public library cards carrying unique computer-readable labels. Though the report does not specify it, no doubt staff members must do the same. The youngest students, who previously had to wait until they could print their names before they could borrow materials, no longer are so restricted. Once a library card with its machine-readable label is issued to them, they can borrow any item in the system. Other immediate benefits are the ability to obtain information about all the school's materials and clients instantly and the ability to manipulate the data automatically.

Books, magazines, and other unspecified nonbook materials are mentioned as part of Fairfax's holdings. However, the computer makes it possible for Fairfax clients to imagine all the resources in the database as available to them, especially when they can determine whether the items are on the shelf or out in circulation as easily for the other thirty-six libraries' materials as for their own. They do not have to go to another library hoping to find an item that Fairfax either does not own or does not have on the shelf, only to find that it was not owned or had been checked out to a client of that library.

The report states that the computerized circulation system keeps track of fines and printed overdue notices automatically.[37] Thus, it can be assumed that, unlike other schools, Fairfax Elementary School has monetary penalties for nonreturns. In addition, the school library media specialist uses the computer to teach students to fulfill their responsibilities to the public libraries outside the school as well. According to the report,

While students are checking out their school library books, the computer shows us any fines that are owed by that student at any other libraries on the system. We remind students to pay their public library fines. Occasionally a student who transfers into Fairfax already has a [Cleveland Public Library] card and if any delinquencies appear on the screen we can confront the student (and/or parents) about clearing the record before new materials are charged out.[38]

One cannot help but wonder whether special policies have been developed to handle instances where members of the teaching staff are "beeped" by the computer because of their outstanding debts to the public library.

Apparently, before the advent of the computerized circulation system, overdue notices were read to students from signed book cards in their classrooms. Volunteer circulation clerks were expected to discuss problems with the children when classes came to the library. Despite all these efforts, precomputer overdues were said to be in the hundreds each week. The combination of automatic production of notices and "beeping" any time the student borrows materials, plus the computer's greater accuracy in charging and discharging materials, has succeeded in overcoming most problems of this sort. The report claims that overdues have dropped to thirty-eight in the count for the week preceding its preparation.[39]

In addition to individual loans, classroom collections are furnished to teachers, and the library is responsible for monitoring their use. No further details about loan periods, renewals, fine charges, or other specifics are supplied by the report.

While Fairfax Elementary School's media center is unique among the participants in this survey (and, surely, unusual in the universe of school libraries/media centers) in being a full participant in a large urban-suburban network, its circulation policies exhibit some familiar characteristics. The great concern about overdues—though mostly predating the computer—is typical of all the schools described in this chapter. Less typical is the policy of charging overdues. The focus of the media center on students, first and foremost, is also typical. Staff are mentioned primarily in connection with classroom services—perhaps not because direct services to individual teachers were lacking (indeed, direct services are mentioned, too), but because more effective classroom services result from use of the computer system.

Unfortunately, no specifics about hours of service, loan periods, types of circulating materials, fines and other penalties, or other client services were given. No doubt these will ultimately be affected, too, by the larger context of service provided by the computer network. In its closing paragraphs, the report states:

Along with sharing human resources, information, and materials, we have come to share a sense of common purpose with our public libraries that has never been so deeply felt before. We consider the project at Fairfax to be a resounding success. We will certainly consider expansion of the project to our other schools in the future.[40]

While it is not unusual for a school library to automate, multitype networking with other libraries is relatively rare and, for many participants including this one, is still in the experimental stages. Called a trend by many hopeful observers despite extremely slow gains, this kind of multitype networking cannot help but gain credence for its proponents from the experiences at Fairfax Elementary School, described above.

SUMMARY OF SCHOOL LIBRARY POLICIES

Simplicity is the most obvious characteristic running through the circulation policies from these six schools, including four secondary schools and two elementary schools/school districts. There appear to be many fewer problems with client identification and registration, partly because the client group is limited in most places to students and teachers of the school or district, but also because, for this primary client group, identification could be so easily confirmed if it was ever in doubt. Since most schools have fewer than 500 students and faculty, librarians can be expected to know everyone. Only two of the libraries/media centers reported that they serve the general public, but others extend borrowing privileges to students and teachers from other schools within their district. The fact that all but one of the libraries reported being open only on regularly scheduled school days and keeping hours that approximated the hours of school makes them less appealing to outsiders—either the general public or even students or faculty from neighboring schools. Even Wichita's System Media Center, the only library that remains open all year and operates with the longest schedule, closes before 5:00 P.M. and has no weekend hours.

Because of the well-publicized involvement of schools with audiovisual aids and instructional materials in nonbook formats, they were expected to have a great variety of nonbook materials in their collections, yet two of the schools whose policies are described in this chapter circulated only books or books and magazines. However, even in places where a great number of different forms of material are part of the collection and are circulated, the number of loan periods tend to be limited, making the whole operation far less complicated. In fact, the Wichita Public School District's System Media Center, which lists the most different types of material, has only one loan period for everything. In general, reserve collections (for which the details of circulation policy were given by only one librarian) and/or classroom collections have limited loans. Reserve materials circulate overnight in the one library that furnished this information. In the others, it was not clear whether reserve or classroom collection materials could be borrowed. Current issues of magazines are another category of material that has been singled out for limited loans—overnight in one school.

Loan periods tend to be short; two weeks is mentioned most frequently. One week is the loan period for one school. Limits on the number of items that can be taken at once appear to be extremely low—from one or two items to a maximum of five. Possibly, the idea is to protect young people from taking more materials than they can read in a loan period, but it could also be attributed to concern that a variety of titles in all subjects might not always be available.

Teachers have even more privileges in school libraries than they do in colleges and universities. The documents of two schools discuss allowing students to check out materials for teachers, as well as equipment for nonbook materials. Indefinite loan periods are common in the libraries that gave that information. Telephone requests are honored in two places, and telephone renewals, even for students, are mentioned, too.

All but one school describe elaborate systems for generating overdue notices, far more than is characteristic of academic or public library policies. Indeed, some academic and public libraries have pulled back from sending as many notices as they once did, and several stated that sending notices was a courtesy to the client, not an obligation of the library. The duty to notify students about their overdue materials and keep reminding them until they are brought back, is, perhaps, the most important circulation obligation of the majority of school librarians/media specialists. Four of the schools declare that no fines are charged for overdue materials. Perhaps that is why there is so much emphasis on notices. In the one library using an automated circulation system, the rate of nonreturns was said to have been brought under control, but notices had not been eliminated—they were automatically produced by the computer.

Policies tend to be written in simpler language using more familiar terminology with simple, straightforward constructions. Whereas the language in some of the public library policies appears to have been made up by lawyers or legislators, the language in school policies sometimes seems to be the product of elementary school students. Nevertheless, they accomplish every bit as much as the more sophisticated policy statements in providing a framework of rules within which library circulation operates.

School library/media centers seem to accept a great many limits as axiomatic to their operations concerning who they may serve, what may be borrowed from their collections, and how it may be done. Yet, without much trouble (other than the planning and effort, of course), the Fairfax Elementary School joined an automated network with two giant colleagues, the Cleveland Public Library and the Cleveland Heights—University Heights Public Library, proving the viability, in this homely context, of David Stam's admonition to librarians to "think globally and act locally."[41] Fairfax began using its computer network to think differently about available materials and to act differently about borrowing them. Students must have wondered, sometimes, if "Big Brother" was, indeed, watching them, especially if they were "beeped" as they tried to get a book past the desk when owing fines. But someone finding a book that was desperately needed for a project waiting on the shelf in a remote public library branch might appreciate the power of this new system. Fairfax appears to be at the cutting edge of library service in schools, with new answers to client questions and new resources to satisfy their needs.

The next chapter will examine the answers of school librarians to the survey questionnaire concerning circulation systems, policy issues, current problems, and plans for the future.

NOTES

1. "Daily Routines," (Morristown, N.J.: Morristown High School Library, n.d.), 3 p.

2. In this school, the term attendance teacher was used to describe the faculty member responsible for a student's records. Others use homeroom teacher, class adviser, or other terms. In this chapter, the term given in the documents is used.

3. "Daily Routines," p. 1. (Emphasis added.) It is extremely interesting to find this statement that all public school libraries have a *closed* membership or strictly limited clientele as an axiom of service. It is possible that such limits are, indeed, written into public school regulations; however, one might question the universality of written legal limits on school library clienteles. Perhaps these limits are merely customary or traditional, rather than written into school district charters.

4. "Daily Routines," p. 1.

5. "Daily Routines," p. 1.

6. "Daily Routines," p. 1.

7. "Daily Routines," p. 1.

8. "Daily Routines," p. 1.

9. "Library Media Center Policy and Procedure," (Silver Spring, Md.: Montgomery Blair High School, n.d.), 4 p. Identified by Judith M. King, Library Media Specialist, as excerpted from the school's Faculty Handbook.

10. "Circulation," (MCPS/Department of Instructional Resources Circulation Policy and Procedure, n.d.), 3 p. (Page 2 is numbered 42.)

11. Both slips require the name, grade, and homeroom section of the borrower but otherwise are geared to the type of material they cover. The yellow vertical file circulation slip asks for the subject and number of items taken and for the titles or numbers. The green magazine request slip asks for the title, date, and page numbers of the desired item, followed by a series of alternative outcomes, e.g., in circulation, lost, not received, and so forth, with a box so that the ultimate result can be checked.

12. "Library Media Center Policy," p. 1.

13. "Library Media Center Policy," p. 1.

14. "Library Media Center Policy," p. 2.

15. "Library Media Center Policy," p. 1.

16. "Library Circulation Policy," (Stamford, Conn.: J. M. Wright Technical School, 1984), 1 p.

17. Selda Arnoff, response to "Survey of Circulation Policies and Practices" (New York, 1983).

18. Geraldine Clark, "Standards for Unified Media Programs," (Brooklyn, N.Y.: Division of Educational Planning and Support, Board of Education of the City of New York, 1978), ca. 15 p. (Pages are numbered in several sequences.)

19. "Standards," pp. 8-9.

20. Response to "Survey."

21. Response to "Survey."

22. "Standards," p. 8. (Emphasis added.)

23. "Standards," p. 8.

24. "Standards," p. 8.

25. "Wichita Library Media Services," (Wichita, Kans.: Library Media Services Department, Division of Curriculum Services, Wichita Public Schools, n.d.), 5 p.

26. "Library Media Services Department," (Wichita, Kans.: Division of

Curriculum Services, Wichita Public Schools, 1983), 2 p.

27. "Library Media Services Department," p. 1.

28. "Wichita Library Media Services," p. 3. Maximum usage, of course, does not always refer to circulation, something that should be kept in mind when reviewing not only these, but all school library policies.

29. "Wichita Library Media Services," p. 5.

30. "Wichita Library Media Services," p. 3; "Library Media Services Department," p. 1.

31. "Library Media Services Department," p. 1.

32. "Library Media Services Department," p. 1.

33. "Report on the Library Automation Pilot Project at Fairfax Elementary School Media Center," (Cleveland Heights, Ohio: Cleveland Heights–University Heights School District, 1983), 5 p.

34. "Report," p. 1.

35. This does not mean that 12,000 titles were entered, but that 12,000 *copies* of a smaller number of titles were labelled. Since virtually all libraries have more than one copy of some titles, the total number of titles is always less than the number of copies—or items—they represent.

36. "Report," p. 1.

37. "Report," p. 4.

38. "Report," p. 4.

39. "Report," p. 4.

40. "Report," p. 5.

41. David Stam, "Think Globally—Act Locally: Collection Development and Resource Sharing," *Collection Building* (Spring 1983): 18-21.

     SCHOOL LIBRARY RESPONSES
TO THE CIRCULATION
QUESTIONNAIRE

Twelve responses to the survey questionnaire, representing one school district, one high school, three junior high schools, and seven elementary schools, were received in addition to those from the six school libraries and districts whose policy documents were analyzed in Chapter 6, for a total of eighteen.

Thirteen of the eighteen responding schools and school districts are located in the northeastern United States (New York, New Jersey, Connecticut, and Massachusetts). The schools represented, nevertheless, a variety of community sizes and life-styles, large and small urban areas as well as suburban and rural communities. A fourteenth response came from the suburbs of a more southern East Coast city. The other three responses came from the Midwest, two from suburban communities, and the third from a relatively large city (for its locale). Some respondents at the district level distinguished between answers representing the policies and practices of their individual schools and those applicable to district-level libraries or media centers. In some of these districts, the grade levels of the schools concerned were limited to elementary and junior high schools; but two people specified that their replies applied to all the public schools in the district at all grade levels, i.e., elementary, intermediate, and high school or, in school jargon, K through 12.

From the small total number of replies and the large proportion of these concentrated in one region of the country, it was expected that a large proportion of the responses would exhibit very little variation. This was the case in most, but not all, of the questions and issues addressed by the survey.

As in Chapters 3 and 5, this chapter is divided into four main sections, covering descriptions of the circulation systems in use, policy formulation practice, current problems and policy issues being addressed in the school libraries, and plans for the future. A fifth section provides a summary and some observations.

THE CIRCULATION SYSTEM

Signed book cards were a big favorite with schools, even more popular than they were in the libraries serving post-secondary academic institutions. Out of a total of twenty charging systems in use in the eighteen schools and districts, fifteen schools/school districts used signed book cards for some or all of their circulation transactions. One of the fifteen said that signed book cards were employed only in the circulation of nonbook materials and a Gaylord system was used for books. Another person who reported using more than one kind of circulation system said that signed book cards were used only in the elementary and junior high schools, but that the high school in her district was "implementing BOOK TRAK [in] 1984-85 (Follett's bar wand microcomputer stand-alone circulation system)."

One of the other two respondents said that computers were used exclusively in her library. The other, from a school district, said that the high school used a Demco charging system and the other schools had unspecified manual systems.

One difference among users of signed book cards seemed to be in their use (or lack of use) of library cards instead of or in addition to other types of identification—school ID cards, class rosters, or simply the recognition of students' faces by the librarians. The simplicity of using a signed book card system is offset to some degree by the additional work needed to issue library cards; nevertheless, one librarian described her method of issuing library cards in some detail. Another reply said that self-service, after identifying signed book cards, was the method of circulating materials. In the self-charging system, identification would not be necessary once clients had access to the library.

Another variation in the use of signed book cards was the choice of using the same card for all materials or different ones for the various collections, media, or other categories of materials. Filing practices also differed, with some libraries keeping all circulating materials in one file and others dividing them by medium, collection or other parameter. One librarian wrote, "We used signed book cards, Magazine and Vertical File slips," while another explained,

The signed book cards of materials out on loan are arranged in one file by classification and signalled with clips indicating month of due date over a period of five months (September to January or February to June).

Some libraries used color-coded slips to identify different kinds of material.

Libraries at the district level, which serve schools as well as individual persons, had a slightly different concern. They needed to accommodate secondary loans at the individual school level for materials borrowed by schools. In one school district media center, this was solved by having a three-card system.

Patrons sign the top white card which is kept in the [center] and filed under the author's last name. Print and nonprint [materials] sent to schools are stamped with the school name on the top white card. The two remaining cards may be used by the receiving schools for recirculation. Both the Library Media Specialist and classroom teacher thus have a record.

The homogeneity in the circulation systems used by this group of libraries to record transactions was predictable, given the small number of schools and the lack of variety encountered in their regulations, described in the previous chapter. The large proportion of schools using the same signed book card circulation system—fifteen out of eighteen schools, or 83 percent—was unique among the three types of libraries surveyed. Less predictable was the limited use of library cards, with only three schools mentioning them or using systems that required them. Systems such as Demco or Gaylord, which substitute cards with unique identifiers for client signatures and can make deciphering transaction records much easier for school librarians, did not appear to have had much impact, at least among this group of schools.

Computers were used by only two schools for recording transactions, and these two systems were quite different. One was a stand-alone microcomputer-based system; the other was part of a large, shared network to which the school was connected only by terminal, the computer itself being based elsewhere. Interestingly, both systems employed wand scanners, so, to the person performing the circulation transaction, both kinds of systems would appear to be very much alike. A third school was using a computer program to produce its overdue notices, although its circulation transactions were recorded manually, using signed book cards.

POLICY-MAKING IN THE INSTITUTION

In two of the schools surveyed, policy-making was the responsibility of the librarian/media specialist alone, although one of them added the following comment: "If I make drastic changes I would ask for input from students—faculty—administration."

Seven librarians replied that policy-making was a joint venture involving various library staff members, although one said, "as needs changed, so have our policies changed. Administrators, teachers, students and parents have proposed changes which the staff has welcomed—they have been appropriate, reasonable and workable." In the other libraries and districts, the group of people making circulation policy decisions included more than just library staff members, i.e., school administrators, students, and/or faculty participated as well. In one school district in this last group, cooperative programs with public librarians included consultation with them on circulation policy formulation, too.

In one reply it was reported that a committee with wide representation formulated policy for the school district. Though it was not the only instance in which a committee was mentioned as the mechanism whereby the several groups involved in making policy were brought together, it was the only one said to be meeting currently. Another librarian explained,

We have had an advisory committee of library staff, teachers and students. It was abandoned last year due to lack of interest by teachers and students. We believe that it was due to satisfaction with our policies. We will announce a meeting again next fall and contact faculty and Student Government.

The impression given by the others indicated that the interaction between the different groups of people was initiated and directed by library staff members. In some cases, this might have been informal consultation, but in others, there appeared to be a need to have changes in policy approved by administrators or other authorities. One description stated that policy was made by

Library Media Staff and Central Administration for total district plan (implementing computerized systems—also general policy for fines (none), cut-off circulation dates at end-of-year, etc.). Each building library media specialist will establish circulation period, overdue notice schedule, etc. with approval of principal.

Authority was not concentrated universally in the hands of school administrators, as might have been supposed. Indeed, a great deal of independent authority appeared to reside with individual school librarians.

A sharp division appeared in the responses to questions about policy review. Eight librarians said that reviews were not regular or formal but were conducted on an as-needed basis. Other comments from these eight included the following:

There is no set time.

Occasionally, circulation problems will be discussed at a district-wide staff meeting, but there is no formal, periodic review.

As the need arises—which really hasn't been often.

Eight other librarians said that circulation policies were reviewed regularly. Two of them conducted annual reviews, at the beginning of the school year, and three of them reviewed policies at the start of every semester. One said,

When required, "on-the-spot" changes may be instituted for critical materials, e.g., limiting one title per student in heavy-demand areas of particular topics or even temporarily changing materials which normally circulate to reference.

Among these replies was one from a school district which gave separate responses from each of six schools. Despite their geographic unity and membership in a single district unit, they, too, split right down the middle. Three said reviews were made on an as-needed basis, and three had regular periodic reviews. Two of them performed their reviews once a year, and the third had two reviews annually, at the beginning and end of each school year.

Examining these factors at the district level only, three out of four districts involved people from different groups within the educational community—library staff members, faculty, students, and administrators—in the process of policy formulation. All four reported having no formal, regularly scheduled review of policies. Looking at the responses now from individual schools only, nine out of thirteen (or 69 percent) reported that policies were made only by members of the library staff. As for reviews, seven had regular periodic reviews, and five did not. (One of the individual school respondents did not reply to this question.)

One might conclude from this distribution of answers that policy-making practice differed considerably depending on the institutional level at which it occurred. District-level policy-making tended to be more diffuse and less formal than those same processes within individual school buildings. This is probably not unusual, considering that district-level staff frequently include among their prerogatives, the coordination of activities with both internal and external groups. In individual schools, on the other hand, coordination among the various groups within the school tends to be the responsibility of the principal, not teachers, students, or library staff members. Unless the impetus for a more diffuse kind of policy-making came from a higher level in the hierarchy, one would not expect librarians to initiate it. Nonetheless, librarians tended to share their authority over policy, democratically, among their entire staffs, as evidenced by the following comment: "Media staff—Specialist, LTA, clerk. Suggestion by library clerk very pertinent as she handles the daily circulation."

Understanding and interpreting the contrast in policy review practices between districts and individual school units, however, is not easy. Why the higher level bodies seemed disinterested in regular reviews is not immediately obvious. Perhaps because the individual schools concerned themselves with ongoing policy review, higher level staff did not feel obligated to duplicate the process unless problems emerged that required attention at district levels. Comments from some of the individual schools reflected the attention they paid to the revision of circulation policies:

A general review is made each semester in order to make required modifications for improving ease and efficiency of operation while better serving the students.

Each year before the beginning of school the library staff reviews policies and procedures.

We review and try out new ideas as they are presented by any of the [staff]; but find our present system well stream-lined by now.

Thus, districts may well find it unnecessary to evaluate policy or initiate policy changes regularly. The autonomy of individual school librarians appeared to be widespread.

PROBLEMS CURRENTLY FACING CIRCULATION DEPARTMENTS

Only one librarian responded that there were currently no problems facing her in administering circulation. (Schools are rarely large enough to warrant separate circulation departments, at least at the individual school level.) Interestingly, this reply came from the elementary school that had recently computerized its circulation system. Another library, at a secondary school, that used data processing to produce its overdue notices said, "The computer program that we use has helped with the return of materials and the clearance of students." They still complained, however, of having a fairly high transient student population which was problematic.

One district-level librarian responsible for lending collections of materials as well as single items complained of the difficulty of contacting the individual school librarians by telephone in order to retrieve collections requested by other teachers or librarians. Telephoning school buildings is often a frustrating task because classrooms and libraries may have no extensions. Thus, to reach a teacher or librarian, messages might have to be given to general office staff members (sometimes student aides), who must relay them to the appropriate individuals. Rapid message service is not usually a high priority in schools. The solution anticipated by that librarian was installation of more telephone lines in the district media center. The two principal problems facing most of the school library circulation operations, however, were more prosaic: first and most critical, the nonreturn of materials and second, the difficulty of getting notices out to borrowers. Nonreturns were mentioned as their worst problem (or one of their worst problems) by thirteen people. The inability to supply overdue notices promptly was named by five. Many of the comments revealed real frustration over the limitations of the library staff to deal successfully with these two problems:

Books not returned on time—[two-thirds] of school [is] on overdue list. Many wait for list to come out before they return books. Still others wait until librarian visits classroom to give back books. Even though school is small, it is too far to carry books to library!

Our biggest problem is the high rate of non-returns. . . . A particular problem in this regard for our library arises from the loss of specialized materials which quickly go out of print.

Non-returns—willingness to pay fine $1 to $2 max[imum] and keep the material.

Overdues and they are not chronic.

Overdues: too many—very time consuming to write and collect.

The biggest circulation problem is retrieving overdue books. A considerable amount of clerical staff time is spent in writing notices of overdue books and later typing lists for homeroom teachers. We do not charge fines—for long overdue books. We hold report cards.

One district librarian commented on the difference between the kinds of problems encountered in her elementary and secondary schools:

At the elementary level, circulation figures are very high. There is not enough clerical help to get notices out often enough. This problem causes backlog of non-returns. Computerizing system should greatly improve the situation. Circulation drops off dramatically at secondary level but there is a greater need to control overdues.

Two people mentioned lack of time to do an adequate job of following up on overdue materials, and one of them added there was not enough time to collect fines either. Others, in schools where fines were not levied, indicated that they thought such penalties might help. If the comment above about willingness to pay fines is typical of student attitudes, however, in order to be effective, the fines would have to be relatively high. Fine levels in many public and academic libraries were not substantially higher than those quoted above, and one might have limited confidence in their ability to make much of an impact. On the other hand, the libraries using computerized data processing for their notices expressed satisfaction over the improvements they realized in recovering materials more promptly. Indeed, the only library to have no current problems of sufficient importance to report had a completely computerized circulation system. Fines had much less to do with their success than the additional information provided by the computer as well as production of notices and the ability to identify delinquents, thus preventing continued abuse of borrowing privileges.

Borrowing books without checking them out (some people might call this stealing) was named as a problem in one high school library. This same library also had a high rate of nonreturns. The librarian saw the "inability to identify items checked out by student name" as a third circulation problem after nonreturns and stolen books. It is more likely that this lack of information was closely related to the large number (large to the librarian, at least) of overdues. This library used a Gaylord system in which a unique number identified each client. Translating the numbers into names is an additional step that signed book card systems do not require. With a limited number of overdues, it might not be a particular problem, but, as the number of overdues rises, even this small amount of extra work becomes significant.

Librarians responding to the survey were also asked to identify those areas in their circulation policies that were in the process of revision. A majority of respondents, ten people in all, said no changes were being made, and an eleventh gave no reply to this question. Three librarians mentioned investigations of automation in connection with revising policy; however, that would appear to be more a revision of operations than policies.

Five problem areas in policy were identified. In one school, the inability to make interlibrary loans outside the school district had become a problem. The school in which this policy—a common one among schools—was being revised had entered into a multitype computer network. Librarians found that their traditional policies were preventing them from cooperating fully with their nonschool library partners.

Two policy changes related to overdues—the libraries' worst circulation problems. In one school, the intention was to alter the pattern of sending notices, except for overnight loans and requested materials, until the end of a marking period. In a second school, the librarian was contemplating beginning to charge fines for student overdues.

The fourth report of policy revision, from a school district librarian, said that a loss of space had initiated unspecified changes in the filing of circulation cards.

The fifth and final positive reply said that an examination of current practice was intended to insure that practice matched library policies. This problem, well known among corporate and governmental agencies, is less frequently discussed in the field of library and information service. Nevertheless, without adequate supervision, practices may diverge— sometimes rather dramatically—from policies. Evaluation of practices in terms of stated policy objectives is an ongoing need that this library did not intend to overlook.

School librarians appeared to have a smaller variety of problems than were expressed by academic and public librarians. Clearly, the worst problem in school libraries was a basic and simple one—the nonreturn of materials. Other operations relating to nonreturns, such as the need to send a large number of overdue notices, became problematic, too, and were intensified by the limited staff resources available to deal with them.

School library clients had a greater variety of complaints than the librarians. Many of them were already familiar, although there are some new wrinkles on the old themes:

Not enough copies of certain books to meet the demand.

Students complain most about their classmates not returning books on time.

The biggest complaint of our patrons is the unavailability of needed materials. This results to a large extent from the non-return of materials.

Echoes of those same complaints were heard from four more librarians, but some of the others had different problems to report:

We are not able to tell patrons what and how many items they have checked out nor when the items are due except by authors or titles.

Thinking they've returned a book; but, in fact, they haven't.

Lack of recall capability.

We won't let them borrow materials until a lost book is paid for or returned.

Complaints about overnight reserve system for materials needed for major curriculum projects.

Reference books do not all go out. (There are no fines)

Errors in sending out overdue notices (difficulty in reading names and room #'s) and not sending them out often enough.

Only four librarians had no client complaints to report. One explained, "They don't complain about much—we try to secure the titles they recommend." Another of the four said, simply, "We don't seem to have any, currently."

The largest number of client complaints related to overdues and nonreturns, although there were a good many other kinds of problems. Nevertheless, these matched the librarians' worst problems rather closely. These complaints might be related to the small size of school library collections compared to those in academic and public libraries.

Looking at the responses from the different perspectives of districts and individual schools, the picture changes. Of the four districts, only one had no client problems to report, and the three who did respond did not list nonreturns as the primary client problem. Not enough multiple copies to satisfy demand and the inability to satisfy demand *immediately* were each mentioned twice. Other complaints included lack of information on borrowed materials and clients, clients claiming that they returned materials which were still missing, and overdue notices that were inaccurate or too infrequently produced and distributed.

Five out of thirteen librarians from individual schools had no client complaints to report, a much larger proportion. Three said that nonreturns were causing the problem of unavailable materials, and a fourth said that lack of a recall system was his clients' biggest problem. One librarian mentioned not enough copies of books to meet demand; another talked about the problem of overnight loans for reserve materials needed for student projects; and one more reported that clients with outstanding materials did not like being denied borrowing privileges. Lack of control over borrowed materials was identified more often as a problem at the individual school level. Concern over sufficiency of collections was seen as more critical at the district level.

FUTURE PLANS FOR CIRCULATION

Answers to questions about school libraries' future plans—for changes in the circulation systems, policies, and services that might be offered in the future—are explored in this section. Interest in automation was high among school librarians, as it was among those in public and academic libraries. Nine people discussed some form of computer processing for circulation as part of future plans. Individual responses, however, indicated that the libraries were scattered at very different points along the road to automation, as can be seen from the following excerpts from their replies:

Will expand [existing] connections . . . [This comment came from a library already enjoying the benefits of computerized circulation.]

Our district's primary goal has been to improve access to the collection(s) by replacing the book catalog (12 yrs. old) with stand-alone OPACs; the circulation will be computerized as part of the available package (secondary goal).

[We are] currently investigating library automation which would include a circulation system.

We would *like* a computerized check-out system with light-pen. However, since our school is scheduled to close in 1987, I doubt that this conversion will be made.

We are in the process of studying a computerized system and are looking into several. . . . The district has been on-line with OCLC since 1974, so a part of our collection is in machine readable form. The district owns a Hewlett Packard, and we are also looking into the feasibility of using this main frame. Hewlett Packard does have a circulation program as well as other library applications. . . . We are presently using Apple II's and Apple IIE's in our school libraries for administrative purposes; i.e., overdues, order files, generating orders, generating bibliography of new acquisitions for staff, etc. How we can use the Apple II for circulation is also being considered. Computerizing a circulation system can have a major positive impact on a library—a "ready-made" inventory system, access to a larger data base right in one's own library, easier to update materials—bibliographies, etc., clerical time-saver, etc.—so that is why we are interested.

Integrated Circulation System with Public Access Terminals—is what we hope to have in place within 5 years. CLSI may be used. Public library has included schools (at H.S.) in multi-type network. LSCA funded automation project.

Would like to get a computerized system.
We are adding a computer this fall.

This group of responses included some libraries at the beginning of a planning cycle, some at the end of their implementation phase, and still others who were either somewhere in the middle or who had not yet begun to do active planning. Interestingly, several librarians were familiar with the use of data processing for administrative services and expected that its application to library services was only a matter of the time it would take to study and select appropriate alternatives.

Initiation by public libraries of local multitype networks that included school libraries figured in the plans of two schools in this small group. Affiliation with a bibliographic utility, while occurring at the district level, was also a factor in facilitating the plans of schools to automate circulation services, whether by joining a larger group of libraries in a circulation network or by using the data generated by the utility in implementing a locally owned, locally controlled, stand-alone system.

Two librarians had not yet reached the stage of active planning for a computer system, and one of them doubted they ever would since the school was scheduled to be closed.

Three librarians mentioned circulation as just one module of an integrated system of technical services. In these integrated systems, the catalog was the primary function to be automated, and computerizing circulation was a secondary goal. That integrated systems were not the aim of more people was somewhat surprising but understandable in terms of the limited resources of individual schools. Indeed, school districts were more likely to lead the way, particularly in the contemplation of larger or more complex systems.

Five librarians reported that no changes to their circulation systems were being considered or planned, although one of them said, "We might experiment with elimination of borrowers' cards if a better, and reliable, system can be found." Two others were thinking about changing to different systems from signed book cards, one to a Gaylord and the other to a Winnebago system. The Gaylord system would eliminate the need for clients to sign their names and addresses or class identification for each item borrowed. The additional work for library staff members of issuing library cards and later looking up the names and locations of persons with overdue materials was not expected to outweigh the advantages of automatic charging with a Gaylord machine. The librarian hoping to switch to the Winnebago system said his reason was twofold: "to ascertain the number of books that each student has charged out; to expedite the prompt distribution of overdue notices especially at the end of the school year."

One of the most striking features about these plans for change was the small number of variations in the kinds of changes being sought. Automation was the only system change desired by more than one library. Another interesting fact was the relatively large number of libraries in which there were no plans under consideration for any changes at all to the circulation system.

Making changes in policies was another way of altering circulation operations. Eight respondents either did not reply at all or said they did not believe any part of their policies were in need of change. One person offered this comment: "Our present system works well for us. It is simple yet does take time."

Many of the positive replies, however, were quite specific and emphasized more service:

For many students, a longer loan period might be helpful, and the introduction of a system of over-night loans might be worthy of exploration.

The distribution of periodicals.

Lack of interlibrary loans; a record of patron loans by patron name as well as author/title and due date; a notification system for use with patrons.[1]

(1) Turning out overdue lists is time-consuming. Therefore, we produce only 4 or 5 a year. I would like to be able to produce a list every two weeks.

(2) Notifying students of books they have reserved. We send notice to homeroom teacher. If student not in homeroom that day, teacher forgets to give it.

The comments in this last quotation were echoed by others. Two others mentioned policies on overdues as being most in need of change, and one other person said that policies for dissemination of reserve information needed attention.

One response was more general, but it pinpointed a problem which can have major effects on library functions: "The lack of planning and defining policy has characterized the manual system in each building. A need to plan for effects of computerization." This remark, from a district supervisor, may reflect a not unusual perception of the division of responsibilities in schools—policies are made at the higher levels and are merely carried out by the staff in individual schools. True or not, this perception may stifle decision making on the part of individual school librarians. In actuality, librarians in individual schools all have a certain amount of independence (more or less depending on the rules of the district and the relationships between district and schools) which can be accepted and addressed with careful thought or can be ignored. The introduction of a computer often is the catalyst for better planning at all levels, but especially at local levels.

Survey respondents were asked what new circulation services they would like to be able to provide. The answers indicated that, for many schools, new services were going to be a long time in coming because none were desired. One reply said, "We are satisfied with the services we are offering—we just wish we could improve the existing ones." Another said, "We prefer to keep our strict control in the elementary school," as if adding new services would be possible only if the school were to relinquish control over their operations. In all, eight people did not even reply to this question, and two gave the negative replies already quoted.

Positive replies named services many academic and public libraries took for granted, as evidenced by the following comments:

Circulation, rather than withdrawal, of some superseded reference works would, I believe, appeal to our students.

When our budget provides for purchase of new encyclopedias, we may experiment with such a plan.

Reserves (automated) and more extensive interlibrary loans.

Several more replies were dependent on having automated systems, including one that said, only, "We would like to have a computerized system." Another was more specific about services:

1. Improved system of overdue notices—send out more often, more accurately.
2. Access to individual student's record of circulation.
3. Access to circulation statistics—by grade, by month, year, etc.

The last reply declared with great practicality:

All of the services mentioned above [i.e., examples of new services suggested in the question] are exciting and have great possibilities. However, a school system must be practical financially and these services cost a great deal. If I had such money available, I'd be putting it into other services—like ERIC, BRS, etc.

What conclusions may be drawn from librarians' statements about plans for change? First, there is a relatively large proportion of people who are not seeking change in their systems, policies, or services, or who do not perceive pressing problems either on the part of staff members or clients that should be addressed. Many school library staff members are satisfied with their efforts and tend to be critical primarily of students who do not return material on time. Others expressed just a little frustration at the rather narrow limits within which small information centers can operate to realize any fundamental changes, such as might be possible with a computer system. Although plans to computerize circulation operations were expressed by nine survey respondents, several of them were still in the preliminary planning stages or had not yet reached an active planning mode, and they were merely hoping for the start of planning or anticipating its initiation.

Interlibrary loan was mentioned by several people as a future improvement. Two of them wanted interlibrary loans to extend beyond the boundaries of their school district. This was especially understandable in the case of the elementary school which had joined a large, automated multitype network and wished to exchange materials with its partners no matter where they were located. To be effective, interlibrary loan depends on mutual access to bibliographic information for materials in all collections in the participant group. Computers have been able to provide this speedily (actually, instantaneously) and, once implemented, inexpensively. The schools, whose traditional interlibrary loan policies were formulated in the absence of widespread sharing of bibliographic data, face the problem of amending policies so that opportunities for expanding available resources are not lost.

Future plans appeared rather limited in nature in some schools, providing very small changes in operations or services, for example, allowing for the continued use of superseded reference materials, or lengthening of some loan periods. Nonetheless, for a small library in a small school, these might have significant impact on both clients and staff. Experimentation with self-charging, saving staff time that could then be invested in greater attention to overdues, did not appeal to any of the respondents. (A notable exception was one library for which self-charging was the current norm.) The vision to dream of bigger and better services seemed lacking except at the district level, exemplified by one librarian's desire to bring online databases into individual school libraries.

SUMMARY AND OBSERVATIONS

Generally, there was very little variation in most aspects of the circulation systems operating in the schools that participated in the survey, either current or planned. While this result was expected in light of the small sample, the possibility that it could be true of more of the school library community bears additional thought and investigation.

The greatest proportion of respondents (83 percent) used signed book cards to circulate books. One librarian allowed students to check out materials themselves. Only one person using signed book cards specified issuing library cards, but others used Gaylord or Demco transaction systems that required cards.

The most important concerns among school librarians appeared to be nonreturns and overdues, without much anticipation of being able to make any dramatic changes. Expansion of services did not seem likely or feasible within the framework of the individual school library, though a few improvements were under consideration, including experimentation with longer loan periods, different periodical distribution, and better dissemination of information. A librarian who was using signed book cards was distressed by the lack of a recall system, yet it would not have been difficult to establish one with that kind of circulation system.

Two libraries in the survey sample used computers to perform their circulation operations, and a third processed its overdue notices with a computer program. One of the librarians using an automated system for circulation reported that with computer applications in place, problems with control diminished and were replaced by more and better service. The other librarian believed that access rather than control was the overriding problem and looked forward to implementing integrated systems supporting both catalogs and circulation services in more schools in her district. In the third, a partially automated library, overdue notices were produced using the computer, and the librarian was satisfied that materials were being returned in greater numbers. A fourth librarian reported expecting to have a computer in the near future to produce notices but not to record borrowing transactions.

Policy formulation and review were the areas of inquiry in which the schools surveyed differed considerably. In two schools, only the librarian made changes in policy; in seven, all members of the library staff were involved; in the rest, librarians were joined by other school staff members—teachers and administrators—as well as students and/or parents in the decision-making process.

Circulation policy reviews were performed regularly by some schools and informally or on an as-needed basis by others. District-level librarians tended to have much less formal review procedures than did individual school librarians.

Problems of school librarians focused on the nonreturn of materials and the production of overdue notices. Other problems mentioned by one or two people included lack of time to follow up on overdues and/or fines, restrictions on ILL, difficulties in contacting individual schools to recall materials needed by others (this, from a district-level librarian), theft, and lack of needed information. One librarian said her library had no circulation problems.

Some client problems echoed those of the librarians, centering on the unavailability of wanted materials because of the high rate of non-returns. While the lack of desired materials was undoubtedly an important problem, client distress over nonreturns on the part of their fellows, reported by more than one librarian, might have been an inadvertent transfer of respondents' own concerns to their clients. The lack of multiple copies of high-demand titles was also mentioned as a client complaint by several librarians, along with the inability to supply wanted materials *immediately*, insufficient loan periods for reserve materials, inaccurate and infrequently distributed overdue notices, and the inability of librarians to supply information about borrowed materials or requested titles.

Many of these complaints were already familiar, having been encountered among academic and public library clients. In schools, however, they were exacerbated by the typically small size of collections. Access to network partners' larger collections through the computer was recognized as a great asset by the school which was linked to its public library neighbors. Insufficiency of school collections was voiced as a concern most often at the district level, but it was at the individual school level that it should have been most visible. The fact that more school librarians did not make this complaint may reflect their adjustment to the situation.

Changes being made in circulation policies and systems, both those in progress and those being planned, indicated what new procedures and services might be anticipated. Many libraries were not planning any changes, either to policies or systems. Other replies mentioned plans to automate, the single most desired change to school library circulation systems, but a number of them were far from the point where implementation was in the foreseeable future. Plans to extend automation were already in progress in the two places where circulation was computerized. In one district, the hope was to have more schools participate in the multitype network system. The individual school in which this pilot project was conducted wanted to add automated reserves and to extend its interlibrary loan capabilities. In the other district, implementation of stand-alone systems was being planned for more schools. A few people wanted integrated systems of technical services as the ultimate goal of their automation plans.

Other changes being contemplated were actually quite minimal. By and large, library staff in individual schools did not seem anxious to consider sweeping changes, and many voiced satisfaction with their systems, procedures, and policies. This was, perhaps, the major difference between this group of libraries and the others analyzed in earlier chapters. They may have been expressing satisfaction with the status quo or resignation to it. In either case, the result was a general lack of fuel to fire searches for solutions to old problems or ways to furnish more services.

NOTE

1. Another librarian wanted to change interlibrary loan policy so that materials could be exchanged with partners outside the school district.

8

A COMPARISON OF CIRCULATION POLICIES, PRACTICES, AND ISSUES AMONG ACADEMIC, PUBLIC, AND SCHOOL LIBRARIES

In the six preceding chapters, circulation policies and practices in a number of academic, public, and school libraries as well as the problems perceived by their librarians and indications of their plans for the future have been examined and described. Although there are many differences between them, which may be directly or indirectly attributable to the differing environments, audiences served, and collecting patterns of the three types of library, there are also many similarities. Surprisingly, there are dramatic differences within type-of-library groups and striking similarities that cut across type-of-library lines. Perhaps the only generalization that holds true throughout is the lack of completely distinctive patterns for each of the three library types.

This chapter is divided into two main sections followed by a summary section. In the first section, the most significant features of policy and practice are summarized for each type of library group, answering the questions: Who may borrow? What may be borrowed? How may materials be borrowed? To some degree, the more detailed and complex descriptions from earlier chapters are necessarily compressed and simplified in the summaries.

The second section of the chapter explores the differences and similarities between the three groups concerning notions about current problems and policy issues as well as their future plans. Responses about the future were sometimes vague, either because the librarians responding felt limited as to what they might discuss or because the word "plan" implied some kind of tangible evidence that ideas had already been translated into an organized course of action. As one district librarian pointed out, planning is a task that some librarians avoid because it requires effort and time, knowledge, and vision. Hopefully, many changes that were only plans on paper or even just bright ideas in the heads of those concerned have already been implemented in the interim.

ANSWERS TO THE THREE QUESTIONS OF CIRCULATION

Who Can Borrow?

The most obvious answers to this question were, as might be expected, that those who constitute the primary borrowing groups are students and faculty in academic libraries, the "public" in public libraries, and students in school libraries. Looking more closely at the composition of these primary user groups and beyond to their privileges, however, revealed some interesting details.

In academic libraries, faculty privileges usually extended far beyond those of students, but they were carefully monitored by circulation department heads resentful of continuing abuses. In some places, responses to the situation have been to limit the privileges, particularly when evidence (sometimes the result of automated circulation systems) could be produced to substantiate the abuses. More egalitarian ideas about service to students and faculty existed in some places, e.g., at the University of North Florida, Pima Community College, and Mankato State University.

The academic libraries differed substantially in their willingness to serve secondary client groups or nonaffiliated borrowers. Definitions of secondary and outside client groups also differed from one institution to another. Some libraries treated alumni and spouses of affiliates as insiders (though not part of the primary user groups) while others treated them as outsiders. As noted in Chapter 2, some private schools (e.g., the University of Bridgeport) were willing to serve outside borrowers though most did not; some public schools (e.g., the State University of New York at Stony Brook) excluded virtually all outsiders although several librarians from public institutions expressed a perceived obligation to serve members of the taxpaying public even if they had no affiliation with the college or university.

Occasionally membership in a network or other cooperative program included the obligation to serve affiliates of fellow institutions. Columbia University Libraries extended some services to other RLIN library users and accepted referrals from METRO, a local cooperative. There were a number of restrictions on both kinds of users, however, and neither enjoyed full service. Libraries of branch campuses in large university systems sometimes extended full service to students and faculty from other branches, though not always to all of them.

Campuses with large commuter and/or part-time student populations (e.g., Queens College, SUNY at Stony Brook, and Pima Community College) developed rules for students not currently enrolled in courses, but there was no universally accepted method of dealing with them during these periods. Some libraries treated them as if they were outsiders, but others extended service anyway.

One of the respondents to the survey for this book reported on a survey that had been conducted by staff members from her library among seventy-two academic libraries about extending service to nonaffiliates for fees. A large majority of the replies—51, or 71 percent—indicated that service to outsiders was provided free of charge. Where fees were charged they were minimal; $25 was reported as the average annual fee paid for borrowing privileges. They also reported that libraries in public institutions were more likely than those in private institutions to participate in reciprocal borrowing programs; nevertheless, more than half of the private institutions did participate in such programs.

The academic librarians did not report contemplating extending their services to additional secondary or unaffiliated user groups, but several said they were considering limiting the privileges that were currently in force or instituting fees for continuing the service, including the one that had conducted the survey on fee-based services. Service to unaffiliated borrowers was almost always limited to people beyond the 12th grade in school, but there was one exception to this, too—Pima Community College allowed younger students to use its materials.

The number of client categories in the fourteen academic libraries described ranged from two to seven. In the three institutions where only two client categories were reported, if outsiders were served, they were given privileges similar to those given to students. Three client categories were reported by five libraries, four categories by one library, five categories by two libraries, and seven categories by one library. In this last library, located in a school of education, laboratory school students, their teachers, and parents were added to the usual mix of students of the college, faculty, administrators, and other staff. Alumni, affiliates of reciprocal borrowing partners, and nonaffiliates were singled out for special rules in various institutions. In all, nine of the fourteen libraries served some type of nonaffiliate.

Public libraries defined their primary user group, for the most part, as adult residents. Children and young adults (an in-between age category distinguished in some places) were served free of charge, also, but were usually distinguished in some way from adult residents and, in all but one library, had to obtain an adult sponsor in order to be served. In a similar manner, adults who paid taxes within the boundaries of a public library's service area, but did not reside within it, were also given borrowing privileges free of charge. One might call resident-children and nonresident-taxpayers *auxiliary primary* user groups for they almost always had some special requirements to fulfill in order to obtain service.

Different age levels were selected in the various public libraries for dividing child (and young adult, where applicable) clients from adults. Fourteen years of age seemed to be one of the most popular transition points to full adult borrowing status, mentioned in the policies of four libraries. Two libraries used twelve as the cutoff point, and one library waited until clients reached sixteen years of age before granting them adult status. One library used grade level instead of age, with adult status beginning at the sixth grade—approximately twelve years of age. In three institutions, child and/or young adult client categories were described without furnishing their specifications. In some policies, children's cards carried limitations on what could be borrowed, but, in a few, children could borrow any library materials without discrimination unless their parents (or other sponsors) specified that their privileges be limited to children's materials.

Most public libraries named one or more special categories of borrowers. These special groups fell into two main categories: persons with special characteristics or needs (teachers, temporary residents, handicapped persons, government officials) and nonpersonal cardholders (schools, businesses, or other community organizations). In addition to these groups, most policies described a special category for fee-paying clients who did not live, pay taxes, or work in the library's service area and who did not qualify for service in any of the other groups already named. These fees tended to be relatively low with special discounts sometimes extended to older people or students whose length of residence was confined to the academic year.

Several of the policies mentioned statewide borrowing programs in which the library cards of any public library in the state were honored at any other public library. More than one policy went beyond this, including cardholders from academic libraries, too, and one library cooperative added corporate and institutional library cardholders to their list of eligible clients.

In general, public libraries appeared more than willing to encourage secondary and outside borrowers to apply for service. While adding special requirements, restrictions, fees, or other qualifications either to their eligibility, services, or both, on the whole they were not viewed negatively as a burden that had to be borne. On the contrary, these client groups appeared to be welcome additions to the library's public, enriching its coffers with their fees and expanding total statistics for services rendered.

School library clients were, for the most part, composed of students in the individual schools in which the libraries were located. Fewer school library policies mentioned serving members of faculties or administrative staffs as one of their primary objectives than did their counterparts in colleges and universities. One exception to this was the policies pertaining to classroom collections, i.e., collections of library materials intended to be kept for a term or some part of a term in a classroom for use by a particular teacher's students. Use of school library materials by teachers for their own professional development or general information needs, however, was not emphasized by any of the schools in the survey.

School libraries had, without doubt, the most homogeneous of all service populations. Nevertheless, there were a few schools and district-level agencies that served parents, students from other schools, or members of the community at large.

There was no mention of fee-paying clients in the school library policies, even in the district libraries serving persons not affiliated with the schools. No doubt, one of the factors inhibiting use of school libraries by outsiders was the hours of service usually maintained, which tended to coincide with the hours that school buildings were in use for classes. Although in some schools the library was opened a little earlier and closed a little later than the schedule of classes, library and class hours were very nearly the same, and libraries were usually closed on weekends and during vacation periods. Year-round service was maintained by only one survey respondent— Wichita Library Media Services.

Not unexpectedly, methods of coping with demands for borrowing privileges by people from outside the schools did not figure in the policy statements examined. On the other hand, several mentioned special privileges for teachers and other staff just as other academic library policies did. Few school libraries issued library cards to clients but relied on other methods of identifying them. Proof of eligibility was less problematic in schools than in the other types of libraries since it can be easily established by class registers.

What May Be Borrowed?

Academic library policies concentrated mainly on the lending of *stack books*, i.e., older printed monographs not designated as reserve room materials (which would have necessitated their removal from the stacks for a period of time). New books were often distinguished from stack books by their location in special shelving areas as well as by the application of different loan policies. Other material categories described in many of the policy statements were reserve room materials, periodicals and other serials, audiovisual materials and equipment, microforms, and other specialized types of materials. These other materials were also governed by different—usually more restrictive—policies.

A minority group among the academic libraries emphasized (or, at least, they did not deemphasize) the use of nonbook materials such as audiovisual software, periodicals, microforms, and hardware. In several of the institutions surveyed, these materials were excluded entirely from circulation except to faculty or under special circumstances. Periodicals, whether current issues or bound volumes, tended not to circulate or to circulate for extremely short periods.

The number of material categories reported in the academic library circulation policies ranged from only one (in three libraries) to twenty-five (in one library). Most policies dealt with several types of materials (two to seven material types were reported by more than half of the libraries) who grouped or divided them in various ways. Stack books, periodicals, audiovisuals, and reserve materials were mentioned most frequently.

Public library policies were also concerned primarily with books, especially adult books, and they were divided into several different categories. The first basic division of adult books was into fiction and nonfiction. Public librarians typically kept their new fiction in separate areas and limited the amount of time clients could keep them; but new nonfiction was usually not so differentiated and could be borrowed for the longer loan periods unless it was a popular title. Paperback books were another category of book, however, and some of these were cataloged and shelved with other books (fiction or nonfiction, as appropriate) while others were not cataloged and were maintained in a separate collection. In one library, a separate collection of gift paperbacks was maintained for use by any client.

Children's books were usually all treated alike, whether the content was fiction or nonfiction. Picture books were often shelved separately, but they, too, were generally circulated in the same way as other juvenile books. Children's paperbacks were usually a separate material category and were often uncataloged.

Periodicals were mentioned in most public library policies and usually circulated except the current issues, which were shelved apart from back issues and bound volumes. Other nonbook materials mentioned included vertical file materials, sound recordings, films and videos (frequently owned by county, state, or regional cooperatives, not by individual libraries), framed art works, and, less often, maps, music, slides, filmstrips, toys and games, and hardware. Encyclopedias and other reference works were sometimes grouped in a category separate from other books when they circulated. In some libraries these were superseded volumes, but in others they were duplicate copies purchased especially so they could be circulated.

All things considered, public libraries seemed to have a great variety of offerings in many media, although book collections were almost always mentioned first and appeared to be foremost in every policy statement.

Contrary to expectations, school library policies did not exhibit concern with as large a variety of materials as were discussed in the policies of many public and academic libraries. In fact, books and periodicals were the only circulating materials mentioned in two of the school library policies analyzed.

Some school library media centers were, indeed, providers of all kinds of book and nonbook materials. The main media center serving Wichita's public schools, for example, included among its lending collections pamphlets, clippings, sound recordings on disc and tape, filmstrips, art prints, film loops, slides, and realia as well as books, book jackets, and magazines. Montgomery Blair High School Library Media Center also listed kits, transparencies, and microforms in addition to sound recordings, film loops, and filmstrips in its collection of 10,000 nonbook materials along with 280 pieces of equipment. Another Wichita center specialized in materials for the blind, which included Braille, large-print books, and tactile objects. (Although they were not described, Library of Congress sound recordings of books, circulated with their hardware free of charge to the visually impaired, may also have been part of this collection, as they are in many public libraries which do not specify them in their policies.)

In general, however, the policies analyzed in this survey focused mainly on traditional resources, i.e., books and printed periodicals. These categories of material were often divided further into reserve collections, ordinary circulating collections, classroom collections, and reference collections. Periodicals, too, were usually separated into current and back issues, with different rules governing their use.

Interestingly, none of the school policies mentioned videorecordings or computer software. Though the survey was small and some of the policies were dated 1983 or earlier, this gap was surprising in view of the perception in the field that collection of educational software was extremely widespread.

How May Materials Be Borrowed?

Stack books circulated to students in seven of the academic libraries for about a month, which was sometimes counted as four weeks and some-times as one month. Three other academic institutions had three-week borrowing periods for ordinary stack books, and four more lent them for two weeks. Faculty in half of these academic libraries, on the other hand, could borrow stack books for a term—quarter or semester—and in two more, faculty loans were longer than a term. Five of the schools were more restrictive about faculty loans, allowing them the same loans as students or extending them only for a short time beyond the normal borrowing period.

Policies on loans of reserve materials varied quite a bit, with the hourly loans that were typically permitted for these items being extended to overnight loans as closing time approached. Several libraries permitted reserve materials to be borrowed for a day, three days, or a week, although how the different loan periods were determined was not spelled out.

Renewals were generally permitted in academic libraries, sometimes only once and sometimes for as many times as a client liked, provided no one else had requested the item. On the other hand, few places would execute renewals by telephone or mail, insisting that the materials be brought in to be recharged.

Fines for overdue materials were generally low, ranging between five cents and $2, with ten cents the amount charged per day most frequently (six libraries of the eleven that specified their overdue charges charged ten cents per day). Only three institutions had daily charges of $1 or more. One university simply charged for the price of the item plus $5 if it was held overdue for too long a period of time. One university did not charge any fines.

Charges for lost books (or books held overdue for exceptionally long periods of time) were more significant than overdue fines. These charges ranged from a low of $15 in one library to "all costs" in another. Replacement costs plus a processing fee was typical, and one university circulation department charged the accumulated overdue fine in addition to both of these. In some libraries, fines were not paid to the library but to university financial offices or, if collected by the library, were turned over to general funds. By doing this, the library might not receive these funds directly for its own purposes, but they also did not have to invest the time and energy into collection operations and record keeping. Libraries that did their own collections sometimes offered discounts of up to 50 percent to those who paid up, in full, on the spot.

The number of notices that were sent to inform academic library clients about their overdue materials varied from one (in four libraries) to three (in one library); however, most of them did not specify how many notices were sent (seven libraries). The presence of computer systems that automatically produced notices did not guarantee that more notices would be sent, and one college library with a fully automated circulation control system sent just one overdue notice. Another policy, which did not specify the number of notices furnished to clients, stated that notices were a courtesy, not a duty, a comment echoed by public library policy statements.

Typical penalties for students who did not comply with the rules were threefold: if they were about to graduate, diplomas and transcripts were withheld; if they were continuing students, they were not allowed to register for the next term. A few policies mentioned penalties for faculty designed to embarrass them into returning overdue materials, such as letters appealing to their sense of responsibility and good will or letters to their deans or department chairs asking for their help in obtaining compliance with the rules. A small number of libraries went so far as to withdraw faculty borrowing privileges, but most stopped short of that drastic step. In general, faculty privileges were sacrosanct.

Public library policies generally geared their loan periods to the relative popularity and/or supply vs. demand balance of various kinds of material. New adult fiction and periodicals, films and videos—all of which tended to be in shorter supply than the demand for them—were usually given shorter loan periods; children's materials, older adult books, and nonfiction—usually available in more than adequate supplies—were allowed longer loan periods. Shorter loans were usually one week; the longer ones were usually three weeks. Often, renewals were denied for the shorter loans and limited to a single renewal for the others. Extended loans for vacationers, teachers, and the homebound were frequently made, nevertheless, and almost every library that circulated them had long loans for framed art works.

Public library daily overdue charges were nominal, too—two to five cents a day for children's materials and five to ten cents a day for adults—and there were low ceilings on the amounts that could accumulate. Special materials such as films and videorecordings, periodicals, and other audiovisual software or hardware often incurred high daily or hourly fines, but even they rarely accumulated to more than $10. Replacement fees for lost or damaged materials in public libraries were less likely to be augmented by a processing fee than in academic libraries, but some followed that practice.

Several public library policies laid out a series of steps for obtaining the return of materials and/or fines ending with sending the bills to a collection agency and, sometimes, threats of litigation. The signatures of cardholders on their applications and, certainly, parent signatures on children's applications, were considered their legally binding assent to observe circulation rules. Withdrawal of borrowing privileges from persons who were delinquent in returning materials or paying their bills was also used to deal with problem clients before their debts reached more massive proportions. There were no client categories explicitly given special privileges similar to faculty members in academic libraries. (One exception to this rule were those places where the library's staff or board members were given extraordinary treatment. They were not, however, explicitly stated in the policy documents examined.)

School libraries/media centers had the fewest number of loan periods, even in those places where there were a great many different types of borrowable materials, for example, a media center with one of the most diverse collections mentioned only one loan period in its policy statement. The length of most school loan periods was short, however; loans of two weeks were most common.

School libraries provided teachers and students with *classroom collections* in addition to use of their ordinary stack books, periodicals, and reserve collections—sometimes called *closed reserves*—but exactly what constituted classroom collections and closed reserves was never specified.

Periodicals usually circulated, except for current issues.

Perhaps the greatest distinction between the way circulation transactions operated in school libraries and in other types of libraries was that fines—even token fines—for overdue materials were rarely encountered in school libraries and media centers.

In academic and public library policies, a great deal of space was devoted to descriptions of fine structures and the application of penalties. Variations by type of client and type of material abounded. One of the most important exceptions to academic library fines and other penalties—faculty members—was the basis of one of librarians' biggest problems. The majority of school libraries, however, survived without exacting any monetary tolls for the nonreturn of materials, although at least one respondent to the survey reported that inauguration of a fine policy for overdues was being considered.

A second sharp contrast between school policies and those of other types of libraries was the attitude of librarians toward overdue notices. Unlike many academic and public librarians who considered notices a courtesy and who held clients responsible for their overdue materials, school librarians seemed extremely concerned that they could not produce notices more frequently and regularly. Their logic was that production of more notices would result in a smaller proportion of nonreturns.

There was another quite different issue on which school policies differed from those of other types of libraries: interlibrary loans. While many academic and public libraries were involved in many cooperative programs on local, regional, and national levels, school libraries took a more parochial view of interlibrary lending. One elementary school library that was linked by computer to a multitype library network found itself unable to reciprocate with its public library partners located outside the district boundaries. This policy was not initiated by the local school but by its district; nevertheless, the school had to abide by it. Even though the elementary school library could borrow materials from public libraries outside the district, it could not lend to them. The school hoped to change the policy which antedated its participation in the computer network.

Summary

What conclusions can be drawn from these policy statements? First, there were few surprises regarding *who* was allowed to borrow materials:

- *Academic libraries* had no clear-cut patterns concerning secondary or outside user groups (e.g., alumni, nonmatriculants, families of affiliates, affiliates of sister institutions, local or regional cooperatives, or the general public).
- Whether an institution of higher learning was public or private did not seem to

affect its decisions to serve (or not to serve) persons beyond the primary user groups.

- Reciprocal borrowing privileges were not always encouraged by academic libraries among its neighbors in a region, college or university system, or network cooperative.

- Faculty borrowing privileges were shrinking in a few places, but, in general, they were still clearly superior to those of students and other borrowers.

- *Public libraries* really defined their primary user group as *residents,* although taxpaying nonresidents were universally served free of charge, too.

- Adults received preferred treatment over children, who had to have the signature of a responsible adult before being served (the age of transition ranged from twelve to sixteen).

- A broad range of special category user groups were served by public libraries including teachers, schools, businesses, the handicapped or homebound, senior citizens, and nonresident students, workers, and others.

- Several public libraries participated in local or statewide reciprocal borrowing programs, and many saw their users in a very wide context.

- *School libraries* did not usually serve many people beyond their primary user groups, i.e., students and teachers (two schools permitted nonaffiliates to use materials, and others mentioned serving affiliates of other schools in the district).

- Hours of service were almost invariably linked to the hours that schools were in session (there was one exception to this rule).

- *All types of libraries* with automated systems did not issue more notices but used the information provided by the computers to identify delinquent clients in order to withhold new cards or even ordinary borrowing privileges.

Second, regarding *what* could be borrowed:

- In most libraries, regardless of type of library, *stack books*—the older and less popular books—were the primary type of circulating material.

- New books were singled out as a special category of material and given special rules for circulation.

- Both academic and public library policies discussed a large variety of nonbook materials, but many of these circulated for limited loan periods or did not circulate at all (e.g., current periodicals, equipment, microforms, etc.).

- Periodicals were categorized by their form, which varied, i.e., loose issues (current or back issues), bound volumes, and microform; books were categorized by their age (in all types of libraries) and content (by public libraries).

- Films and videorecordings, circulated primarily by public libraries, were often held in county, state, or regional cooperative collections, not in the collections of individual libraries.

Third, concerning *how* materials circulated:

- Stack books were permitted the longest loan period by academic and school libraries, but not by public libraries.

- Typical loans for stack books ranged between two and four weeks (sometimes, one month) in most libraries, regardless of the type of library.

- Periodicals were universally held by all types of libraries, but back issues often did not circulate at all in academic libraries, while in public and school libraries they usually did unless they were bound, in which case they sometimes did not.

- Most nonbook materials and equipment were loaned for shorter periods than stack books, as were new books (except for nonfiction in public libraries) and periodicals, although there were a few notable exceptions.

- Especially long loans were given to faculty by libraries in academic institutions and schools and to people with special needs (teachers, vacationers, handicapped) by public libraries.

- Materials almost always given special treatment of unusually long or short loans included art prints (long loans by public libraries), materials for the blind (long), films and videorecordings (short), reference works (short), and reserve collection items (short).

- Modest daily fines for overdue materials were almost always charged by academic and public libraries but not by school libraries.

- Academic libraries often charged processing fees for lost books in addition to the cost of the book; public libraries sometimes did, too; but schools rarely mentioned such a policy.

- Several academic and public libraries warned their clients that notices were only a courtesy not an obligation of the library, but most school libraries worried about not producing enough timely notices.

- Some academic and public libraries were extremely careful to spell out expected obligations of the client and legal recourse to which the library would resort if clients were delinquent.

These conclusions indicate several current trends in circulation policies:

1. Perceptions of eligible clients seemed to be broadening in public libraries and narrowing in a few academic libraries.

2. There were few changes in circulating materials: Books were still very much the primary material dealt with in all types of libraries. Special types of books, including new books, reference books, and reserve materials and nonbook materials and equipment, could be borrowed in many libraries, especially in the public libraries, but not for the loan period given for stack books.

3. Some libraries withdrew borrowing privileges if accounts were not settled quickly. Legal actions for nonreturn of materials were being written into circulation policies by several public and a few academic libraries. Delinquency, though treated as an ever-present evil by school libraries, was being attacked through both of these means by academic and public libraries.

4. Lost book fees were often enlarged by hefty processing fees and, occasionally, by the addition of fines, but daily fine charges were not increasing significantly.

5. Automation of circulation was not resulting in the distribution of more overdue
   notices but in supplying more up-to-date information about clients and materials
   for use by circulation departments.

A COMPARISON OF CIRCULATION POLICIES, PRACTICES, AND ISSUES FOR CIRCULATION

Circulation Systems

Many academic librarians participating in this survey complained about their charging operations. The majority of them were employing manual circulation systems based on signed cards or slips. Several libraries used more than one system simultaneously. Of those systems that were specifically named, the McBee keysort was most popular (four libraries), followed by Gaylord (three libraries), Demco (two libraries), and Brodart (one library). Only seven libraries used computers in their operations, three of them were offline batch-processing systems and four were online, interactive real-time systems.

In contrast, the majority of public librarians in this sample, or twelve out of seventeen, employed computer-based circulation systems, although three of them also used manual charging systems for some portion of their operations. The automated systems all used minicomputers and were turnkey, stand-alone online systems. Only one of the public libraries doing manual charging used the McBee keysort system that was so popular among academic libraries, and photocharging was the most popular type of noncomputerized charging system. Other manual charging based on signed book cards, aside from the one mentioned, were absent.

All but one of the libraries relying entirely on manual operations and five of the libraries using computers were planning changes to their systems. Some of the changes were simply extensions of previously purchased systems that had not been fully implemented at the time of the survey, and some of the changes were part of ongoing enhancements of existing systems. Others acknowledged satisfaction with their existing systems but felt that technology had progressed to the point where newer systems could link with or supersede the older systems then in place. Only one public librarian expressed dissatisfaction with the current computerized system and sought to improve the situation by changing to a new one.

Most school librarians had the simplest kind of manual charging systems based on signed cards or slips. Two reported using computer-based systems, one a stand-alone and the other a large network system. Both of these librarians were satisfied that automation had resolved most of their circulation problems and offered other benefits. A third school was employing a computer to generate overdue notices, and a fourth was about to do so. Only three schools used charging systems other than these. The lack of variation in charging systems, while mildly surprising, might be attributed to the small sample of school libraries, or it could be an accurate reflection of the general situation. Plans to change to new systems, particularly computer-based systems, were afoot in several of the schools. Those who seemed closest to implementation were already familiar with the application of computers in their district, for administrative operations in their schools or in local public libraries.

Complaints of Circulation Staff Members

Complaints by academic librarians about their manual systems focused on the time it took clients to write names, addresses, and bibliographic information on the charging slips as well as the difficulty staff had in deciphering the data when the slips were used to recall material or send overdue notices. The tedium of manual operations and the lack of information the systems supplied were motivating them to contemplate new systems. Only three of these libraries had no plans to change their charging system, only one of these because they were satisfied with it. The rest were at some point along the road to acquiring and implementing an online circulation control system, often as part of a larger system of automated technical services and/or with other partners in a consortium or cooperative group.

Other academic library problems named included abuse of their privileges by faculty, materials that were overdue or missing, and their inability to trap delinquent clients.

Public library problems mentioned most frequently were the high rate of nonreturns and the inability to trap delinquents, obtain accurate information, and produce overdue notices promptly—all complaints attributable to libraries operating manual systems. A host of other problems were named once or twice including problems that computers could not affect, such as insufficient budgets, annoyance with the demand for new materials, and materials clients claimed had been returned.

School library problems were as homogeneous as their circulation systems, focusing primarily on nonreturn of materials. Several librarians said they wished they had the time to produce overdue notices promptly and frequently, presumably because they felt it would lead to a better return rate. The pervasiveness of delinquency in one school was shocking, as reported by the librarian who claimed that two-thirds of the students were on the overdue list. Although daily overdue fines were not levied in most school libraries, some withdrew borrowing privileges until overdue books were returned or lost materials were paid for.

Client Complaints

Client complaints in academic libraries overlapped those of staff members. The principal client problem was a lack of desired information about materials they wanted to borrow or materials they already had charged out. Reserve room limits and restrictions on renewals—both the number of renewals permitted and the inability to make renewals by telephone—were other problems voiced by clients, along with disgust over the tedium of manual charging procedures and overly strict application of circulation rules.

The complaints of public library clients were, most frequently, that there were not enough desired titles available and that they were not notified about their overdues. Clients also chafed at short loan periods, limited renewals, fines, and the use of collection agencies. They did not like waiting for anything—library cards or popular titles—nor did they welcome inaccurate information, confusing procedures, or receipt of notices for items already returned. Keeping track of borrowed materials was a client problem that computers could help resolve, as they could for several of the others; nevertheless, automated libraries had the same complaints at the top of their lists. The largest number of client complaints focused on matters of policy.

Students, who formed virtually the entire school library client population, had complaints similar to those of public library clients, mainly, that the materials they wanted were not available. They wanted information about the materials they had already borrowed, and they disliked receiving overdue notices for materials they believed they had returned. Like clients of other types of libraries, they were annoyed by limited loan periods and restrictions on their privileges—issues that were largely a matter of policy and had little to do with circulation systems or operations.

The Policy-Making Process and Recent Policy Issues

Policy formulation was not uniform throughout the group of academic libraries but varied widely. Some of them involved all possible groups within the institution including circulation staff, library administration, students, faculty, and others. Most, however, limited policy-making to the circulation staff—especially the department head—and the library administrators. Seven librarians reported conducting regular policy reviews, usually annually; five had no review mechanism at all. The rest examined their policies on an as-needed basis, in response to complaints or perceived problems.

Changes in circulation policies in response to the introduction of automated systems often included a different schedule of overdue notices. Grace periods were often added to loan periods to account for the time lag between returns and check-in or to avoid the automatic generation of notices for items returned only a day or two overdue. Loan periods were adjusted, sometimes to standardize them among several libraries sharing a computer. Individual comments indicated that the changes served to extend services some of the time, but, at other times, they resulted in limitations in service.

Policy formulation in public libraries was divided between those libraries where administrators were the primary policymakers and those where committees made the decisions. Committees tended to include both administrators and library staff members. Less frequently, members of library boards and representatives of the general public sat on committees, too. All the respondents claimed to conduct regular reviews of circulation policies; however, the frequency with which they were conducted varied from those who claimed to review policies continuously to those who did it once a year, and many people did not specify. Approval by the library board of new policies was also mentioned in some descriptions of the policy-making process.

Revisions to policies in progress in some of the libraries at the time of the survey were intended to accommodate new automated systems, including the harmonizing of policies of different agencies that planned to share one circulation system or the necessity of maintaining both automated and manual systems side by side. Other libraries were dealing with their departmental manuals, statistics, and/or data management systems, as well as re-registering clients and examining a variety of measures to encourage better return rates and fewer abuses. Two librarians said their intentions were to liberalize policies or otherwise extend services. The others were looking at restrictive measures such as increasing fines or strengthening identification requirements for transients in order to address the problem of nonreturns.

Policy formulation in school libraries was most often the province of library staff members. Sometimes, teachers and school administrators were included, too, as well as students and parents. Consultation with these groups seemed to be initiated by the librarians, rather than being imposed from outside the library. Policy-making committees were encountered, too, but only one of them was said to be active at the time of the survey.

Policy changes were being sought in one school library to initiate daily overdue fines and, in another, to alter the pattern of overdue notices—both to address the problem of nonreturns. An elementary school library that became part of a large network system hoped to change its interlibrary loan policies in order to serve its partners more effectively, having benefitted from their ILL services. Filing procedures were changing in one school district that had lost part of its space. One district was launching an investigation of practices in individual schools to ensure that they were in keeping with established policies. Most school libraries, however, were not revising their policies at all.

Future Plans for Circulation

Future plans for circulation departments, regardless of the type of library in which they were located, focused on automating operations or extending computer applications that were already in place. More ambitious libraries, some with sophisticated circulation control systems already in place, anticipated integrated or linked systems of technical services, providing opportunities to add status information to catalogs, permit access to circulation information from remote sites, or otherwise increase or enhance the information available about materials and clients. They were also interested in adding new services for staff members and clients or new methods of delivering them. Less ambitious libraries simply wanted a better method of controlling ordinary circulation operations, although several indicated their ultimate automation goals were more complex than this.

Policy issues that circulation librarians wanted to address, for the most part, dealt with methodologies and devices to improve return rates or, conversely, limit nonreturns. Some of the specific intentions were to change loan periods, limit the privileges of special clients, and add more registration or card renewal requirements to trap persons owing fines or materials to the library. Very few librarians expressed a desire to raise fines, although there were some. Even in those libraries where fines had been raised in the recent past, there seemed to be a lack of confidence that this alone was effective in deterring nonreturns. Much more interest was expressed in obtaining the facts—irrefutable proof that alleged overdues were, indeed, overdue—that justified remedial actions such as withholding borrowing privileges.

School librarians were concerned about increasing their production of overdue notices, but academic and public librarians were generally not as interested in this as they were in trapping delinquents at the chargeout and registration desks. Many academic and public librarians were beginning to view overdue notices as a courtesy, putting the burden of responsibility for materials clearly and completely on clients' shoulders. The perspective that the library was accountable to higher authorities was expressed in several public library policy statements. This was reflected in several academic library policy statements, too. It was the rationale underlying recourse to legal action taken against clients. The threat of turning over uncollected debts to collection agencies (and the subsequent impact on a person's credit rating) was not widely applied at the time of the survey, but those who employed it seemed pleased with the policy.

Several librarians, a minority of the whole group, were happy with their circulation systems and policies just as they were at the time of the survey. This group planned no changes in operations at all. The largest proportion of such satisfied respondents were in the school sector; the smallest proportion was in the academic sector.

By and large, the librarians who claimed to have succeeded in improving returns *and* services were those who had computerized their operations and combined the added capabilities of their automated system with other policy changes that eliminated any slack in dealing with delinquency, particularly by developing responses to the problem with "teeth" in them. This did not mean that no changes were in progress, but that changes were not attacking endemic delinquency in the client population, a problem that had already been successfully addressed. Rather, changes were being sought to extend services, though not necessarily to liberalize privileges. Several of these libraries were part of reciprocal borrowing programs and other cooperative networks. It appeared that their effectiveness was attributable as much to their more businesslike attitude as it was to the computer system providing the information that made it possible.

A FEW FINAL WORDS

Several new ideas about circulation policy, particularly in an automated environment, emerged from the analysis of these documents and survey responses. Among these were the following observations:

1. The most important feature of effective circulation policies and procedures was the presence of clearly defined objectives underpinning cohesive policies and procedures.

2. Automating operations, by itself, was not enough to provide libraries with successful circulation departments. The way automated systems were used was much more important than the implementation of a computer.

3. While policies of automated libraries were often more detailed and stricter in their application, many of them encouraged a broad range of clients—both affiliated and nonaffiliated—to borrow materials.

4. Capabilities of automated systems in operation at the time of the survey were not sophisticated enough to accomplish all the things circulation librarians felt were important. The principal lack was integration with other functional components of technical and public services.

5. Provision of new services was far less important to librarians than more effective execution of services already being rendered, although *new* and *old* tended to differ depending on whether services were already automated.

The *who* of circulation was expanding dramatically in many places, particularly where universal borrowing was being implemented as a part of statewide library policies. This expansion appeared to be linked, to a certain degree, with state or regional automation activities. In some areas, either in addition to statewide programs or in their absence, local borrowing networks were springing up—clearly the result of computerizing circulation. The network might be the result of a joint automation project, as it was in the case of the LEAP libraries in Connecticut. None of LEAP's constituent libraries was large enough to support the project alone (at least, not at the time it was established); but, together they were able to purchase their computer system and institute better controls simultaneously with enhanced resource sharing. The network might be a multitype system, as it was in the Cleveland-University Heights area where an elementary school joined with public library neighbors in what was reported as an extremely successful experiment. (LEAP, too, was joined by a high school library some years after its founding.) In fact, reciprocity between public libraries and local academic libraries also appeared to be successful in more than one locale. The vision of broadened access seemed to be on the rise in these institutions.

On the other hand, some of the larger academic libraries, both public and private, appeared to be focusing inward on their own primary client groups at the expense of virtually all nonaffiliated borrowers. Whether this was a response to a belief that the libraries were unable to function effectively in the broader context, or, perhaps, because of a belief that outsiders had abused privileges previously extended to them by the institutions, was not clear. It was a sharp contrast to those areas where universal borrowing included academic as well as school and public library participants.

The *what* of circulation was not startlingly different than expected. That is to say, older books were the *typical* material dealt with in circulation policies. Everything else—new books, nonbook materials, equipment, periodicals, and other serials—was considered special. In fact, it was actually disappointing to find a few school libraries that described circulating only books and printed periodicals—the most traditional materials. Library literature would lead one to believe that school libraries generally were the possessors of rich and varied nonbook media resources, collected since the 1960s. It is possible that some schools had separate learning resource centers for nonbook media or that the survey predated the introduction of collections of such cutting-edge technologies as video or microcomputer materials.

Cooperative lending programs added materials not owned by a particular library to those available from its own holdings. Small schools often relied on centralized district facilities to provide the variety of media forms and titles no individual school could afford to buy. This is the model we saw in Wichita, and it is a familiar one. More disappointing than the lack of variety in the holdings of any particular collection, however, was the absence of any indication of a trend toward more eclectic collecting in these institutions. As a group, public libraries lent the largest variety of materials. Videorecordings and films were usually subject to stricter regulations than other nonbook (or book) items, however, particularly for those that did not belong to the individual libraries but to central film services.

The *how* of circulation was changing. Loans were being monitored more carefully, and swift responses to delinquency were designed to limit library losses and insure that clients who maintained their good standing were better served. The increased control over materials and transactions resulting from computerizing circulation information offered an efficient mode of enforcement.

None of the libraries surveyed had aggressive fine policies, whether or not they had computerized circulation operations. For the most part, the few cents a day charged for an overdue item was far too low to represent more than a token penalty. Ceilings on accumulations limited the impact of overdue charges even further. The emphasis shifted from fining borrowers as punishment to stopping them altogether, at least in the libraries where delinquents could be identified. Although as a group, school libraries appeared to be the least aggressive as well as the least successful in bringing about an end to continued delinquency, the two school libraries with computerized circulation systems were notable exceptions.

Only school libraries still set great store by multiple overdue notices and accepted full responsibility for producing and sending them. Members of the other library groups were beginning to express the notion that it was not the library's but the client's responsibility to monitor due dates. Clients of several libraries in the survey were told that overdue notices were only a courtesy. This was happening particularly in libraries where computer systems could produce overdue notices automatically.

Indeed, increased control over materials and transactions resulting from computerizing circulation information was the critical component in changing policies. It was a catalyst in the extension of client access to materials beyond the boundaries of geography or the barriers of affiliation. Without doubt, librarians working with fully automated systems were delighted with the results. They seemed to concentrate more on services than materials. But they were also far more likely to demand that clients be accountable, too, and take responsibility for their actions.

After all is said and done, client access is really the ultimate purpose of circulation services. The measure of library services in the future may well depend on how far the limits of circulation services can continue to expand and enrich access.

APPENDIX 1: SURVEY OF CIRCULATION POLICIES AND PRACTICES

Sheila S. Intner, Investigator

PLEASE RESPOND to the questions below in your own words and in as much detail as you wish. If you need more space, feel free to use the back of the questionnaire or add more sheets of your own. Also, feel free to add your own comments at the end.

1. What kind of charging or circulation system do you use? Indicate separate reserve book room systems, if applicable. (For example: CLSI, Gaylord, photocharging, signed book cards, etc.)

2. If you have a computerized system, have your circulation policies changed because of its introduction and how? If not, skip this question and go on to Question 3.

3. Do you plan to purchase, develop, or implement a different circulation system in the foreseeable future? What kind of new system are you planning and why?

4. What circulation services not currently offered would you most like to be able to provide for the public? (For example: self-service charging, materials by mail, selective dissemination of information, etc.)

5. What part(s) of your current policies for circulation do you believe are most in need of change?

6. Who contributes to the formulation of circulation policies? (For example: administrators, circulation staff, the public, a designated committee, etc.)

7. Do you regularly review circulation policies and procedures, and, if so, how often? Who does this review?

8. Are you currently in the process of revising your circulation policies, and, if so, toward what ends?

9. What is your biggest circulation problem? (For example: high rate of nonreturns, difficulty collecting fines, problems getting notices out, etc.)

10. What is your patrons' biggest complaint? (For example: length of borrowing period too short, fines too high, lack of recall capability, etc.)

ADD YOUR COMMENTS PLEASE!

APPENDIX 2: *PARTICIPATING INSTITUTIONS*

The list that follows includes all the institutions that sent documents describing their policies and procedures in addition to filling out the survey questionnaire. Librarians from twenty-five more libraries—eight academic, five public, and twelve school—who responded by filling out only the survey questionnaire were promised anonymity and, therefore, cannot be named.

ACADEMIC LIBRARIES

Agnes Scott College, Decatur, Georgia
Bank Street College of Education, New York, New York
Columbia University, New York, New York
Emory University, Atlanta, Georgia
Graduate School of Education, Harvard University, Cambridge, Massachusetts
Mankato State University, Mankato, Minnesota
Nazareth College of Rochester, Rochester, New York
Pima Community College, Tucson, Arizona
Queens College of the City University of New York, Flushing, New York
State University of New York at Stony Brook, Stony Brook, New York
University of Bridgeport, Bridgeport, Connecticut
University of North Florida, Jacksonville, Florida
University of Wisconsin, Whitewater, Wisconsin
Whitworth College, Spokane, Washington

PUBLIC LIBRARIES

Atlanta-Fulton Public Library, Atlanta, Georgia
Baltimore County Public Library, Towson, Maryland
Burlingame Public Library, Burlingame, California
Elmhurst Public Library, Elmhurst, Illinois
Free Library of Philadelphia, Philadelphia, Pennsylvania
Great Neck Library, Great Neck, New York
Hamden Library, Hamden, Connecticut
Hays Public Library, Hays, Kansas
Library Exchange Aids Patrons, Hamden, Connecticut
Los Angeles Public Library, Los Angeles, California
Menlo Park Public Library, Menlo Park, California
Pasadena Public Library, Pasadena, California
Peninsula Library System, Belmont, California
San Bruno Public Library, San Bruno, California
San Mateo City Libraries, San Mateo, California
Tacoma Public Library, Tacoma, Washington
Washoe County Library, Reno, Nevada

SCHOOL LIBRARIES

Fairfax Elementary School, University Heights, Ohio
High School of Graphic Communication Arts, New York, New York
J. M. Wright Technical School, Stamford, Connecticut
Montgomery Blair High School, Silver Spring, Maryland
Morristown High School, Morristown, New Jersey
Wichita Public Schools, Wichita, Kansas

SELECTED BIBLIOGRAPHY

The bibliography that follows is not intended to be comprehensive. Rather, it lists readings that provide a jumping-off point for someone interested in pursuing the topics covered by this book in greater depth. Annotations, some lengthy, are included for many titles. If the author was unable to peruse an item, it is listed without comment.

POLICY ISSUES: HISTORICAL BACKGROUND

American Library Association, Library Administration Division, Circulation Services Section, Circulation Control Committee. *Circulation Policies of Academic Libraries in the United States, 1968 A Report.* Chicago: American Library Association, 1970.

Bobinski, George S. "A Survey of Faculty Loan Policies." *College and Research Libraries* 24 (Nov., 1963): 483-86.

In the introduction to his article, Bobinski notes how little on this topic has appeared in the literature for the previous thirty years. His survey had an extremely high response rate, revealing great concern from practicing librarians. Bobinski found that policies were not always written; indefinite loans were the most popular for books although limited loans, if any, were given for periodicals, reference books, and reserve books; recalls did not differ; and fines were rarely imposed (only one out of 108 libraries). Despite a pervasive feeling of "hopelessness," librarians felt faculty should have extended privileges—but not beyond a year, after which librarians believed professors should buy their own copies.

Brown, Charles Harvey, and H. G. Bousfield. *Circulation Work in College and University Libraries.* Chicago: American Library Association, 1933.

> This companion volume to Flexner's work on public libraries followed a few years later. It begins by discussing the differences between college and public libraries affecting circulation and proceeds to cover much of the same territory from its own perspective. The authors attribute the differences between public and college library circulation work to more detailed administrative control of college libraries, more homogeneous clientele, greater demand for nonfiction, more "insistent demands for certain books," (p. 12) greater emphasis on preservation, and less uniform loan methods. Special topics include reserve collections and periodical rooms. No separate chapter covers personnel but sections in Chapter 4, "Organization and Activities of the Loan Department," discuss the qualifications and duties of "loan and reference librarians," clericals, and student assistants. Illustrations, though few, are practical including sample forms, suggested floor plans, etc. Closed stacks are assumed, but a limit of three minutes' waiting time for a book to be paged is recommended. Among the issues discussed by Brown and Bousfield are "retention by faculty members of books needed by students" (p. 75). They observe that "these practices are not conducive to good library service. . . . Unfortunately, they seem quite general" (p. 76). This book gives thorough coverage to its subject, but its approach and style are quite different than Flexner's, reflecting the orientation of academic libraries toward circulation services.

Flexner, Jennie M. *Circulation Work in Public Libraries.* Chicago: American Library Association, 1927.

> This 320-page book is a classic work on circulation services, covering all the major components of the function in depth. It defines circulation as "that activity of the library which through personal contact and a system of records supplies the reader with the books wanted," (p. 1) and goes on to discuss borrower registration, charging systems, privileges, fees, desk routines, statistics and reports, and other relevant topics. A pragmatic and people-oriented work, it has two chapters about circulation personnel. Chapter 12 is devoted to administering a circulation department, beginning with a section on policies. Flexner feels the basis for circulation policies is "the size of the library, the resources available, a survey of immediate library and community needs, and of possible future demands," (p. 254) and adds, "No organization should be accepted as final, no matter how effective" (p. 256). In Chapter 5, different types of borrower categories are explored, as well as the length of regular and special loans, renewals, reserves, rentals, returns, restrictions, and interloans. She urges attention to the relative cost effectiveness of various policies. In fact, the book sounds remarkably up to date in its approach and emphasis on flexibility and staff involvement as keys to success.

CHARGING SYSTEMS: BEFORE THE EIGHTIES

Bahr, Alice Harrison. *Automated Library Circulation Systems 1979-80.* White Plains, N.Y.: Knowledge Industry Publications, 1979.

Boss, Richard W. "Circulation Systems: The Options." *Library Technology Reports*, 15 (Jan., 1979): 7-105.

Geer, Helen Thornton. *Charging Systems*. Chicago: American Library Association, 1955.

Illustrated descriptions are given of the equipment used and routines followed for charging, discharging, renewals, overdues, reserves (i.e., holds), and statistics for seventeen charging systems. Following each description is a valuable analysis of the advantages and disadvantages of the system. An extensive bibliography (pp. 169-77) offers a backward look at the literature and lists libraries using fourteen of the systems—a valuable appendix at the time of publication.

George Fry & Associates, Inc. *Study of Circulation Control Systems: Public Libraries, College and University Libraries, Special Libraries*. Chicago: Library Technology Project of the American Library Association and the Council on Library Resources, 1961.

This landmark study of circulation systems and operations was performed by a team of professional management consultants at a time when the library world stood at the door of the computer age. The organization of this book is quite different from most. Text is kept to a minimum, with an overview of the entire study and its recommendations comprising only 30 out of 138 pages. Brief descriptions of twenty-eight different systems are given. Central to the study are tables, graphs and analyses of the masses of data collected comparing features, costs, and operation of these systems in 104 libraries. Three sections at the end of the book are system selection manuals in workbook form for each library type. They provide a method of selecting the best of the systems for one's own library and comparing their costs with the current system. For the first time, alternative policies are clearly defined, and priorities are recommended for the various functions of a circulation system.

Scholz, William H. "Computer-Based Circulation Systems—A Current Review and Evaluation," *Library Technology Reports* 13 (May, 1977): 231-325.

Tauber, Maurice F. *Technical Services in Libraries*. New York: Columbia University Press, 1954.

CHARGING SYSTEMS: CURRENT LITERATURE

Boss, Richard W., and Judith McQueen. "Automated Circulation Control Systems." *Library Technology Reports* 18 (Mar./Apr., 1982): 3-126.

Matthews, Joseph R. "Automated Circulation: Planning for a Region." *LJ Special Report*, 19 (1981).

______. "Automated Circulation System Marketplace: Active and Heating Up." *Library Journal*, 107 (1 Feb., 1982): 233-35.

Pope, Nolan F. *Microcomputers for Library Circulation Control*. Indianapolis: INCOLSA, 1984.

Rush, James E. Associates. *Library Systems Evaluation Guide: Circulation Control*. Powell, Ohio: JERA, 1984.

One of a series of *Guides* on specific library functions intended to serve as an evaluation workbook for libraries automating these functions. This book contains listings and descriptions of currently available computerized circulation systems with names, addresses, and phone numbers of persons to contact. In addition, it lists and describes all the functions of an ideal circulation control system.

Thomason, Nevada Wallis. *Circulation Systems for School Library Media Centers.* Littleton, Colo.: Libraries Unlimited, 1985.

POLICY ISSUES: CONTEMPORARY LITERATURE

Anderson, A. J. "How Do You Manage? Faculty Borrowing Privileges." *Library Journal* 109 (1 Sep., 1984): 1611-13.

This case study describes the efforts of a library's middle managers to persuade their director to allow them to pressure faculty members into returning overdue books. Responding to Anderson's hypothetical case, Nancy R. John, University of Illinois at Chicago, suggested that staff members document the problem and develop several solutions from which the director can select an appropriate strategy. Alice S. Clark, University of New Mexico, Albuquerque, suggested something similar, with staff members studying how many requests were made for titles that faculty had overdue. If a real problem was observed, Clark believed the onus for addressing it should rest not only with the library director but include informing the university administration and involve library users in developing a solution.

Anthony, Rose Marie. "No Signature, No Library: A Primary Teacher Asks Why Young Children Must Print Legibly to Use the Library." *American Libraries* 15 (Sep., 1984): 567-68.

An experienced teacher and children's specialist makes a case for eliminating the requirement that children sign their names on library application forms before receiving their own cards. She points out that there is not enough room for the large letters children typically make, that tiny library pencils are hard to manipulate, and that the hand-eye coordination required to sign a name is not related to the ability to enjoy a book. Furthermore, the parent must cosign and is actually the responsible party. A survey of five public libraries by *American Libraries* editor Edith McCormick found all of them had the requirement, but one felt uncomfortable about it and two more were quite liberal about what they accepted. Two said they "did not discriminate" between clients. Four of the five said a child should be able to understand the importance and responsibility attached to having a card.

Burr, Robert L. "Toward a General Theory of Circulation." Master's thesis, University of Illinois, 1977.

Frohnberg, Katherine A. *Research on the Impact of a Computerized Circulation System on the Performance of a Large College Library.* Oberlin, Ohio: Oberlin College Library, 1983.

Haka, Clifford H., and Nancy Ursery. "University Faculties and Library Lending Codes: A Survey and Analysis." *College & Research Libraries* 42 (July, 1981): 369-73.

This survey was launched by circulation staff members at the University of Kansas who, upon imposing fines on faculty members, were angrily told that such penalties were not applied at other institutions. All ninety-eight of the ARL libraries contacted responded. The authors found that not quite half of the libraries do impose *some* irrevocable fine. More than half of those who do not, use "other punitive measures." More than half of those who do, cannot legally force payment. The University of Kansas librarians, thus, found "ample precedent for the introduction of library penalties against faculty members" (p. 372).

Hansel, Patsy, and Robert Burgin, eds. "Library Overdues: Analysis, Strategies and Solutions to the Problem." *Library & Archival Security* 6 (Summer/Fall, 1984), 135 p.

This double issue of Haworth Press' quarterly journal offers fourteen articles by authors from different types and sizes of libraries on topics relating, for the most part, to policy issues. (One or two articles deal exclusively with methodologies based on new technology.) Particularly relevant articles are "Baltimore County Public Library and the Delinquent Borrower" by Marilyn Murray; "Overdues and Academic Libraries: Matters of Access and Collection Control" by Jean Walter Farrington; and "The Fines—No Fines Debate" and "Overdues and the Library's Image" by Barbara Anderson. In addition, an annotated bibliography is included by Terry Bossley for fifty-seven items on six topics: fine/no fine, helpful hints, collection agencies, legal action, research studies, and overdues in general.

Kohl, David F. *Circulation, Interlibrary Loan, Patron Use, and Collection Maintenance.* Santa Barbara, Calif.: ABC-Clio Information Services, 1985.

Lyons, Amy Gische. "Circulation Policies, Overdues, and Fines: Results of a Survey of Academic Health Sciences Libraries." *Bulletin of the Medical Library Association* 69 (July, 1981): 326-30.

This survey reported responses from 134 libraries and explored the length of loan periods, policy about notices, fines and bills, and enforcement practices. Similarities emerged about loan periods for various types of materials. Generally, faculty and student loans were the same, and most allowed renewals though the number varied. A majority sent out three notices before moving to the next step of enforcement. The authors believed a trend toward no-fine policies was emerging though "many institutions fined both faculty and students. Some . . . did not fine faculty" (p. 329). They found circulation policies undergo frequent change, attributing it to efforts to meet client needs.

Stratton, Peter J. *A Regression Study of Demand, Cost and Pricing Public Library Circulation Services.* Arlington, Virginia: Computer Microfilm International, 1978.

Truett, Carol. "To Fine or Not to Fine: One School Library's Experience." *Top of the News* (Spring, 1981): 277-80.

Truett reports a successful experiment with eliminating fines for overdue materials in a middle school library. Book losses went down overall, and much of the library's bookkeeping duties were eliminated. In addition, the number of lost books for which the library was not paid went down a spectacular 51 percent. Another benefit was an improvement in the library's public relations.

MISCELLANEOUS TOPICS

Lomonosoff, F. *Study of Reciprocal Borrowing Privileges in the Patchogue Library.* Patchogue, N.Y.: the Library, 1969.

Trochim, Mary Kane. *Measuring the Circulation Use of a Small Academic Library Collection.* Washington, D.C.: Office of Management Studies, Association of Research Libraries, 1985.

Zelkind, Irving, and Joseph Sprug. "Increased Control Through Decreased Controls: A Motivational Approach to a Library Circulation Problem." *College & Research Libraries* 32 (May, 1971): 222-26.

A psychology professor's report analyzes why students take library books without checking them out and describes his subsequent success (with the college librarian) of changing to a more convenient, do-it-yourself charging system. The professor's hypothesis was "that a person-oriented approach concerned with psychological factors would produce better control at lower cost than the object-oriented approach which is conventional" (p. 222).

INDEX

About the Author

SHEILA S. INTNER is an Assistant Professor in the Graduate School of Library and Information Science at Simmons College, Boston. Her earlier works include *Access to Media: A Guide to Integrating and Computerizing Catalogs*, and she has contributed numerous articles and reviews to *American Libraries*, *Library Journal*, *RQ*, and *Information Technology and Libraries*, among others.